D0008205

Four Wars, Five Presidents

Four Wars, Five Presidents

A Reporter's Journey from Jerusalem to Saigon to the White House

Terence Smith

ROWMAN & LITTLEFIELD
Lanham • Boulder • New York • London

Published by Rowman & Littlefield
An imprint of The Rowman & Littlefield Publishing Group, Inc.
4501 Forbes Boulevard, Suite 200, Lanham, Maryland 20706
www.rowman.com

86-90 Paul Street, London EC2A 4NE, United Kingdom

Copyright © 2021 by The Rowman & Littlefield Publishing Group, Inc.

All rights reserved. No part of this book may be reproduced in any form or by
any electronic or mechanical means, including information storage and retrieval
systems, without written permission from the publisher, except by a reviewer who
may quote passages in a review.

British Library Cataloguing in Publication Information Available

Library of Congress Cataloging-in-Publication Data
978-1-5381-6061-9 (cloth)
978-1-5381-6062-6 (electronic)

♾™ The paper used in this publication meets the minimum requirements of
American National Standard for Information Sciences—Permanence of Paper
for Printed Library Materials, ANSI/NISO Z39.48-1992.

To Grand Daughters three: Scout, Neva and Saylor

"Writing is easy: just sit down, open a vein and bleed."

—Red Smith

Contents

1

Here We Go

The Six-Day War between Israel and her Arab neighbors erupted on the morning of June 5, 1967, when Israeli warplanes streaked across Egypt's Mediterranean coastline and smashed most of the Egyptian Air Force on the ground.

For me, the war began with a phone call and a hangover.

I was a newly assigned and breathtakingly green, twenty-eight-year-old correspondent for the *New York Times* in Jerusalem. I had arrived in Israel on my first foreign assignment ten days earlier. It is astonishing to recall how little I knew and how unprepared I was for what was about to unfold.

The hangover was the result of gin and tonics at a party the night before at the home of the outgoing *New York Times* correspondent, Jim Feron. We geniuses in the foreign press had foolishly believed Moshe Dayan, the Israeli defense minister, when he had announced at a news conference that Israel was going to give diplomacy more time to resolve the three-week-old standoff with Egypt. Suggestion: whenever a military officer or defense minister says he is going to give diplomacy more time, grab your flak jacket.

It seemed a good time for a party. And it was a good party, ostensibly to welcome Flora Lewis, the foreign-affairs columnist, who had crossed through the Mandelbaum Gate from Jordan to Israel the night before—the last person to use the gate. As the junior Timesman on the scene, I had driven to the gate to greet her. It was a ramshackle affair: Israeli and Jordanian guard posts separated by barbed wire and a barren no-man's-space, used mainly by United Nations personnel. Flora trudged across in the evening light, slightly stooped, carrying her own luggage, a poignant but determined figure. The gate on the Israeli side closed behind her, never to open again.

The phone call, which came just after dawn on that hot, dry June morning as I slept in my room in the King David Hotel, was from Michael Elkins, the resident correspondent for *Newsweek* and the BBC. Elkins had been at the party, too, but his exceptional sources in Israeli intelligence had woken him with a tip that full-scale war was underway. "This is the real thing," he growled into the phone. His real message was, "Get your ass out of bed, Smith; you've got work to do!"

I thanked Mike and quickly called the military spokesman at the Government Press Office. He said he'd just been handed the communiqué, which began, "Since the early hours of this morning, heavy fighting has been taking place on the southern front between Egyptian armored and aerial forces, which moved against Israel and our forces, which went into action in order to check them . . ."

Moved against Israel? Went into action in order to check them? Not exactly. In fact, Israel's military commanders had finally persuaded their hesitant political leadership to seize the moment and launch a surprise, preemptive attack against Egypt. President Gamal Abdel Nasser had certainly provided sufficient provocation by closing the vital Straits of Tiran, cutting off Israel's access to the Red Sea, and by dispatching United Nations peacekeepers from Gaza. Launching its air raid that morning, catching the Egyptian Air Force off guard and, ultimately, those of Syria and Jordan, Israel took command of the skies of the Middle East and effectively won the greatest military triumph in its short modern history.

I didn't know that, of course, but I knew enough to get going. My hangover evaporated. I tumbled out of bed and headed down to the King David's high-ceilinged lobby. It was empty, except for the manager, Zvi Avrami, a gregarious bear of a man who had already changed from his dark hotelier's suit to olive drab fatigues and boots. I hadn't even known that Zvi was in the reserves, but there he was, standing all alone in the lobby, with a colonel's insignia on his collar and an urgent, excited look on his face. I told him I needed to use the telex machine behind the front desk to get word of the fighting to the paper in New York. It was about 8:30 a.m. Jerusalem time, 1:30 a.m. New York time, and if I moved quickly I could still make the final edition of that day's paper.

It was strictly illegal for Avrami to let me use the hotel telex. Those were the days of mandatory military censorship in Israel. Foreign correspondents were supposed to take their copy to the censor's office, get it cleared and stamped, and then deliver it to the telegraph office, where it would be sent by telex. That would take an hour or more, and I would miss the final edition.

I looked hungrily at the telex. Zvi followed my eyes, grinned, and said, "I'm looking the other way."

In twenty minutes of furious typing, I sent what I had been able to learn from the communiqué, Mike Elkins, and a phone call to a government source. It wasn't much—maybe six to eight paragraphs. But at least the paper had something from their correspondent on the scene. It was splashed across page one, with a subhead that read, "EACH SIDE ACCUSES OTHER OF MAKING FIRST ASSAULT." Evidently, the Egyptians had put out a communiqué with their version as well.

Hard as it is to imagine today, that was all I could do at the moment. There were no satellite phones, no computers, no Internet, no Facebook, no Twitter, no new media of any kind—social or antisocial. The phone call to New York that I had placed from my room earlier would not come through for at least another hour. Compared to today's instant satellite telecommunications, it was the dark ages.

Back in my third-floor room, I walked out onto the stone balcony. I had a great view to the east, across the rubble-strewn no-man's-land that separated the Israeli and Jordanian sides of Jerusalem, over the barbed wire and antitank barriers on the hillside, and up to the Old City wall, built by Suleiman the Magnificent in the 1500s. I could see the conical roof of the Dormition Abbey inside the Old City and, through the hot, morning haze, a Jordanian Arab League gun emplacement atop a corner of the wall.

It was surreal. War had begun. Only a few hundred yards separated me from the front line of a hostile Arab state and yet, it was utterly quiet. I could hear a donkey braying in the valley to the south, but little else. No sirens, no guns. Jordan had stayed out of the fight during the Suez Crisis in 1956. Would it do so again?

Just then, the phone rang. It was my call to New York. The paper's final edition had closed, so there was nothing I could add to the abbreviated piece I had filed, but I was glad to be able to talk to Alan Oser, the

night editor on the foreign desk. I pulled the phone to the balcony door
and described what I could see.

"You won't believe this, Alan," I said, "but it is completely peaceful.
No traffic, no noise—nothing. There's full-scale war in the Sinai. But
at this point, at least, no fighting with Jordan."

Just then I heard the burp-burp-burp of a heavy machine gun, then
another burst, then the thump of a mortar, then more machine gun fire.

"Check that, Alan," I said, stepping back from the exposed doorway
and feeling especially stupid. "Check that. It looks like we've got a
two-front war."

Today, a correspondent would immediately update the paper's web-
site, post a blog item, and record a brief video of the eruption of the
battle that would ultimately cost Jordan its control of East Jerusalem,
the West Bank, and half of the Hashemite Kingdom. The report would
go viral in minutes. NPR would be calling for a live account. The reporter would probably post a tweet, put something up on Facebook, and
transmit a cell-phone video. But in 1967, all I could do was describe the
scene to the night reporter on the foreign desk, who had already put the
paper to bed. I looked at my watch. It was 11:20 a.m. Jerusalem time,
4:20 a.m. in New York.

What I didn't know then and didn't learn until secret US intercepts
were released years later, was that Nasser was calling King Hussein of
Jordan about that time, urging him to join in the fighting. Even after
the Israeli Air Force had destroyed Egypt's best fighter-bombers on the
ground and launched a three-pronged attack on Egyptian troops in the
Sinai, Nasser was doing a full-throated con job on Hussein. Egypt was
already on the ropes, and doubtless Nasser knew it. But the self-appointed
leader of the Pan-Arab world told Hussein that triumph was inevitable
and that he had better join in the glorious battle or be left behind.

At the same time, Israel was sending secret messages to Hussein,
urging him not to join the fighting and promising not to attack Jordan
if he stayed out of it.

Nonetheless, to his eternal regret, Hussein took Nasser's bait and,
over the next few days, paid the price. By the time the shooting stopped,
he would lose half his kingdom and, crucially, control of the eastern
half of Jerusalem and dominion over the Holy Places.

It was time to get moving. I hung up the phone, grabbed my notebook
and camera, and headed out the door to cover the battle for Jerusalem.

2

From New York to Jerusalem

Journalism, at least working for a newspaper, was a natural path for me. I grew up in a newspapering family. At one point in the 1960s, all the working males in the extended Smith family were working for New York newspapers. I was covering politics at the *New York Herald Tribune*; my father, Red Smith, was the celebrated sportswriter at the *Trib*, where he was writing his Views of Sport column six days a week; my uncle Art, Red's brother, was writing the rod and gun column, Pavement's End, for the *Trib*; and my cousin Pat, Art's son, was writing sports at the *New York World-Telegram and the Sun*. Later, Art's daughter, Georgia, would become a featured writer for the *Times*. Needless to say, a citywide New York newspaper strike, which came along periodically in those days, put a nasty dent in the collective family income. There was even a point in 1964 when all of us were writing for the *Trib*, when Stanley Woodward—the great sports editor, who had hired my father and was his biggest fan—saw three of us chatting in the office together, shook his head, and said dryly, "This has got to stop!"

Despite their labor troubles, newspapers were the powerhouse media organizations in the 1960s. New York alone had eight major dailies at the beginning of the decade, including the mass-circulation *New York Daily News*, the *New York Daily Mirror*, the *New York Post*, the *New York Journal-American*, and the *Wall Street Journal*, in addition to the *Times*, *Trib*, and *World-Telegram*. By the end of the decade, it was down to four, after the *Trib*, *World-Telegram*, and *Journal-American* collapsed into the *World Journal Tribune*, nicknamed the Widget, a hapless product that folded altogether in 1967. The Hearst Corporation closed the *New York Daily Mirror* in 1963.

5

Despite the ongoing, inevitable shrinkage, newspapers counted. They had prestige, influence, and reach. Their editorial-page endorsements mattered. Politicians and candidates courted their favor. Television was on the rise but didn't yet compete as an opinion-shaping, agenda-setting medium. Advertisers, especially the city's big department stores, had no comparable way to reach their customers. In hindsight, the 1960s were the beginning of the end of the golden age of New York City newspapers, but that was far from obvious at the time.

My father did not urge me to go into newspapers. In fact, he pointed out that I could almost surely make more money doing other things. Practically any other thing. Again and again, he said I should follow my own passions and pursue what interested me. But the pure pleasure he took in reporting and writing, and in the newspaper life, was conspicuous and, for me, contagious.

Growing into my teenage years, I would tag along when he went to the ballpark or racetrack, when he covered a major football game or headed up to the Catskills to watch Rocky Marciano or Floyd Patterson prepare for a big fight. We'd go to the track together at dawn to watch the morning works, then hang around the barns behind the backstretch where, on the good days, the famous trainer "Sunny Jim" Fitzsimmons cooked pancakes for all comers. I loved it.

The annual sports calendar set the family agenda. We'd be in Louisville for the Derby, Baltimore for the Preakness, and at Belmont for the final jewel in the Triple Crown. August found our whole family at the races in Saratoga. If the World Series was in Yankee Stadium, as it so often was in that era, we'd be there. After a big game or a heavyweight-championship fight, we'd repair to Toots Shor's legendary saloon, where "the writers" were celebrated almost as much as the athletes.

Joe DiMaggio would walk in with his vicuña coat and Marilyn Monroe on his arm, and my sister, Kit, and I would gawk. Toots would walk up to my father and smother him in a bear hug and bellow, "Hiya, crumb-bum." The world's best saloonkeeper would sweep us to table number one, just to the left, inside the dining room, past the circular bar, where my father would trade stories with a parade of writers, politicians, mobsters, athletes, actors, and hangers-on. My mother would smoke and drink martinis and smile at the stories, a lot of which she'd heard before. Sometimes Toots would dismiss the bill with a wave of his arm; other times my father would pick it up. Financial security, my father would say in those days, is having enough money to snatch the check at Shor's without putting us all on the dole.

It did not take a genius to realize that this was a pretty good life. I also bought into the notion that observing and reporting on the world around you was a worthwhile thing to do—not just in the high school civics sense of empowering voters to make good decisions, valid as that is, but as a way of portraying the human condition and, conceivably, improving it. I'm not sure I dwelled on this, but I believed it then and believe it now.

So, in the summer between my sophomore and junior years in college, I marched down to the *Stamford Advocate*, in Stamford, Connecticut, where we lived, and applied for a job. The *Advocate* was an afternoon daily, owned by a wealthy local family who also owned the *Greenwich Time*, in nearby Greenwich. The *Advocate* was a tidy little gold mine, on which the owners spent as little as possible and collected a nice profit.

The editor was Ed McCullough, a gruff, silver-haired, pot-bellied, suspendered, cigar-smoking character straight out of *The Front Page*, Ben Hecht and Charles MacArthur's classic play about rough-and-tumble Chicago newspapering in the 1920s. We hadn't met, but McCullough knew my family and who I was.

"If you're half as good as your father," he growled through a cloud of cigar smoke in his office just off the newsroom, "you'll be fine. With the little I'm going to be paying you, it's not much of a gamble anyway. Report to sports, and get to work." McCullough's "little" turned out to be fifty dollars a week. Not a fortune, perhaps, but not bad for a summer job for a kid with zero experience in 1958. I was delighted.

I went home and told my father I was a newspaperman.

"Oh, lord," he said in mock horror. "Another wasted life! You could have been a doctor or a lawyer or something useful—at least something that paid better. Wait 'til your mother hears!"

He was delighted, too.

With that, I became one half of the *Advocate*'s sports staff, covering everything from the local ball teams and golf tournaments to the fitting-out of twelve-meter America's Cup contenders at the boatyards on Long Island Sound. I had to scramble to prove to the sports editor that I could do the job, but it was fun, and I learned fast. Good thing, too, because I had everything to learn. I came back to the *Advocate* the following summer and for a year after graduation from Notre Dame, this time covering straight news, from zoning-board hearings to the police beat to city hall. I enjoyed sports, but politics seemed an even better game. Now and then, I scored a scoop at city hall, and that raced my motor. The *Stamford Advocate* may not have won any Pulitzers in those days, but it was an excellent laboratory to learn the business.

I had ambitions to swim in a bigger pond, but my first, absurdly over-the-top attempt failed spectacularly. I was in Paris, bumming around Europe in the summer after graduation from Notre Dame, where, through my father, I met Bernard Cutler, then the editor of the *Paris Trib*—which became the *International Herald Tribune* and then the *International New York Times* and is today the *New York Times International Edition*. Paris was magic to me and the idea of working for the *Paris Trib* was romantic beyond belief. I could envision myself living on the Left Bank, sleeping with glamorous French women, and prowling Europe in a trench coat. I implored Cutler for a job, any job that would keep me in Paris, but Cutler said no.

"I actually have an opening on the copy desk," he said, rubbing salt in the wound. "But I'm going to do you a favor and not give it to you. If you want Paris, go back to the US, work for some papers bigger and better than the *Advocate*, and come back as a full-fledged foreign correspondent. Do it right!"

"No," I whined, "don't do me that favor! Give me a job!"

But Cutler was firm (and right, of course). As soon as my summer money ran out, I headed home and was back at the *Advocate*, covering city hall. At age twenty-two, with my student exemption expired, the Selective Service System—aka the draft—was stalking me. When I passed the induction physical, I joined a local unit of the Army Reserve to avoid the two-year draft commitment. I served six months of active duty defending Fort Dix, New Jersey, against Soviet invasion. (You'll note that, with me pulling mostly KP and guard duty, working for the weekly newspaper, the *Fort Dix Post*, and spending weekends on the beach at the Jersey Shore, the Russian Bear did not dare attack.) I was bored in the peacetime army, where the greatest danger was weekend sunburn, but it was not a total loss: they taught me to touch-type, and I came out of basic training and advanced infantry training in the best physical shape of my life, then or since.

Mustered out in the early winter of 1962, I couldn't wait to leave Stamford behind and get to the Big Apple. In my gall, I applied to both the *Times* and the *Trib*, and, astonishingly, there were openings at both. That's the stark difference in the news business between then and now: the better newspapers were thriving and expanding. Today they are shrinking and cutting jobs, thinning the product, and losing readers and advertisers. Most new reporters head straight to online operations. Print seems a dead end to them.

As it was, I was offered an entry-level job in the *Times'* sports department under editor Jim Roach, an old family friend, and a reporting slot on the city desk of the *Trib*. Even more amazingly, the job at the financially struggling *Trib* paid twenty dollars more, or a gilded two hundred dollars a week. I took it, partly on the belief that there were already enough Smith family members writing sports at the time, partly because I found politics more fun than sports, and partly because the *Trib* was a "writer's paper," smaller, scrappier, less formal, with more opportunities for a new boy, to say nothing of the extra twenty dollars.

In the process, I got a lasting lesson about connections in the newspaper business. Knowing people, as I did through my father, will get you in the front door. It certainly did me. It will help you get a job if there is an opening, but it won't guarantee anything after that. On a newspaper, you are quite literally as good as your last story, and bloodlines do not produce bylines. You have to perform. An editor will cut you loose without a second thought if you do not. I'm sure it is the same in other businesses, like banking or the law or medicine or selling insurance. But in the news business, your product comes out in black-and-white on a daily basis for all to see. You'd better have the right stuff—or learn it very quickly.

In my case, I had a resident editor at home. Even though I had moved to Manhattan at this point, sharing an apartment with two other bachelors, my father would read what I wrote and tell me what he thought. He had sharpened his own style over the years and had become, arguably, the most widely read and literary of America's sportswriters. *Newsweek* put him on its cover and dubbed him "STAR OF THE PRESS BOX." The awards stacked up, and his column was syndicated in hundreds of papers across the country. His writing made him a genuine celebrity. But as an editor, his was a light pencil. Mostly, he talked to me about the importance of description, of placing the reader at the scene, of conveying the essence of an event through detail, of dialogue as the spine of any good story. He told me how to listen in an interview or press conference for the distinctive turn of phrase, whether from a ball-player or a politician. It was great advice, and I tried to incorporate it without overtly mimicking his distinctive, witty style.

In the process, I was learning what other offspring of well-known people had learned before me. Especially those who choose to go into the same business.

A famous name (although *Smith* is pretty anonymous), is both a blessing and a curse if you choose to follow the same professional path. You get a boost at the beginning of a career, but you are inevitably com-pared, and, worse yet, you tend to compare yourself to your celebrated parent. For some, this is a crippling burden. There are any number of examples in politics or public life or media or entertainment where the blood has thinned dramatically.

Comparisons from one generation to the next may be unfair, but they are inescapable. Over the years, I have often been approached by people who want to tell me how much they admired my father's writing. They mean it as praise for him, not as a put-down of me. And I take it as such. But it left me with an empty feeling, as though I didn't really exist, that all my work to "make it" in the big time was just that . . . making it, nothing more. In any event, in my case, the advantages of the advice and encouragement I got from my father far outweighed any invidious comparisons I, or others, may have made. He was a great teacher and role model. The only real downside for me was that I probably spent too much time and energy scrambling to prove that I was good enough for the jobs that came my way. I suppose I felt more pressure than the next guy to succeed, but I didn't spend a lot of time consciously wor-rying about it.

Besides, if I needed competition, I certainly had it all around me when I arrived in the newsroom of the *New York Herald Tribune* in the early 1960s. Tom Wolfe, resplendent in his three-piece white suits and spectator shoes, sat a few desks away. He would shortly depart and create the celebrated "New Journalism" and turn out best-selling novels that captured an era. Charles Portis—who would make it big as a nov-elist later with his iconic Western, *True Grit*—was next to me. Jimmy Breslin was writing his column, William Whitworth, who would go on to the *New Yorker* and to edit the *Atlantic Monthly*, was on the reporting staff. So were Richard Reeves, James Clarity, and other outstanding writers. This younger talent augmented the paper's established stars, like Art Buchwald, Walter Lippmann, John Crosby—who wrote the television column—and the distinguished theater critic, Walter Kerr. The irony was that, just as the owner, John Hay Whitney, and his moneymen were moving to curb the *Trib*'s financial losses, James Bellows, the editor, was assembling one of the best writing staffs anywhere. But the money people and the news people were working on different tracks and, as it would turn out, cross-purposes. Of course, the money won.

My Brilliant Career at the *Trib* got off to an inauspicious start. I accepted the job as a reporter on the city desk and was scheduled to report for work on December 8, 1962, barely a month after I got out of the army. But at 11:59 on December 7—a day that will live in infamy in New York newspaper lore—the printers went on strike, shutting down all the citywide newspapers in the longest and most costly work stoppage in newspaper history. It was a bitter, existential dispute over the introduction of automatic typesetting. The printers' union knew it was the end of the protected, featherbedded existence they had enjoyed for a long time. Down the road, it would lead to the introduction of cold type, the computerized revolution that transformed the business. The stakes were huge for labor and management, nothing less than survival, and both sides knew it.

I was locked out before I could get in the door. Unemployed and ineligible for strike benefits—I hadn't had time to join the Newspaper Guild—but with a one-third share of the rent coming due each month on an apartment on East Seventy-Ninth Street, I scuffled for freelance and other work for the next 114 days. I wrote features for a newspaper-of-the-air that started up on local radio and television during the strike and for six weeks worked for General Motors' New York office updating their press-contact list. One way or another, I managed to pay the bills through the winter and into the spring, and finally, on April 1, 1963, the strike was settled, and the papers reappeared. The *Trib*'s banner headline expressed management's view: "READ ALL ABOUT IT: OH, WHAT A BEAUTIFUL MORNING!" I couldn't have agreed more. Finally, I reported for work and could claim to be what I had set out to be: a big-city reporter.

My first year at the *Trib* was spent writing allegedly bright, eminently forgettable features. I shudder to read them today. Parades and festivals seemed to be my specialty. This was an era when every ethnic group in melting-pot New York seemed to march up and down Fifth Avenue on one holiday or another, and there I would be, notebook in hand, trying to pull a lively quote out of some drunken Irishman in a leprechaun costume as the marching band from the Faithful Sons of this or that marked time noisily behind us.

The newsroom at the *Trib* was a vast, open space cluttered with ancient desks and scuffed wooden chairs, teletype machines, and, in the center, the U-shaped copy desk. There was no air conditioning, and in the hot weather the tall windows on the Fortieth Street side would be thrown open day and night. When you arrived in the morning, the floor and desktops would be covered with a fine layer of West Side Manhattan grit that would crunch underfoot. It was all very *Front Page*, and I loved it from the minute I walked in.

I was in the city room on November 22, 1963, when word came through that President John F. Kennedy had been shot in Dallas. Several editors were clustered around the AP and UPI teletype machines, reading the news as it came in line-by-line. I pushed into the knot of editors and read the words as they did . . . *rifle shots . . . grassy knoll . . . Texas Book Depository . . . open limousine speeding to Parkland Memorial Hospital.*

I and a couple of other junior reporters were sent out immediately to get man-on-the-street reaction. On the wide sidewalk in front of the New York Public Library, I stopped passers-by, asking if they'd heard the news and what they thought. Some were upset, some actually crying at the news that the president had by now died, but others, to my amazement, were angry and bitter. "Serves him right," one man said bitterly. "Good riddance," said another, hustling past me. I was learning about the harsh world of politics quickly.

In the evening, after the 7 p.m. first-edition deadline, the *Trib* editorial staff would repair to Bleeck's, the Artist and Writers Restaurant "downstairs" at 213 West Fortieth Street, immediately next door. It was a hard-drinking bunch, giving rise to the line in a parody at the time, "Drink is the ruin of the *Herald Tribune*, and sex is the curse of the *New York Times*." I would soon learn that neither weakness was exclusive to the other. In fact, at the *Trib* it seemed that everybody was sleeping with everybody. Some of these casual hookups led to lasting relationships and marriages—like that of the author Gail Sheehy and the magazine editor Clay Felker—but most were forgotten the next day.

By 7:30 p.m. of an evening, the reporters and editors would be three deep along Bleeck's famous, forty-two-foot-long bar, with Walt Kelly, the cartoonist creator of the popular strip *Pogo*, challenging all comers to the match game to determine who would pay for the next round. Pogo's famous line "We have met the enemy, and it is us" certainly applied to the denizens of Bleeck's.

Jimmy Breslin would hold forth with his stories of the mobsters and shyster lawyers in the Queens County courthouse, occasionally stumbling backward into the full suit of standing armor that had been liberated from the Metropolitan Opera just down the street. Breslin would regale us with tales of Marvin the Torch, who, for a modest fee, could burn your business down for the insurance money, and his colorful cast of semifictional Queens and Brooklyn characters until the bartender shouted last call. It was all pretty silly, but the *Trib* and Bleeck's and the New York newspaper business seemed wildly romantic to twenty-five-year-old me. It was where I wanted to be.

Now and then I'd get a break from my parade beat and be assigned to cover New York City politics, which I relished. This was a vintage era when the Greenwich Village reform movement was challenging the sclerotic Democratic establishment and the third-term administration of Mayor Robert F. Wagner Jr. There were classic ward bosses, like Carmine DeSapio, who ran their neighborhoods like independent fiefdoms, down to the last patronage job. It was corrupt and colorful and made great copy. I must have done alright with those stories, or at least avoided any libel suits, because the city editor, Dick Schaap, sent me to New Hampshire in February 1964 to cover the first-in-the-nation presidential primary.

Senator Barry Goldwater was running for the Republican nomination that he eventually won to run against President Lyndon Johnson, but in a stunning upset, Henry Cabot Lodge Jr., then US ambassador to South Vietnam, halfway across the world in Saigon, won as a write-in candidate. The good people of New Hampshire weren't sure what to think of Goldwater, who was in his shoot-from-the-lip mode, so they chose a safe, familiar name from neighboring Massachusetts. Needless to say, it was a great story and set the hook in me. I wanted to cover politics at home and, when the chance came, go abroad. Paris, needless to say, was still waiting.

Meanwhile, while I had been dating and occasionally sleeping with a few of the young women at the *Trib*, and others I'd met around town, none of those casual relationships amounted to much. At a cocktail party at a private club on lower Park Avenue, I met Ann Charnley, who was working at the Institute of International Education, a nonprofit near the United Nations that helped foreign students coming to the United States on Fulbright Scholarships. She was cute and funny and about as direct as she could be when I asked her what she was doing at the party. "I'm here to get somebody like you to take me to dinner," she said with a laugh. We headed uptown for a hamburger at Martell's, a favorite watering hole on Third Avenue, and had a great evening.

By that time, I was living in a one-bedroom parlor-front apartment in a brownstone at 14 West Ninth Street in Greenwich Village. Ann, it turned out, lived in a large studio at 18 East Tenth Street, just a block up and on the other side of Fifth Avenue. We kept seeing each other, trundling back and forth from one apartment to the other, capping a lot of the evenings with stingers on the rocks at a piano bar one step down on Tenth Street. We skied in Vermont, played tennis in Central Park, and occasionally went out to the track with my parents. Ann had lived in Rome for a year and, importantly to me, was keen to go abroad again. She was also three years older than me and made it clear that this relationship was going to end up at the altar, or just end. Finally, I proposed over dinner at Shor's, and we sealed the deal with a stinger at 21.

We were married on a sultry Saturday, June 20, 1964, at the Church of St. Thomas More in Manhattan. A reception followed at the Westbury Hotel. Among the guests were Henry Luce, founder of the *Time-Life* magazine empire, and his wife, Clare Boothe Luce. Ann's aunt, Dorothy Farmer, was Clare's executive assistant, editor, and confidante. She had introduced us to the Luces, and they had graciously, if erroneously, adopted us as a Bright Young Couple and invited us to join them at dinners and at their weekend estate in Connecticut.

These were dressed-down versions of a weekend at Downton Abbey. Guests would gather for a served and seated Saturday lunch with a lot of table talk about politics, the Catholic Church (Clare was a recent and vocal convert), and the like. Everyone would do their own thing in the afternoon while Clare wrote in her study and Hank, as she called him,

napped or did whatever he did. By six, the group would reassemble for
a long, liquid cocktail hour and dinner. Mr. Luce would grill me about
the perilous economic situation at the *Herald Tribune*, which he probably understood better than I. For a while, I hoped he would get out
his checkbook and save the paper by buying it, but magazines were his
ticket, and he was too smart to take on the crippled *Trib* at that stage in
its life and his.

Clare took it upon herself to introduce me around. When she heard
that I had been assigned to the Republican presidential primary in New
Hampshire, she immediately said, "You've got to meet Teddy White."
At that point, *The Making of a President 1960*, Theodore H. White's
wonderfully readable, narrative account of John F. Kennedy's 1960
presidential campaign, had been a huge best seller that read like a novel
and redefined political reporting. Now he was covering the campaign
for *Time* and gathering material for a sequel. Clare put us in touch, and
I linked up with Teddy in New Hampshire, where we chased after the
candidates in an enormous, rented Lincoln Continental driven by Bob
Healy of the *Boston Globe*, with columnist Mary McGrory riding shot-
gun. No one had a better time, better role models, or a finer introduction
to national politics than I did.

Later that year I got a choice assignment: Robert F. Kennedy, the
attorney general and brother of the assassinated president, declared to
run for the US Senate seat held by Kenneth B. Keating, a silver-haired,
mild-mannered Republican from Rochester. It was a whirlwind, sixty-
day campaign in which Kennedy crisscrossed the state in the family
plane, the *Caroline*, with a few reporters covering him. As the *Trib*'s
man, I went the whole way, competing against two superb political
reporters who rotated for the *Times*: the legendary war correspondent
Homer Bigart, and R. W. "Johnny" Apple Jr. This was competition, and
exposure, on another level for me. I scrambled and in the end broke as
many stories as the *Times* did.

Bob Kennedy was shy and subdued on the campaign, still reeling
from the shock of his brother's assassination the year before. Aboard
the *Caroline*, he would stare morosely out the window, lost in his own
thoughts. But there were some lighter moments along the way. On one
long day of whistle-stop campaigning on the *Caroline*, the traveling
party was joined by W. Averell Harriman, former governor of New
York. When the plane set down at Albany airport in the evening to

refuel before going on to the next stop, about twenty of us, including Governor Harriman, piled into the airport bar for a drink. We all had a round or two, and suddenly the call came to hurry back to the plane. Harriman, immensely wealthy and famously cheap, shocked everyone into silence by asking for the check. Like Kennedy, he rarely carried any cash; some assistant would pay the bill. But this time, sitting at the bar next to Mary McGrory, he pulled a roll of bills from his side pocket and slowly peeled off two twenties to cover the tab. Very softly, he leaned down to Mary and nodded toward the bartender. "Do you tip this fellow?" he asked. Mary nodded yes. Slowly and carefully, he pulled a single dollar from the roll, put it on the bar, and looked inquiringly at Mary. Mary shook her head. Harriman pulled out another single and put it on the bar. Mary again shook her head, no. Finally, with the air of a man who was running out of patience, Harriman put a third dollar on the bar. This time, Mary nodded yes. Harriman looked very pleased with himself and put the rest of the money back in his pocket.

On another night, just a few days before the election, the campaign arrived in Glens Falls, New York, about two or three hours behind schedule. It was dark and cold, well after midnight. We were all exhausted, Kennedy's voice was raspy, and his face was lined with fatigue. But when the bus pulled up to the rally site in a public park, there was a huge crowd cheering and clapping beneath floodlights as Kennedy emerged. Exhilarated, Kennedy gave one of the best speeches of the campaign. Then, he went over the top, promising that if he won, he would come back to Glens Falls the next day to say thank you. The crowd went wild. "Fuck, no!" the press contingent groaned as one. Homer Bigart rolled his eyes and muttered, "The little bastard really is ruthless."

None of us knew it at the time, but this would be the only political campaign that Robert Kennedy would ever complete as a candidate. He would be assassinated in June of 1968, running for the Democratic presidential nomination. But in 1964, Keating, a liberal Republican, never knew what hit him. The Kennedy juggernaut simply rolled him, using the most sophisticated television ads seen to date in a Senate campaign, plus lots of money and glamorous Kennedys and famous celebrities along the campaign trail. It was a vintage campaign, and Kennedy won going away.

Filing copy at that point in the evolution of daily journalism was primitive but surprisingly simple. Most of us would write our pieces aboard the plane on portable typewriters, making at least one carbon copy. If we could find a Western Union operator at the next stop, we'd file, using an office credit card. If not, I would find a phone and call the telephone dictation room at the office and read my piece into a recording device, enunciating carefully and including all punctuation. Fast, accurate stenographers would listen on a dead-key extension, cutting in now and then to clarify anything they didn't understand. They would type the copy and deliver it to the desk in short order. Inserts, new leads, and updates could be phoned in later or dictated to a rewriter if the deadline was close. The advantage of this laborious process was obvious: the copy passed through several hands, including a desk editor and a professional copy editor, and errors and stupidities were often caught before publication.

It was a twenty-four-hour news cycle with one climax: all the reporting, interviewing, and writing went into a single piece that was filed by a 7 p.m. deadline. There was time to think, research, and question what was going on. One time, for example, Homer Bigart decided to check the accuracy of a quote that Kennedy used to finish most of his stump speeches. "As the great poet Dante once wrote," Kennedy would invariably say, "the hottest circles of hell are reserved for those who, in a time of moral crisis, preserve their neutrality." No one was quite sure what it meant, but Kennedy used it all the time, and the crowds loved it. Bigart found a copy of the collected works of Dante and pored over it. No such quotation. Nothing remotely like it. Homer put a zinger about the manufactured Dante quote in his piece in the *Times* the next day, and everybody, except Kennedy, got a laugh out of it. The candidate winced and dropped the line from his subsequent stump speeches.

Today, of course, Homer would be too busy tweeting and blogging and shooting video with a handheld digital camera to check the candidate's Dante scholarship. Is the world better off either way? Not necessarily. Thanks to Google's search engine, a candidate's literary transgressions would likely be exposed soon enough—probably by an alert reader. But the reporter on the beat likely wouldn't have time.

As I covered the campaign, my father's celebrity continued to grow. His column was syndicated, and he became the most widely read sports columnist in the country. "SHAKESPEARE OF THE PRESS BOX," read the over-the-top headline on one magazine cover. He started doing guest spots on television and at one point was asked to testify before Congress on baseball's antitrust exemption. He bathed in the attention, and I enjoyed the reflected spotlight as well. Was I jealous of his success? No, not really; I relished it. But there were times when I felt invisible, more "the son of . . ." than myself, almost an extension of him.

But Pop, as my sister and I called him, remained my biggest fan. He read everything I wrote and commented positively or negatively on it all. If he liked a piece, he'd be on the phone in the morning saying so. If he found another piece lacking, he'd explain why and usually suggest ways to improve it. He'd praise my work to others, and it would often get back to me. He also taught by example. He was a prodigious worker, seven days a week, reporting and writing, always on the go, following the sports beat. As a result, we didn't see as much of each other as I wanted, and I hungered for more of his time and attention. But his schedule and mine made it hard to get.

3

From the *Trib* to the Cathedral

By now, politics was my beat, and the next year brought a mayoral candidate and campaign none of us could have imagined. New York was such a capital-D Democratic town in those days that Republicans were invariably sacrificial also-rans in the mayoral elections. But in 1965 Nelson A. Rockefeller—the wealthy, powerful Republican governor—and the high-roller Republican establishment wanted to change that. They were determined to break the Democratic stranglehold on city hall. Their scheme led to a scoop for me that proved the enduring value of dumb luck.

To put their plan in motion, Rockefeller and Vincent F. Albano Jr., the Manhattan GOP leader, gathered fifteen or twenty top Republican officeholders, consultants, and moneymen in a closed-door meeting in a private meeting room on the mezzanine level of the midtown Roosevelt Hotel to choose what they believed would be a dream candidate for mayor. The 4 p.m. meeting was no secret, but it was closed, and I and the other reporters covering it were kept in the hallway outside the double doors to the room. Some of my thirsty colleagues wandered down to the lobby bar, confident that the meeting would take a while. I decided to wait and found the door to the adjacent meeting room open. It was empty, save for a few straight-backed, stackable chairs. I set one against the temporary wall divider separating the room from the one in which the Republicans were talking and sat down to review my notes.

In the silence of the semidark, empty room, I suddenly realized that I could hear voices coming through a louvered vent in the wall above my head. Familiar voices. I could hear Rockefeller's unmistakable, raspy, nasal tones, Albano's New Yawk accent, and, now and then, John V.

Lindsay's preppy, patrician, Yalie voice. Lindsay was the handsome, young Republican member of Congress from Manhattan's East Side, the so-called Silk Stocking District, a budding Republican Kennedy. And as I listened, he was saying, yes, he'd be willing to give up his safe House seat and run for mayor if Rockefeller and Co. would raise the money for a first-class, fully funded campaign.

I was taking verbatim notes furiously, standing now on the chair to get closer to the air vent, straining to hear as the governor said money would be no problem. Several of the big contributors in the room agreed. Lindsay said in that event, he was in. It was a deal, one that would change the course of New York City politics.

The men in the room—they were all men—agreed to not announce their deal right away. Instead, they spent the next twenty minutes discussing what they would tell the reporters waiting outside. They settled on their story: no decision yet, more discussion needed, but stay tuned, because they had a plan to take back city hall. They rehearsed the statement again and again and then opened the doors to spin the reporters waiting outside.

I raced to a phone booth in the hotel hallway—no cell phones in those days. By now it was close to 6 p.m., with our first-edition deadline just an hour away. I called the city desk and, for the first and last time in my career, told the paper to hold page one. Dan Blum, the cynical, wisecracking assistant city editor, asked if I was kidding or had been drinking. No, I said, hold page one; you won't be disappointed. I'll be in the office in ten minutes.

The *Trib* splashed the story of "THE REPUBLICAN ASSAULT ON CITY HALL" across the top of page one. The piece described Lindsay's hand-picked candidacy, the promised funding, and the campaign strategy in huge headlines. Verbatim quotes from the closed meeting were displayed across the top half of the page, with the exchanges between Lindsay, Rockefeller, and Albano in boldface. The piece caused a huge stir in New York political circles and sent the other papers, including the *Times*, scrambling to catch up. Once again, dumb luck had triumphed.

Vince Albano was furious about the story and embarrassed about being caught lying to the other reporters. Not about lying, mind you—about being caught. He announced publicly that I had bugged the meeting and called for an investigation. No one in authority took him seriously, but, as the organizer of a supposedly confidential meeting, it covered his ass.

As it happened, the next night was the annual dinner of the Inner Circle, the New York equivalent of the Gridiron in Washington, where the town's politicians and reporters cavort in black tie, spoofing each other on a hotel ballroom stage. By this time, Albano himself was laughing about the whole business. "Here's the Bug Man!" he called out when I walked into the hotel lobby, "the Bug Man himself." Later, after a few drinks, he pulled me aside and pressed me to admit that I had bugged the room. How else could you get those quotes, word-for-word? he demanded. "You had to bug it." "Not me, Vince," I said smiling, "not me."

Today, in the era of Murdochian phone hacking, of Wikileaks, of Edward Snowden, of Russian hacks, listening through an air vent seems guilelessly innocent and unbelievably old school. But it got the job done.

John Lindsay's campaign revolutionized New York City politics. Columnist Murray Kempton captured the spirit of Lindsay's race against the drab, diminutive Democratic candidate, City Comptroller Abraham Beame, when he wrote of Lindsay, "He is fresh and everyone else is tired." Running on a so-called fusion ticket with Liberal Party support, Lindsay won by four points and swept into office on January 1, 1966, only to be greeted by a citywide bus and subway strike. As the paralyzed city struggled awake on a cold, clear New Year's Day, an exuberant Lindsay led a contingent of supporters and reporters on a fast-paced, four-mile power walk from his Midtown campaign hotel headquarters to City Hall for his noon swearing in. I remember Sugar Ray Robinson, the great middleweight champion and a Lindsay supporter, jogging along as part of the merry band. At one point, in a slapstick scene straight out of a film, a distracted Sugar Ray walked straight into an open phone booth. He backed up, shook it off like a left hook, and rejoined the procession. It was a chaotic start to a tumultuous term. Fun City, it was dubbed, sardonically.

I covered the mayoral campaign for the *Trib*, except for three weeks in late September and October, when the Newspaper Guild went on strike and closed down all the dailies except the *Post*. The papers came back on the street on October 10, 1965, for a furious final few weeks of campaigning. I scored the occasional beat on the *Times* and just before election day got a call from A. M. Rosenthal, the *Times'* intense, mercurial, and brilliant metropolitan editor, and his tall, arm-waving, gentle deputy, Arthur Gelb, inviting me to lunch at Sardi's. They liked my campaign coverage and said they wanted me to join the *Times'* metropolitan staff and cover Lindsay's first year in office if he won. It was an enviable plum, but Abe had a question for me before I said yes or no.

"What's your eventual ambition at the *Times*?" he asked.

"I want to go overseas," I said. "Paris, if it's available."

"What?" Rosenthal exploded. "I'm the metropolitan editor, not the foreign editor! I'm building the best reporting staff the *Times* has ever seen. I want you to work for me. More than that, I want you to *want* to work for me!"

Both Arthur and I glanced at the nearby tables to see if anyone was listening to this outburst. Sardi's was the *Times'* office saloon—their Bleeck's—and a major gossip mill. I reminded Abe that he had spent years overseas for the *Times*, had won his Pulitzer Prize overseas, and had qualified for his editorship by his foreign coverage. "You're the last person I'd expect to object," I said.

Abe calmed down at that. "Alright, alright, I'll make you a deal," he said, quickly.

"Work for me on the metropolitan staff for one year, and if you still want a foreign assignment, I won't stand in your way."

"Deal!" I said. I hadn't even been hired yet, and already Abe and I had had our first argument. Gelb was smiling. He'd seen this act before, I'm sure. I am equally certain that Abe was supremely confident that a year under his spell would persuade me or anyone with a brain to stick around.

Arthur, the good cop, broke it up at that point. "Take a few days and think it over, and let us know," he said as the three of us stood up and shook hands.

Back at the *Trib*, I went to see James Bellows, the lanky, laconic editor who was trying to save the financially sinking *Tribune*. I didn't think it would be long before he heard about the raised voices at Sardi's, and I wanted to tell him about the offer myself. I told him how much I enjoyed the *Trib* and asked him what my chances were of getting a foreign assignment. He raised his eyebrows and said, "I'm going to be brutally frank with you: right now I have two foreign bureaus outside of London. The question on my desk is, which one do I close first, Moscow or Paris?"

I told him that as much as I loved the paper, as important as the *Trib* was to me and my family, I was going to take the *Times'* offer. His eyes narrowed at that, and his tone hardened.

"Then you'd better go right now," he said. "Leave! I don't want you pulling your punches for us in the last days of the campaign."

Today, in an era when people leaving or being let go by an organization are routinely frog-marched to the parking lot by security, Bellows's reaction doesn't particularly shock me. But the idealistic, cocky twenty-six-year-old me was insulted at the time.

"I'd never do that," I said angrily.

We both cooled off and agreed that I would finish covering the campaign for the *Trib* and then join the *Times*. I did, and to prove Bellows wrong, I never worked harder than I did in the next few weeks.

When I moved to the *Times* on November 15, three days before my twenty-seventh birthday, I decided to change my byline from my nickname to my given name, from Terry Smith to Terence Smith. Terry seemed a bit casual for the Gray Lady, and *Terence* avoided the confusion that had produced letters from readers that began, "Dear Miss Smith . . ." It seems silly now, but either way, my father wasn't going to let me get away with it without a little teasing. "Goodbye, Terry; hello, Terence," he said in a toast at a newsroom going-away party at the *Trib*. "Enjoy the Cathedral." I, of course, used the cathedral line on him several years later when he, too, joined the *Times*.

Covering the first year of an administration—any administration, in New York City Hall or the White House—keeps a reporter busy. It established me as a front-page fixture at the *Times*. I was writing virtually every day and adjusting, gradually, to the culture of a very different paper. The atmosphere at the *Trib* had been light-hearted and irreverent, with the editorial orchestra playing as the ship was sinking financially. It was a writer's paper, where a reporter's style drew as much attention as much as the scoops. It was marvelous fun, but you didn't have to be a financial genius to realize that it couldn't last.

The *Times*, by contrast, had then, as it does today, a great sense of itself as the paper of record and, rightly, as an important, urbane, institutionalist, worldwide news-gathering organization. It had correspondents around the globe and a Washington bureau that rivaled the entire news staffs of most other papers. It was an editor's paper, hierarchical and formal, almost military in its structure. The metropolitan reporters were the enlisted ranks, the national staff the officers, and the foreign correspondents the field-grade officers. The editors ascended to the top of the pyramidal structure. The op-ed page opinion columnists were knights of the realm. The members of the editorial board thought deep thoughts in wood-paneled offices on an upper floor that resembled a fusty men's club. At the apex were the Sulzbergers, generation after generation of public-spirited publishers and owners who respected the famous wall separating the business and editorial sides. They were rich and getting richer by plowing many of the profits back into the product. (Iphigene Sulzberger, the family doyenne, once explained the family's acceptance of narrow profit margins in an interview, saying diffidently, "We're not yachting people.")

The *Times* thought of itself as special, and it was, located just west on Forty-Third Street off Times Square. And, oh yes, it was a man's world in 1965. There were few women on the editorial staff and even fewer Blacks. Gays stayed in the closet. It wasn't exactly a cathedral, but the resemblance to Canterbury was more than passing.

My first year at the *Times* was spent covering the new Lindsay era. In truth, John V. Lindsay was too patrician, too well-bred, to succeed as mayor of in-your-face New York, but he gave it a high-spirited, high-energy, indefatigable try. He brought in bright, gifted deputies and commissioners, took on the most entrenched of the city's unions, and tried to change the culture of cronyism and corruption overnight. It was a formula for failure, of course, but Lindsay had his moments.

In the midst of his first long, hot summer, for example, when race riots were breaking out in neighboring Newark, he walked the streets of East Harlem to defuse the tension. With his tie loosened and the sleeves of his white shirt rolled up, he loped along 118th Street, scooping up litter from the sidewalks and urging the Hispanic and Black kids following him to do the same. "Is this cat serious?" one kid asked when the mayor dumped some paper and bottles into a trash barrel. The crowds welcomed him, but his Tom Sawyer routine fell flat when he urged a heavyset Black man sitting on a stoop to pick up his own street. "Come on, help me clean it up," Lindsay called to him as he scooped more debris. The man just looked at him, without moving a muscle. Finally, he said flatly, "That's what we have a sanitation department for, Mayor."

The cultural chasm may have been too wide for Lindsay to close single-handedly, but his walking tours of the slums of Bedford-Stuyvesant in Brooklyn, South Jamaica in Queens, and Harlem helped keep the lid on New York while other cities were burning.

Ann and I were living in an apartment on East Sixty-Sixth Street and enjoying the city. We had lots of friends, plenty of parties to go to, and, in the winters, weekends at a shared ski house in Vermont.

But when my first year at the *Times* was up, I held Abe Rosenthal to his word and asked the foreign editor, Seymour Topping, for an overseas post. I mentioned that I would be happy with Paris. Top ignored that and suggested Lagos, Nigeria, instead. My heart sank. I had always said I was game to go anywhere, but Africa was so far off my map that, after thinking it over, I asked Top if I would forever forego my chance of a foreign assignment if I turned Lagos down. No, he said, explaining that he wanted to match correspondents with posts they really wanted. "But don't think you can make a habit of turning down assignments," he said. "You can get away with once."

A few months went by, and finally, just as I was wondering if I would ever get another shot, Topping invited me to lunch. He had another proposition: Jerusalem. This was easy. Of course I wanted to go. It was—and is—a great assignment. Especially for the *Times*: a nonstop story that is continuously on page one, a one-person bureau (in those days) where you could be your own boss, based in a magical city. It had history, romance, and breaking news on a daily basis. Nor did it hurt that the *Times'* readership cared deeply about what happened to Israel and its long-running problems with its neighbors. It may not have been Paris, but it was irresistible to me.

There was only one problem. My mother had died a few months earlier after losing a terrible nine-month struggle with pancreatic cancer, and my father, shattered and suddenly alone after decades of marriage, was living by himself in our family home in Stamford, Connecticut. The *Herald Tribune* had folded, and while he was still writing his column for syndication in other papers around the country, he had no outlet in New York. Not being read in New York, he used to say, was like writing his column every day and flushing it down the toilet. He was lonely and, frankly, adrift, spending too much time at the bar in Shor's and driving himself home to the suburbs late at night. I could picture him full of scotch after midnight, running into a bridge abutment on the

Merritt Parkway. Ann and I had tried to persuade him to sell the house and move to an apartment in New York, but he was dragging his feet. My sister, Kit, my only sibling, was married with four children and living her own busy life in Wisconsin. Ann and I were his only immediate family in the area. While he was still traveling on the sports beat, there were a lot of empty nights in Stamford. I was worried about him.

Earlier, after the *Tribune* folded, I had tried to find him another outlet for his column in New York. On my own, I called Vermont Royster, former editor and columnist for the *Wall Street Journal*. How would you like to run the best sports column in America in the *Journal*, I asked. Mr. Royster, whom I did not know, was intrigued. At that point, the *Journal* was a business paper throughout, with no sports department. I thought it could use one. I think he did, too. Let me get back to you, he said. A few days later he called back and said no. He had discussed it with management, he said, and they simply were not prepared to devote the space to a sports column.

"Too bad," he said. "Your father would brighten up our pages." Years later, the *Journal* expanded its coverage to include sports and, needless to say, a sports column.

Eventually, *Women's Wear Daily*, of all papers, picked up my father's column and ran it under the too-precious title "Sportif." Once again he was read in New York. He laughed at the thought of appearing alongside the fashion pages but in truth was grateful, even if *WWD* did not have a lot of subscribers among the characters who hung around Shor's or went to the ballpark. Years later, when an opening developed at the *Times*, Abe Rosenthal, by then executive editor, hired my father to write Sports of the Times. Now I was the grateful one. Red won his Pulitzer Prize for distinguished commentary there in May 1976, at the age of seventy, at "The Cathedral."

But all that was in the future. Now, I had to grapple with the idea of leaving him alone in New York and moving five thousand miles and six time zones away to Jerusalem. While I fretted, Topping wanted an answer. I asked my father to join me for dinner, just the two of us, in New York so we could talk about it.

"Fine," he said. "I'll meet you at Toots's."

"No!" I said. "I can't talk to you there. Too many interruptions." This was a familiar argument between us. I was always the kid, hungry for more time and attention from my father. I doubt he ever realized that.

He was a busy guy who traveled a lot and probably thought he spent a lot of time with me. But I always wanted more—more of him, I guess. If we met for dinner at Toot's, he'd be the center of attention, constantly turning to greet others. I'd be struggling to keep him focused on what I wanted to talk about, which was us—and him. So I suggested another spot to meet.

Over a plate of pasta at a corner table in the cellar at Mama Leone's, in the Theater District, where nobody would bother us, we talked. At least, I tried to talk to him about my concerns about what might happen to him if I took the assignment. As soon as I started to tell him that I was seriously worried about him and about leaving him alone, he cut me off sharply.

"Go, get out of here!" he said, his voice rising. "Don't think twice about it. You've wanted this for years. Don't worry about me. I'll be fine."

To put my mind at ease, he promised to get an apartment in the city, which he never did, and to visit us in Jerusalem, which he did.

4

The Holy Land

My plane landed at Lod—Israel's international airport, now Ben Gurion International—at dusk. There were soldiers in combat gear guarding the runways and tanks positioned outside the terminal. The neighborhood and countryside around airport was quiet and, it seemed to me, oddly, strangely, unaccountably dark.

I had left the US in a hurry. Originally, I had been scheduled to arrive in Israel in late June and overlap for a few weeks with Jim Feron, the outgoing correspondent, who would show me around and introduce me to some of his contacts. But when Nasser closed the Straits of Tiran to Israeli shipping on May 22, cutting off Israel's access to the Red Sea, events started to move fast.

I was in Washington that day, getting a briefing at the State Department about the situation in Cyprus, which is part of the coverage area of the Jerusalem bureau, when Abe Rosenthal called from New York. He read me the wires from the Middle East and asked how quickly I could leave for Israel. Neither he nor I knew for sure whether war was imminent, but it seemed likely.

"Can you go tonight?" he asked.

"Not tonight," I said. "My passport is in New York. But I can go tomorrow."

With that, I headed back to the city, packed in a rush, got several thousand dollars in cash, a camera, and a portable typewriter from the office, and jumped in a cab for the airport. I was leaving Ann in the lurch. She would have to pack up our apartment, ship our goods to Israel, and follow me as soon as possible for what we both expected would be a three-year tour. It would turn out to be a month before she could even get to Israel.

Jim Feron was waiting for me at Lod. At my request, the Israeli immigration official pounded my entry stamp on a separate piece of paper and tucked it inside my passport. If I were to travel to neighboring Arab countries, as I hoped, the passport would have to be clean of any evidence of Israeli entry.

Jim and I talked fast during the hour-long drive to Jerusalem He filled me in on the latest developments and sketched out some pieces I might work on for the first few days. The army had laid on a bus for the next morning to take foreign press to the Negev, where newly mobilized troops had assembled opposite Egypt's forces. "Might as well get you started seeing the country right away," said Jim. "The bus leaves at 6 a.m."

As Jim talked and drove, outside the car the countryside seemed ominously dark. A partial blackout? No, Jim said, the country is mostly mobilized, but no blackouts yet. This was Israel, not New York—a nineteen-year-old teenager of an independent nation, not nearly as developed as the United States I had left behind. There simply weren't as many lights. But as we entered Jerusalem, the city where I would live for five of the next nine years, the streets were bright and busy with cars, the sidewalks full of people. Hardly a wartime scene. I relaxed a bit.

Instead of going to the King David Hotel, where I would be staying, Jim drove to an apartment where a large, noisy party was going full tilt. "There are some people here you're going to need to know," Jim said, leading me inside. Moments later, a drink in hand, I met Ronnie Medzini, the government spokesperson, some other Israeli officials, and half a dozen US and British reporters stationed in Jerusalem. Total immersion, ninety minutes after touchdown.

At dawn the next day, I was indeed on a bus heading south, seated next to an attractive brunette from Scarsdale, New York. Scarsdale? Where the hell was I? She turned out to be Beth Elon, the American wife of Amos Elon, one of Israel's leading journalists and authors. She was telling me about her life in Israel when suddenly the bus jerked to a stop just outside Beersheba, in the Negev, alongside a mobilized unit of Israeli soldiers. Beth let out a shriek, bolted off the bus, and threw herself into the arms of a wiry, bespectacled soldier by the side of the road. It was Amos, who had been mobilized a few days earlier. Beth almost knocked him over, covering him with kisses. I began to get an idea of just how small this country was.

One of the first official Israelis I met was Teddy Kollek, the ebullient, fast-talking, irrepressible mayor of Jerusalem. When he heard that a new *New York Times* correspondent was in town, he called personally and suggested a get-acquainted tour. "I'm visiting some neighborhoods this afternoon," he said. "I'll pick you up at 2:30." This was typical Kollek, who seemed to be on a first-name basis with most of the top editors at the paper, and a vintage Kollek welcome for anyone from the *Times*. It was my first indication of the special status the *Times* enjoyed in Israel, a standing that I would learn could sometimes be a help, sometimes a hindrance.

Teddy—everyone called him that—arrived at the hotel in a green Dodge sedan. He had a driver, who was probably packing, but no other security. Among other stops, he took me to the Israeli side of the Mandelbaum Gate, pulled up, and explained that diplomatic personnel from the United Nations and embassies could use it, along with some correspondents traveling between Jordan and Israel, but no Israelis and no Jordanians. The gate was named after a hapless Mr. Mandelbaum, whose now-deserted two-story stone house had the misfortune of sitting astride the armistice line when the fighting had stopped in 1948. Today it is a museum, with displays that document the division of the ancient city from 1948 to 1967. It was here that I would greet Flora Lewis in a few days, and two days after that the gate that symbolized the division would be leveled by bulldozers as Israeli forces rolled into East Jerusalem.

What struck me was the intimacy of Jerusalem, the way Israelis and Jordanians, Jews and Arabs were living so close to each other, at gunpoint but without firing at each other, for nineteen years, separated only by the no-man's-land that meandered through the heart of the city. All that was about to change.

I filed a piece about my mayoral tour and several more over the next few days as I traveled to Israeli villages on the eastern edge of the Sea of Galilee in the shadow of Syrian artillery on the Golan Heights, to the Lebanese border, to Haifa, and to Tel Aviv. I tried, in those early pieces from Israel, to follow my father's advice to put the reader in my place, to see what I was seeing, and to hear what I heard. The country was so compact that you could drive anywhere and be back for dinner in Jerusalem. Everywhere I went, I saw people getting ready for war, but no one was sure whether it would come, or when.

5

The Battle for Jerusalem

When war did come to Jerusalem, on that sunny Monday morning in June, I had no time to waste. Camera and notebook in hand, I headed out the front door of the King David Hotel. Jordanian artillery was already lobbing shells across the no-man's-land into the western, or Israeli, half of the city. One landed with a crash in the garden of the big stone building across the street that housed the YMCA, splintering a palm tree. I had played a game of tennis with an American diplomat in that garden a couple of days earlier.

In the curved driveway of the hotel, an excited American couple—apparently the last two nonjournalist guests in the King David—were piling into the back seat of a cab they had persuaded to take them to the airport. The man spotted me and shouted, "Tell them back home that the Bermans of Brooklyn are okay!" He waved, and the car sped off.

I jumped in my rented car and raced toward the Government Press Office in the old Russian Orthodox Church compound in the center of the city. By now, the Jordanian artillery barrage had intensified, buildings were being shelled, and ambulances were racing through the streets. Some nine hundred buildings would be hit over the next two days by six thousand Jordanian shells. About two dozen Israeli civilians would be killed and one thousand wounded.

There were a dozen foreign reporters in the Government Press Office along with Ronnie Medzini, the press spokesperson I had met at the party on my first night in Jerusalem. Tall, slim, and sardonic, he was now mobilized and wearing an olive drab Israeli army uniform. "This should keep you busy," he said, handing me a half-dozen army communiqués summarizing the initial fighting in the Gaza Strip and

33

the Sinai. They were sketchy at best and had nothing about the battle for Jerusalem, which was my story. Jim Feron had already departed for the military headquarters in Tel Aviv to report on the big picture. By midday and early afternoon, the fight for Jerusalem was fully underway, with Israeli units beginning a wide pincer movement around the northern and southern perimeters of the Old City and an Arab Legion battalion advancing toward Government House, the United Nations headquarters on the prominent hill to the south known as the Mount of Evil Counsel, so named because it is described in the New Testament as the spot where the high priest Caiaphas decided to arrest Jesus.

The Jordanians initially took the hill, which dominates Jerusalem from the south, and dug in around Government House, firing mortars and recoilless rifles at the Jewish neighborhood of Ramat Rachel and the nearby Allenby Barracks. They even established a machine gun placement at a second-floor window of the huge, white Government House, which housed the British high commissioner during the days of the Palestinian mandate. But the skeleton UN observer detachment under General Odd Bull threw them out, arguing archly that it was neutral territory and that neither side had any business there.

Two Israeli infantry companies led by eight tanks begged to differ. They mounted a counteroffensive, charging up the hill from the west. Hearing about this at the Government Press Office, I drove my rented car up the hill behind them—not the smartest move in retrospect, but it gave me a front-row seat. The advance halted as fast as it began when the Jordanians knocked out the two leading Israeli tanks, sending me into a ditch for cover. Artillery shells landed in front of me and behind. Stones shattered, and trees toppled. Dust and smoke everywhere. Three Israeli tanks bogged down in mud in Ramat Rachel, but the infantry continued up the hill behind armored personnel carriers, broke through western gate of the compound, and started clearing the building with grenades. I got as close as I could to Government House and watched the battle unfold. After three hours of fighting, some of it hand-to-hand, the Israelis took control of Government House and the adjacent Antenna Hill. The Jordanians fell back to the east, the Israelis dug into the side of the hill, and General Bull, still protesting loudly that this was neutral ground, got his headquarters back.

I had a story to tell, so I drove back into town, passing an apartment building where one wall had been blasted away, exposing a kitchen on the third floor. Bottles and cans were still on the shelves, and water from a broken pipe cascaded into the street below. Whoever lived in that flat was gone, or dead.

I filed a description of the first day's fighting and the battle for Government House that ran on page one under the headline, "TROOPS AND ARMOR CLASH IN JERUSALEM." I even managed to include a line about the Bermans of Brooklyn being okay. That piece, like everything I filed through the Jerusalem telegraph office, had to be submitted to the Israel Defense Forces military censors, who maintained a small office in the Government Press Office. Young English-speaking officers would pour through your copy, line-by-line, deleting any references to troop movements, specific casualty figures, damage reports that might tell the Jordanians where their artillery had hit home, and the like. I had no objection to scrubbing the copy of tactical military information; any army would want to do that. But often the Israeli military censoring went beyond the strictly tactical, straying into issues of morale and image. Any reports that depicted Israeli troops in a bad light—especially during the subsequent occupation of the Palestinian communities of the West Bank—would be blanked out of the copy before it was delivered to the telegraph office.

With today's open, instant communications, such strict copy control would be impossible. But in 1967, the Israeli government controlled and monitored the pipeline to the outside world. It had the leverage and didn't hesitate to use it. An individual reporter could argue a point with a censor, even appeal it to a superior officer, but in the end it was the army's call. The only effective way to evade censorship in those days was to leave the country and file from abroad—hardly practical with news breaking all around you.

The censorship actually dated back to emergency regulations imposed during the British mandate that administered Palestine prior to 1948. The Israelis kept many of those rules on the books once the state became independent and uses some of them, like administrative detention, to this day. The rationale is that the country is at war, which arguably it is, despite the peace treaties signed subsequently with Egypt and Jordan. The downside is that censorship erodes Israel's carefully cultivated image as a democracy that defends free speech.

Certainly Israel was at war on that evening of June 5, 1967, as I made my way back to the King David under now-continuous Jordanian shelling and Israeli return fire. The sky was bright with tracer fire, and the night rocked with explosions on both sides. The streets and sidewalks were empty as I drove, headlights out, to the hotel. The Israelis had mounted huge searchlights atop the Histadrut labor-federation building, the tallest in western Jerusalem, and used them to expose and blind Jordanians in their positions just across the no-man's-land. Clever. They hadn't taught us that trick during basic at Fort Dix.

From the balcony outside my room, illumination flares periodically bathed the Old City walls and the Tower of David in an eerie, white light. I had an astonishing front-row seat as the fighting continued to build. Suddenly, around midnight, an Israeli shell ignited the steep, conical roof of the Dormition Abby, built on the spot where tradition has it that Mary spent her last night on earth and Jesus held the Last Supper. The wooden roof burst into flame and burned through the night like a huge, too-perfect bonfire. Israeli jets streaked overhead, strafing targets east of the city. The grassy embankment leading up to the Old City walls caught fire as well, lighting the entire scene, which looked like a Hollywood production. Today, a reporter with that extraordinary vantage would be beaming pictures back home and describing it live, via satellite phone. As it was, I took notes and snapped a few still pictures for the next day's paper.

There was a wider war to cover, of course. While I focused on the Battle for Jerusalem, Jim Feron had raced to Tel Aviv, where the defense ministry and Israel Defense Forces general headquarters were located. From there he could get updates on the big picture, the fighting in the Gaza Strip and Sinai, and the Israeli Air Force assaults on Egypt, Syria, and Jordan proper. He also wrote about Israel's air strikes against bases in western Iraq and the shooting down of a single Lebanese Air Force fighter. James "Scotty" Reston, the *Times'* great columnist, was in Tel Aviv as well, having arrived a few days earlier. The paper was also getting excellent reporting from Eric Pace in Cairo, Max Frankel in Washington, and Drew Middleton at the United Nations in New York, among others.

But Jerusalem was my story, and an incredible story it was. By dawn on Tuesday morning, June 6, the battle for the holy city was roaring. The Harel Brigade and units of Israeli paratroopers supported by tanks under Colonel Mordechai Gur had launched a wide, encircling movement around the northern side of the city, blasting their way across the no-man's-land at the Mandelbaum Gate and assaulting Arab Legion positions dug into trenches on Ammunition Hill, a major fortification built by the British in the 1930s to store ammo for the nearby police academy, a stone fortress in itself.

The Jordanians fought back fiercely, first retreating to the police academy and then falling back from there. Both sides suffered grievously. The fighting ended by midmorning, with thirty-six Israeli soldiers and all the officers but two company commanders killed. In all, seventy-one Jordanians died there. Scores more were wounded.

I could see and report some of this from high ground on the Israeli side. At one point, I watched as Israeli paratroopers moved up a broad street behind a marching wall of mortar fire and two tanks. Before long, they fought their way up to Mount Scopus, the Israeli enclave that housed the original Hadassah Hospital and Hebrew University campus. It had been cut off since 1948 and resupplied by UN convoys over the years. Now, as Israeli soldiers poured in, it was reconnected by an open corridor to the rest of Israeli Jerusalem. Beyond its symbolic value, Mount Scopus gave the Israelis a commanding military position overlooking the Old City.

Meanwhile, other Israeli units took out Jordanian positions near the American Colony Hotel and moved down Nablus Road toward the Old City. It was brutal, face-to-face street fighting. The Israelis leveled the barrels of their tanks and fired directly down the city street. The Jordanians fought back stubbornly but slowly pulled back to the east in the face of greater Israeli firepower.

Unbeknownst to me, the Israeli troops had been ordered to stop short of the walled Old City, the ancient, densely packed warren of narrow streets and stone walkways that is home to the Church of the Holy Sepulcher, the Western Wall, Al-Aqsa Mosque, and the Dome of the Rock. In all, twenty-one of the most revered religious sites of three major religions are located within the sixteenth-century walls. Apparently, the defense minister, Moshe Dayan, had consulted with David Ben-Gurion, the former prime minister, and shared his concern that Israel would incur fierce international backlash if it blasted its way inside the Old City. Dayan guessed they would likely have to give up the territory, which was going to come at a price. Ben-Gurion agreed with Dayan, and for that evening anyway the Israeli troops held their ground outside the Old City.

At a news conference that evening, Mayor Kollek admitted that he was amazed how quickly the Israelis had established control over most of the city. "Nobody expected this," he said. He reported that most of the Jordanian units had withdrawn from the Old City and that Ahmad al-Shukeiri, chairman of the Palestine Liberation Organization, had fled. Asked what the Israelis would do about the Old City, Kollek shook his head. "Its not for me to say," he said. "To talk about it at this point would be like cutting up the bear rug before you skin the bear."

The bear skinning started first thing the next morning, Wednesday, June 7. Moshe Dayan, alarmed at new efforts at the UN headquarters in New York to impose an immediate cease-fire, reversed himself and authorized the Israeli units outside the walls to take the Old City.

The Fifty-Fifth Paratroopers Brigade under Colonel Gur maneuvered around the city walls, and at 9:45 a.m., Sherman tanks blasted their way through the barricaded Lions' Gate on the east side, and Israeli paratroopers charged inside. They came under fire from isolated Jordanian gunners but quickly confirmed that the bulk of the Arab Legion forces had withdrawn to the east during the night. Other Israeli units entered the Old City from gates on the south and west sides and encountered only scattered opposition. All of the Israelis converged on the open, tree-shaded courtyard that surrounds the Dome of the Rock and Al-Aqsa Mosque. To Muslims, it is the Haram al-Sharif, or Noble Sanctuary, one of the holiest sites in Islam; to Jews, it is the Temple Mount, the site of the First and Second Temples. The huge retaining Western Wall of the mount, or Wailing Wall, is revered as a remnant of the Second Temple and is Judaism's most sacred site. This is the spiritual heart of Jerusalem, the Holy of Holies, where Jewish tradition holds that Isaac, son of Abraham, was bound. The Noble Sanctuary is also where Muslims believe Muḥammad ascended to heaven. The revered Al-Aqsa is regarded as the third-most-sacred site in Islam.

The open plaza was Colonel Gur's objective as his troops turned first this way and then that in the narrow, twisted, stone-paved streets of the Old City, quickly getting lost. Confused, Gur stopped and asked an old Arab resident for directions to the Haram al-Sharif. This way, said the man, as though he were giving a tourist directions to a shop or museum. White flags of surrender hung from the houses as the paratroopers made their way upward to the high ground surrounding the Dome of the Rock and atop the Western Wall. There was a brief firefight with Jordanian soldiers, and then everything was quiet. Gur famously radioed his commander a simple message that quickly became part of Israeli military lore: "The Temple Mount is in our hands."

About this time, Ronnie Medzini, the government spokesperson, commandeered an open jeep in West Jerusalem and raced east with Jim Feron and me hanging on as he dodged shell holes and burned-out vehicles. We raced through the Mandelbaum Gate and up to Sheikh Jarrah, a wealthy Palestinian neighborhood on a hill immediately north of the Old City. Dozens of Palestinian prisoners were handcuffed and crouching along the honey-colored walls under the watchful eye of Israeli guards with Uzis. The sun was already high and hot in a cloudless blue sky. We drove around the Old City walls to the Lions' Gate, ditched the jeep outside the entrance, and headed inside in the footsteps of Colonel Gur's units. I could hear occasional sniper fire, but it was quiet by the time we emerged into the bright, hot, midday sun on the Noble Sanctuary. A few bullets had splintered the lovely blue tile walls on the outside of the Dome of the Rock, and the glass entrance door had been shattered, but the shrine was intact. Inside it was cool and quiet. Even the broken glass had been swept into a pile by the door. Exhausted Israeli soldiers sat slumped against the outside walls, seeking relief in the narrow band of shade. They showed no interest in the emotional scene unfolding a couple hundred yards away at the Western Wall.

Several dozen Israeli soldiers had squeezed into the narrow space between the wall and the rundown Arab squatter houses that had been built in the nineteen years since Israelis had last visited this spot. I got there, pushing through the narrow Mughrabi Gate just south of the wall about noon, and hurried down the stone steps.

The scene before me was amazing. Some soldiers, clearly deeply moved by the historical and spiritual moment, were weeping and praying. Following a tradition that they had been denied for most of their young lives, they wrote prayers on scraps of paper and stuffed them in the cracks between the giant stones. Others stood back, taking in the scene, indifferent to the religious significance of the moment, holding their weapons and keeping a wary eye on the rooftops for the few snipers still shooting. An observant Israeli corporal, chanting and davening at the base of the wall, was cut down as he prayed by a remaining Arab sniper. His was the only death reported by Israeli forces after they entered the Old City.

Suddenly, there was a commotion, and a short, stocky man with a full, white beard rushed down the steps from the Mughrabi Gate and stood at the base of the wall. It was General Shlomo Goren, chief rabbi of the Israel Defense Forces. Gathering a knot of soldiers around him, he led them in prayer and blew a long, loud blast on his shofar, or ram's horn. Clutching a Torah scroll to his chest, he said excitedly, "I made this Torah in 1948. I had it with me in the Sinai in 1956, and I carried it into Gaza with the troops yesterday."

The words came tumbling out in a mixture of Hebrew and English: "We are now realizing the dreams of Jews for two thousand years!" he shouted, with soldiers trying to hold his arms to calm him. "We are entering the Messianic Era. We shall never leave this place!"

At that point, someone hoisted a blue-and-white Israeli flag with the Star of David, and, apparently silently acknowledging defeat, the Arab snipers ceased firing and melted away.

About 2:30 p.m., in a scene clearly meant to be photographed, Defense Minister Dayan—wearing a combat uniform and net-covered helmet, flanked on his right by Uzi Narkiss, commander of the Jerusalem sector, in a cloth fatigue cap, and on his left by a helmeted Yitzhak Rabin, chief of the general staff of the Israel Defense Forces—arrived at the arched entrance to the Lions' Gate. Once the photographers and camera operators were in position, Dayan motioned with a hand and the three marched dramatically up the street, setting off a clatter of camera shutters. The pictures of that procession splashed across front pages throughout the world as the enduring symbol of the Israeli capture of Jerusalem.

When Dayan reached the wall, he, too, wrote a short prayer and stuffed it in between the stones. Turning to the soldiers and reporters around him, he said, "We have returned to the holiest of our holy places, never to depart from it again. To our Arab neighbors, we offer, even now, our hand in peace."

Rabin, more phlegmatic, spoke in his deep baritone of the "countless generations of Jews murdered, martyred, and massacred for the sake of Jerusalem." His face was impassive, but later he recalled, "This was the peak of my life. For years I had secretly harbored the dream that I might play a role in restoring the Western Wall to the Jewish people. Now that dream had come true."

It was an incredible scene, and I hurried back to West Jerusalem to describe it as best I could for the next day's paper. The story ran at the top of page one, beneath a picture of the soldiers praying at the Wall. "ISRAELIS WEEP AND PRAY BESIDE THE WAILING WALL" read the headline. Inside was another photo of an Israeli tank rumbling through the wreckage of the Mandelbaum Gate. The dateline was Jerusalem, June 7, 1967. It had taken the Israelis just forty-eight hours to capture the ancient city. According to historians, it was the forty-fourth time control of Jerusalem had changed hands in war in the city's long, turbulent history.

6

Six Days in June

"**Y**our Graces, your Beatitudes, your Excellencies, your Eminences," the urbane former brigadier general Chaim Herzog began in English as he addressed an assemblage of Greek Orthodox, Roman Catholic, and other Christian leaders the next day in the Ambassador Hotel on the Jordanian side of the Mandelbaum Gate. The newly appointed military governor of the West Bank had called the clerics together to assure them that their sacred sites in the Old City would be protected. The only room large enough to hold the assemblage was the hotel bar. I sat in the back taking notes as the religious leaders listened in armchairs arranged in a broad half-circle beneath a gaudy mural of an Arab belly dancer slipping out of her veils. They kept their eyes firmly on Governor Herzog.

Prime Minister Eshkol had already met with Muslim officials in the Old City to give them similar assurances. Mayor Kollek had called in Jordanian civic administrators to restore water and electricity to the eastern half of the city, and the Israeli city council, in a special meeting, voted to expand the Jerusalem master plan to include the entire city. The council also voted to establish the Jerusalem Fund, with a goal of fifty million dollars to finance the reconstruction of historic sites in the Jewish Quarter of the Old City. The war was still underway in the Sinai—and about to begin in the north—but Israelis were wasting no time in making it clear that, whatever the future of the West Bank, they intended to keep control of all of Jerusalem.

While Mordechai Gur's forces were taking the Old City, other Israeli units were sweeping eastward across the West Bank, pursuing the retreating Arab Legion. They took Nablus in the north, Bethlehem and

Hebron to the south, and Jericho to the east and soon found themselves along the banks of the Jordan River. Tens of thousands of West Bank Palestinians had already fled to the East Bank and Amman, and Israeli engineers quickly destroyed the bridges across the Jordan River to ensure that there would be no counterattack or mass return of the refugees.

I drove down the wide, gently winding road that descends from East Jerusalem, which sits at about 2,600 feet, to Jericho, some several hundred feet below sea level, on the floor of the Jordan Valley at the north end of the Dead Sea. The scene along the road was a devastating illustration of Israeli airpower. Both sides were littered with the burned-out hulks of Jordanian tanks, armored personnel carriers, cars, and trucks, some still smoking, some with corpses of Jordanian soldiers. An entire mechanized unit of the Arab Legion, trying to come up to help in the defense of East Jerusalem, had been wiped out by Israeli strafing runs the day before.

Jericho itself was sleepy and quiet in the baking midday sun when I got there. A thermometer read 104 degrees. A few Israeli tanks were posted at intersections, but most of the population of seventy-two thousand appeared to have fled. The Allenby Bridge, the principal crossing of the Jordan River, had been deliberately taken out by an Israeli airstrike and was collapsed in a tangle of twisted metal in the brown, muddy waters. Refugees with bundles and cartons on their heads were wading across to the Jordanian side in knee-deep water. In truth, I could hardly believe that this narrow, muddy stream was the mighty Jordan.

When I got to Bethlehem the next day, it was similarly quiet. The Israelis had taken it the day before without firing a shot. The Church of the Nativity had received a dozen hits from earlier shelling, leaving a gaping hole in the roof, but there seemed to be little other damage. The tourist shops in Manger Square were coming back to life, selling mother-of-pearl and olive-wood trinkets to Israeli soldiers-turned-tourists. Commerce has always been the soul of Jesus's birthplace, and the Bethlehem merchants were not going to let a little thing like war interfere. On Manger Street, I saw the Three Wise Men souvenir shop, the Holy Manger gift shop, and the King David religious-goods factory, all busy.

Jean Michel, proprietor of the Bethlehem Oriental Store, was groaning theatrically as he completed sale after sale. The Israeli soldiers were paying for their purchases, but not without prolonged haggling sessions.

"I'm losing money on every item," Michel moaned as he stuffed cash into his register.

"Great stuff," my father wired me the next day. "Keep it coming."

The fighting was finished on the West Bank, and life in Jerusalem was slowly returning to something approaching normal, but the war was far from over. Defense Minister Dayan, initially reluctant to open a third front against Syria, relented on Friday, June 9, and authorized the northern command to assault the Golan Heights, from which Syria had been shelling Israeli settlements. Israeli troops scaled the heights, fought hand-to-hand through the Syrian bunkers and fortifications, and rolled east to Quneitra and north to the flanks of the ten thousand-foot-high Mount Hermon. It was brutal, costly fighting, but by 6:30 p.m., Saturday, June 10, when a UN-sponsored cease-fire was finally accepted by all sides, Israel had demolished much of the Syrian Army and eliminated a major strategic threat to the northern part of the country.

The Six-Day War had been fought and won in an incredible 132 hours on three fronts. Israel had conquered forty-two thousand square miles and multiplied its size by three-and-a-half times. An estimated fifteen- to twenty thousand Egyptian soldiers had died, plus seven hundred Jordanians and 450 Syrians. Israel admitted to eight hundred dead. When the fighting was over, Israel held at least five thousand Egyptians as prisoners, plus 550 Jordanians and 365 Syrians. Fifteen Israeli soldiers were prisoners of war, all later exchanged. As usual, the greatest suffering was among civilians. Many had been killed in the crossfire, and an estimated 250,000 Palestinians fled the West Bank for refugee camps in Jordan, adding another quarter-million to the exodus and serial displacement that had begun in 1948.

The victory could hardly have been more swift or total. And yet, at this writing, fifty-four years later, Israel has been unable to convert its military triumph into genuine peace. Treaties have been signed and ambassadors exchanged with Egypt and Jordan, but the two-state solution that is still the key to an effective peace with the Palestinians remains more elusive than ever. Working in concert, former President Donald Trump and former Israeli Prime Minister Benjamin Netanyahu cleared the way for Israeli annexation of its settlements on the West Bank and much of the Jordan Valley. Syria has been embroiled in its own civil war agony. Quneitra remains a ghost town in a demilitarized zone. Generations of refugees remain in squalid camps. Generations of Israelis have spent their army service policing the frequently violent West Bank. Five-plus decades of occupation have hardened the hearts of occupier and occupied alike. Occupation is a dirty business that demeans both sides and benefits neither. Resentment of one side of the other has deteriorated into hatred and contempt. Vast new Israeli settlements have been built throughout the West Bank, most on confiscated Palestinian territory. The several hundred thousand settlers, many religious zealots, have molded into a powerful, right-wing force in Israeli politics, pulling the entire government hard to the right. Israel today is hard for me to recognize as the enlightened, liberal state I encountered in 1967. All of this is the direct consequence of those six days in June 1967.

It is hard to remember now, but peace seemed inevitable in the immediate aftermath of the Six-Day war. It was inconceivable to people on both sides in Jerusalem, for example, that such a devastating and complete outcome could result in anything less than a peace agreement and a new beginning. How could it not?

That answer came quickly. By July 1, less than a month after the start of the war and barely three weeks after the cease-fire, Israeli and Egyptian jet fighters were clashing above the Suez Canal. By the fall of 1967, the Arab nations assembled in a summit conference in Khartoum and agreed on the famous three nos: no peace, no negotiations, no recognition of Israel. Six years later, of course, in 1973, full-scale war would erupt again.

For me, as a neophyte war correspondent, the Six-Day War was the proverbial baptism by fire. It was intense, absorbing, exciting, challenging, frightening, exhilarating, and exhausting, and by the time it was over, less than three weeks after I had first arrived in the country, I felt like a veteran. That was an illusion, of course. Only later, sometimes years later, did I learn about events that had gone on around me that I had known nothing about at the time.

There is a truism about foreign correspondence: after six months in a country, you think you know everything there is to know; after three or four years, you begin to realize how little you actually understand. That underscores the importance of actually stationing correspondents in a given country and having them learn the language and customs and begin, however imperfectly, to understand the place. News organizations understand that, but it is an increasingly costly business. Many have cut back or closed their foreign bureaus altogether. The networks especially fly reporters into a country, parachute them into the heart of a conflict, and pull them out as fast as possible. The result is fragmentary, often shallow coverage and that contributes to a national amnesia about recent events in the rest of the world. Not good for a supposed superpower like the United States that seems these days to be in a state of unending warfare in scattered and remote corners of the globe and rapidly turning inward.

In any event, the Six-Day War turned out to be the first of four wars that I would cover as a correspondent. I never intended that; it simply happened that way.

In the aftermath of the war, I set out to see and write about some of the real estate that Israel had conquered. I drove up to the Golan Heights and prowled through the bombed-out Syrian bunkers, explored the Gaza Strip and Sinai all the way to the eastern bank of the Suez Canal, and flew to the Israeli garrison at Sharm el-Sheik overlooking the Straits of Tiran. International shipping was moving placidly through the narrow straits, some of it heading for the Israeli port of Eilat, but most of it bound for the nearby Jordanian port of Aqaba. The Israeli soldiers guarding the outpost spent most of their time sleeping, eating, and swimming in the incredibly clear, blue waters of the Red Sea. There was no tension. It was hard to believe that the closing of this narrow waterway had been the proximate cause of the war just a few weeks before.

In Beersheba, in the Negev, the Israeli Air Force staged an air show to celebrate their victory and honor their dead. The star of the show was a MiG-21, an advanced Russian-built fighter that an Iraqi defector had flown to Israel before the war. It had been repainted blue and white with a Star of David on the side and the number 007 on its tail. The ten thousand Israelis in the audience roared their approval as an Israeli pilot flew the plane low and fast past the grandstands, igniting the afterburners before climbing into a spotless, blue sky.

The emotional high moment for postwar Israel came on July 9, 1967, when the Israel Philharmonic performed for the first time in twenty-four years at the outdoor amphitheater on Mount Scopus, the original Hebrew University campus in East Jerusalem that had been a UN-supplied enclave since 1948 and was retaken on the second day of the war. Leonard Bernstein, who had flown in from New York, conducted, and Isaac Stern, who was in Israel for six weeks with the orchestra, performed a Mendelssohn concerto and a Mahler symphony.

The setting was spectacular, with the brown Judaean hills falling away to the east and the blue Mediterranean to the west. It was a brilliant, sunny afternoon. The 103-member orchestra and the 110-member philharmonic choir could barely fit on the simple stage, while the audience of 1,400 sat on rough stone seats. When the white-haired David Ben-Gurion and an injured Israeli soldier with one leg in a cast were helped to seats down front, and the orchestra launched into "Hatikvah," the stirring Israeli national anthem, the audience melted. Musically, the concert was a near disaster, with a stiff desert breeze ripping sheet music from the stands and knocking over folding chairs, but Bernstein said later that night that he had loved it. "Everything was against it," he said exuberantly, "the wind, the sun, but somehow, nothing seemed to matter today. What a moment!"

Another singularly Israeli moment occurred two weeks later outside the home of Moshe Dayan in Tzahala, a Tel Aviv suburb where a lot of the senior Israeli military lived. It was a double wedding—Dayan's twenty-eight-year-old daughter, Yaël, was marrying Dov Sion, a colonel in the Israeli army; and Dayan's twenty-four-year-old son, Asaf, was marrying a twenty-two-year-old literature student at Hebrew University. But, inevitably, this being Israel, in the wake of a war and in the midst of internal political turmoil, it was political theater as well. The two thousand guests—including virtually the entire government, most of the 120 members of the Knesset, or parliament, the diplomatic corps, and the high commands of the Israeli army, navy, and air force— gathered in a floodlit garden behind the house and schmoozed and gossiped the night away. The house and garden were decorated with stunning antiquities—urns, jars, carvings and the like—that Dayan had famously "liberated" from ancient sites around the country and in the newly occupied territories. Banks of television cameras captured the scene. Dayan was busy at that moment trying to unseat the premier, Levi Eshkol, but for this night they set their political competition aside long enough to toast the two couples. It was a hellova wedding.

I was covering it all for the *Times*, writing nearly every day, and loving it. Ann joined me about a month after the war, and we lived in a suite in the American Colony Hotel in Jerusalem while we waited for our furniture to clear customs. The American Colony—a converted pasha's house with arched ceilings and spacious, tiled rooms built around a central courtyard—had been ground zero in the battle for East Jerusalem. There were still a few bullet holes in the handsome Armenian tiles that flanked the entrance, but the hotel itself was back in business and thriving, with a clientele of journalists, diplomats, and UN personnel. The owners, Horatio and Valentine Vester, were a marvelous, witty nineteenth-century couple who became our great friends. He was a descendant of the American missionaries who had founded the American Colony in Jerusalem's Old City the 1800s, she the India-born daughter of British diplomats. Cocktails in the lush garden behind their private apartment on the hotel grounds took a perfect page out of the British Mandate days.

Eventually Ann and I moved into an apartment in Rehavia, an upscale neighborhood in West Jerusalem, and settled in for what was supposed to be a three- or four-year assignment. I was scheduled to be bureau chief—chief, that is, of myself in what had been a one-man bureau up to that point. But there was such a steady drumbeat of news, the paper decided, rightly, that it was going to need two correspondents in Israel and the region for the foreseeable future. Jim Feron's next posting was canceled, he stayed on, and he and I covered the country together for the next year. We worked well together and became fast friends in the process.

I also made reporting trips to Cyprus, Turkey, and Greece—all new to me and therefore irresistible. In the fall of 1967, my father made good on his promise to visit us in Jerusalem. The three of us had a grand time sightseeing, touring the country, and relaxing. It was his first vacation since my mother had died the previous February and my first break from daily reporting since my arrival in-country in May. One day, he and I drove down the highway from Jerusalem to Jericho—at 846 feet below sea level, the lowest town on earth—and discovered a dilapidated, windblown shell of a racetrack on the shore of the Dead Sea. Even though he was supposed to be on vacation, the sports columnist/racing fan couldn't help himself, producing a funny column he titled "DEAD SEA DOWNS," which he described as "the lowest gambling hell in the world" and the site of "cheerful debauchery in a region where sin is not exactly an innovation." The track and a nearby gambling casino on the shores of the Dead Sea had flourished before the war, he wrote, where the "beauty and chivalry of the royal court in Jordan had gathered each winter Sunday to play the ponies and the camel race that

concluded each program." It was a terrific piece and proved to me that
he could find a column anywhere.

Continuing our holiday, Pop, Ann, and I flew to Cyprus and checked
into a beach hotel near the picture postcard town of Kyrenia. That was
where I nearly lost him. He and I foolishly went swimming in the surf
after a storm had passed, leaving steep, breaking waves and a riptide behind. We were both strong swimmers, but I was twenty-nine and he was
sixty-two, and before long we were struggling to get back to the beach
against a powerful undertow. It was a losing battle. We exchanged a
desperate look, put our heads down, and ploughed toward the shore.
After an exhausting several minutes, we dragged ourselves onto the
sand, coughing and barely able to catch a breath. Neither said what was
obvious: that was a dumb move.

In early 1968, I spent three months on special assignment in India
and Pakistan. The New Delhi correspondent, Joseph Lelyveld, later
executive editor of the *Times*, had been dreading the prospect of covering an upcoming UN-sponsored international trade and development
conference that was bringing some 1,500 delegates from 132 nations to
the Indian capital for two months of dreadfully serious, doubtless important, but inexpressibly dull talks about trade preferences and the like.
In an inspired bureaucratic maneuver, Lelyveld escaped this journalistic
purgatory by preemptively persuading the *Times* that UNCTAD, as it
was awkwardly known, was so vital, so central to the future of mankind,
that it should have a dedicated correspondent to cover it. The paper
agreed, and I got the call.

This was fine with me: India was another check-off destination, a
missing link in my wanderlust. Ann and I arrived in New Delhi and
checked into the musty-but-grand Ashoka Hotel. After less than two
weeks, and perhaps four or five scintillating stories about international-
trade policies and commodity prices at UNCTAD, I could see it was
going to be weeks before any meaningful decisions were taken. In the
meantime, the endless debates made for mind-numbing copy, every bit
as tedious as Lelyveld had forecast. Nothing was getting done; even the
business-page editors of the paper of record were bored.

Hungry to see something of the subcontinent, I suggested to the foreign desk that we let UNCTAD simmer in its own argumentative juices
for a few weeks while I went looking for stories elsewhere in India and
in Pakistan, where there was no resident *Times* correspondent. New

York agreed, and I was on my way, heading first to Bombay (Mumbai today), where I wrote about everything from the boom in gold smuggling from Dubai to the troubling development of India's allegedly peaceful nuclear program to the betting frenzy that took place every Sunday at Bombay's elegant Mahalaxmi Race Course, home to the Royal Western India Turf Club.

After a week in Bombay's handsome Palace Hotel, I went on to Karachi, the sprawling, traffic-choked, vibrant former capital of Pakistan on the Arabian Sea. If India was exotic and alluring, so was Pakistan, with the added flavor of the wild west. This country was barely two decades old as an independent nation, still reeling from its 1965 war with India over Kashmir, and laboring under the heavy hand of its president, Field Marshal Muhammad Ayub Khan, who had ruled for ten years. It was a rich tapestry in an increasingly important region, and the paper was hungry for whatever reporting it could get.

I was trying, at this point, to use and appear in every section of the paper and every format. My piece on the Bombay Turf Club was featured in the sports section; the UNCTAD stories, dull as they were, were displayed in the business pages; I wrote news analyses, features, breaking news, News of the Week in Review pieces, and a Talk of Karachi that sought to describe what life was like in a city that had grown crazily from three hundred thousand residents to three million in twenty years.

I was still typing the pieces on my portable in those days and filing via telex through Cable and Wireless, the British system, to the *Times London* bureau, which would send the material on to New York via their twenty-four-hour line. When possible, I would illustrate the pieces with my own photos, using a thirty-five-millimeter Nikon. I'd get the pictures developed and wired by United Press International or whatever wire service was available. The *Times*, in its munificence, would pay its correspondents a princely thirty-five dollars for every published picture.

Today, of course, all this would be transmitted wirelessly via satellite. The pictures and copy would be digital and the transmission instant. The communications technology is different today, but the fundamental function of the foreign correspondent is the same: try to penetrate a culture, report how it is evolving, and describe it in terms that make sense to your readers. The *Times* made a specialty of publishing a worldwide report and at that point had about thirty-eight foreign correspondents deployed around the globe. I was one of the newest and least experienced, but I was learning the ropes. This was what I had wanted to do since my abortive attempt at getting a job on the *Paris Trib*. It wasn't Paris, of course, but from a reporter's point of view, where I was placed was vastly better. India and Pakistan and all of Asia were growing in importance and relevance to American readers. It was an era when the United States was expanding its reach economically, diplomatically, and militarily. We were well into the American Century, and international news was more important than ever.

Ever since I had first traveled abroad as a teenager and after college, I had been fascinated by the ways in which people in other countries sorted out their lives, how they chose to be governed, how they solved their problems, how they dealt with one another. Now I was seeing the world, traveling on someone else's nickel and getting paid to write about it. That struck me as a pretty good arrangement. Every now and then, when the mail caught up to me, I'd get a letter from my father saying that he liked what he was reading. That was important to me. Subconsciously I was still trying to prove myself. As what? And to whom? My father's son, I suppose, trying to demonstrate to him—and myself—that I belonged in the big time, that I could make a name and reputation for myself by myself, that I was not a *New York Times* foreign correspondent strictly because I was Red Smith's son. I didn't obsess about this at the time, nor even admit it to myself, but it was part of the motivation.

I kept moving in Pakistan. From Lahore, with its ancient forts, I went on to Rawalpindi, the army's garrison city, and to Islamabad, which was under construction as the new capital. Ayub Khan had moved the capital from Karachi and ordered all the embassies to transfer to Islamabad, which had set off a huge building boom. When I was in Karachi, residents told me sourly that that the president was determined to reduce their city to a backwater as payback because they had voted for his opponents in a recent election. Politics in Pakistan, it seemed, was nothing if not personal. And local.

There were stories everywhere. In Karachi, for example, I met Mahmud Hussain. He and his brother, Zakir, had chosen separate paths in 1947, when the Jewel of the British Empire was split into two separate nations, Pakistan and India, one largely Muslim, the other mostly Hindu. Though Muslim, Zakir had cast his lot with India, rising to become a state governor, then vice president, and finally president of

India. Mahmud, equally urbane and educated, prospered in Pakistan, moving up from parliament to the cabinet and eventually becoming the dean of the faculty of arts at the University of Karachi. Sitting in his book-lined study in a Karachi suburb, Mahmud said sadly that he and his brother rarely talked any more. His was the tale of a painful family split that perfectly illustrated the division of the subcontinent twenty-one years earlier. I thought their bittersweet story explained a lot about the current state of relations between India and Pakistan, so I wrote a piece about my conversation with Mahmud Hussain that the *Times* ran under a headline that read, "A BROTHER'S LAMENT: 'HE OPTED FOR INDIA AND I CHOSE PAKISTAN.'"

Abe Rosenthal, who had served earlier as the *Times'* correspondent in India, sent me an enthusiastic cable applauding the piece as the kind of reporting the *Times* needed. Make it human, he said, like a letter home, and people will understand it. Good advice then, good advice now.

Still traveling, still learning, still fascinated, I continued west from Islamabad to Peshawar, deep into Kipling country, in the North-West Frontier Province, where the laws of Pakistan were treated as mere suggestion. A car and driver took me from Peshawar to the Afghan border, through the Khyber Pass and up the road toward Kabul. This was truly the wild west, rugged, rocky country where clan clearly mattered more than country. Most adult men carried rifles slung across their shoulders. The houses were surrounded by high mud walls with gun slits at the top, and the women were kept out of sight. Pakistani authorities were nowhere to be seen.

In Landi Kotal, in the heart of the Khyber, surrounded by the craggy peaks of the Sulaiman Mountains, I found a sprawling bazaar that offered a little bit of everything: embroidered silks from China, worsted tweeds from Britain, Swiss watches, French perfume, Japanese cameras, Italian sweaters, and American cigarettes—all duty-free, of course. There were no banks as such, but an entire street of money changers displayed stacks of every negotiable currency set out in neat piles on folding tables. Every shopkeeper kept a rifle cradled in his lap and a pistol hidden in his robes. The Pathans, whose tribes ruled on both sides of the largely unmarked border, explained to me with pride that they were, bar none, the best smugglers in the world. Looking at the selection in the bazaar, it was hard to dispute. I took pictures and filed a piece.

It was also hard, driving through that stark, barren Afghan countryside in the spring of 1968, to imagine that the Soviet Union would fight and lose a decade-long war in those hills in the 1980s and, worse yet, that the United States and NATO troops would spend another two decades after 9/11 trying to bring order into a chaotic, untamed land where tribal politics trumped all. Not for nothing is Afghanistan called the graveyard of empires.

All too soon for my taste, I was back in the huge meeting hall in New Delhi, covering the closing days of UNCTAD. To no one's surprise, the conference concluded in deadlock and achieved little. The bottom line of eight weeks of talk was to demonstrate that the wealthy, industrialized nations of the world were not prepared at that point to do much, if anything, to help the less-developed nations and that the emerging countries were in no position to do anything about it. The "news" in the final communiqué was that the participants had decided, in a triumph of hope over experience, to hold a third UNCTAD conference a few years hence.

Ann and I returned to Jerusalem. She was pregnant, and we were awaiting the birth of our first child. Elizabeth Reed Smith, a shiksa sabra, was born on June 15, 1968, in an Israeli maternity clinic, delivered by Dr. Maccabi Salzberger, a fine obstetrician who, though no relation to the Sulzbergers, had delivered the children of previous *New York Times* correspondents in the same clinic. A fertile place, the Holy Land. The Israeli supervising nurse nearly got a knuckle sandwich from Ann upon commenting dryly after Ann produced Elizabeth with a minimum of fuss, "Not bad, for an American."

Ann and I brought Elizabeth home to our apartment in Rehavia. When we got inside, we unwrapped the swaddling clothes and looked with amazement at this newest member of our family. Ten fingers, ten toes—check. All's well.

Friends have wondered in the years since what it was like to have a child in Jerusalem just a year after the war. In fact, while there were some antioccupation demonstrations in Eastern Jerusalem and a handful of terrorist incidents, it was probably quieter there than in the US, which was abroil with riots, assassinations, and furious antiwar (Vietnam) demonstrations. We felt safe and secure by contrast.

A few days later, I registered her birth at the US Consulate in East Jerusalem in the former Jordanian sector, because that is where such paperwork was done in those postwar days. When Elizabeth got her own passport a few months later, it listed her place of birth as Jerusalem. Not Jerusalem, Israel; or Jerusalem, Jordan—just Jerusalem. The US passport office was not about to prejudge the final status of the city, which still remains to be resolved decades later. Israel has formally annexed the whole city and enlarged its boundaries with huge housing complexes and encircled it with a tall security wall; but the United States has never formally and legally recognized the annexation, and neither have most nations, least of all the Palestinians. President Trump moved the US embassy to Jerusalem in 2018 in an empty, pointless, purely symbolic, totally political recognition of the city as Israel's Capital. In fact, the US had long recognized that West Jerusalem was Israel's capital but rightly insisted that the final status of the Holy City would have to be settled in negotiations between the parties. Trump's gesture changed nothing in the legal sense, and neither did his "recognition" of Israeli sovereignty over the portion of the Golan Heights it occupies. The border issues are too fraught to be settled by presidential whim and politics. Diplomacy-by-Twitter is just that: twitter.

On June 5, the first anniversary of the start of the Six Day War, the smoke was clearing from a daylong aerial and artillery battle between Israeli and Jordanian forces on either side of the Jordan River just south of the Sea of Galilee. There were casualties on both sides in the incident, which was the first involving aircraft in nearly four months. But there was a more momentous story developing that same day in Los Angeles, where Senator Robert F. Kennedy was shot and fatally wounded by a Palestinian assassin who decided to commemorate the war's anniversary at gunpoint.

I was stunned by the news. After covering Bob Kennedy's Senate campaign, I had come to like and admire him. He was my senator when I had lived in New York, and I knew his political passion for justice and racial equality was the real deal. We had seen each other a few times and corresponded repeatedly. He had written, sending condolences on my mother's death and later congratulations on my assignment to Israel and again in reaction to something I had written from Jerusalem. That last letter, on his Senate stationary, arrived after he was shot.

The next day, I was attending a cocktail reception at the home of the US ambassador, Walworth Barbour, in Herzliya, near Tel Aviv, when Barbour drew me into his library, closed the door on the party, and told me that the assassin, Sirhan Sirhan, whose name had just been released, had been born and raised in Jerusalem and that his father, Sirhan B. Sirhan, was a Christian Arab living in Taiyiba, a West Bank village outside of Ramallah, now under Israeli occupation.

I thanked the ambassador, left the party, and drove straight to Jerusalem. I picked up a translator and, because the West Bank was still a closed military area at that point, a pass and a two-soldier military escort from the press office and headed to Taiyiba. It was nearly midnight when we got to the darkened Sirhan house on the outskirts of the village. I rapped loudly on the door, and, after a few minutes, Sirhan appeared, pulling a pair of pants over his pajamas. He invited us in and, in the tradition of Arab hospitality, insisted that we sit at his kitchen table while he made coffee. The Israeli soldiers sat outside in their jeep. I told him I was a reporter, not an official of any kind.

Interviewing him in English at the table, I discovered that Sirhan had heard the news about Kennedy but had gone to bed before the assassin's name had been announced. He was clearly puzzled as to why I had come to his house in the middle of the night to talk about it.

I asked Sirhan if he had sons, and he said yes, proudly, five. I pushed my notebook across the table and asked him to write the names of his sons in the order of their birth. He did, including the fourth of the five, Sirhan Bishara Sirhan. I tapped my finger on that name and told him that that was the name of the man who had been identified as the assassin.

Sirhan Sr. gave me a hard, disbelieving look and shook his head for a moment as though he couldn't absorb what he was hearing. He stared into my eyes and could see that I was serious. Now he started to rant and cry, first about how much he admired the Kennedy family, then how his fourth son couldn't have been the shooter.

"He was the best of the boys, the smartest, with the best grades," he said. "I was proudest of him."

Then his face darkened. "If he did this dirty thing, then let them hang him," he said. "Kennedy could have been president; he could have finished what his brother started."

Pausing, he looked at me intently and said, "But it couldn't be. Not Sirhan, not him."

The conversation went on like this for half an hour, back and forth, with Sirhan getting more and more incoherent. He would switch in an instant between what a good son Sirhan Jr. had been to how wrong it was that Kennedy had been cut down at the height of his life. He was crying one moment, angry the next, then silent.

By now it was 1:30 a.m. I raced back to Jerusalem, wrote as quickly as I could, and filed my account of the encounter with Sirhan's father and what I had learned about the assassin's childhood. Thanks to the time difference between Jerusalem and New York, I made the principal late city edition of the June 6 paper. The piece ran at the bottom of page one, which was topped by a triple-decked, eight-column headline that read,

KENNEDY IS DEAD, VICTIM OF ASSASSIN;
SUSPECT, ARAB IMMIGRANT, ARRAIGNED;
JOHNSON APPOINTS PANEL ON VIOLENCE

The one-column headline over my dispatch read, "FATHER OF SUSPECT 'SICKENED' BY NEWS."

The next day, I located Sirhan's former school in the Armenian Quarter of the Old City. It was the Jerusalem Evangelical Lutheran School, and the class records showed young Sirhan to have been a bright, promising student near the top of his class. What the records didn't reveal, the headmaster told me, was the troubled situation in the Sirhan home. The parents had terrible fights, he said. Sirhan Sr., clearly unstable, beat his wife, and the children suffered as a result. The father had been an official with the city water supply who had lost his job after the 1948 war and apparently never recovered. He worked on and off as a plumber and blamed the Israelis for the family's dire straits. The parents finally split up, and the mother, Mary, with help from a Christian missionary group, had taken the children and moved to the United States in 1957. It was not hard to understand how angry the younger Sirhan might have been about his childhood and, ultimately, the Israelis, and even the Kennedy family, whom he apparently saw as supporters of Israel. I never saw Sirhan Sr. again, but I've never forgotten that night or the look of horror in his eyes when he heard the news.

There was still plenty to be covered in Israel. Fighting erupted periodically that June across the cease-fire lines with Egypt and Jordan, the internal political situation was in its customary chaos, the first Israeli settlements were being established on the West Bank, and the restive Arabs of East Jerusalem were staging general strikes and the occasional violent protest.

But there was another event going on several thousand miles to the east that was dominating the front pages and, though I didn't realize it, pulling me in that direction. Vietnam was aflame in the wake of the Tet Offensive, with hundreds of American soldiers dying every week. Tet may have been a military defeat for the North, as military historians have argued, but it ignited the antiwar movement in the United States and was the biggest news story of the time. As a result, I was not totally surprised when Seymour Topping, the *Times'* foreign editor, proposed that I move east. The assignment he was offering was not Saigon but Bangkok. I would succeed Peter Braestrup as the *Times'* Southeast Asia correspondent, responsible for everything from Laos to Indonesia— essentially every country in the region but Vietnam. For someone whose wanderlust was by now clearly incurable, who had never been east of New Delhi, whose visit to the subcontinent had ignited a fascination with Asia, and who could never turn down an offer to go anywhere he hadn't been, the proposition was catnip.

I flew to Bangkok to take over the bureau. Braestrup had already left for his next assignment. What I found was a small two-room office with some battered furniture, a house where the lease had expired and could not be renewed, a gunmetal gray Land Rover as the bureau car, and a young Thai driver named Chemoi who was bemused by these Americans who kept coming and going and wondering what the hell was going to happen to his job. This was going to be a challenge.

Ann stayed behind in Jerusalem until Elizabeth was old enough to get her vaccinations and travel. After a little looking, I managed to rent a marvelous Thai-style house on stilts over the Chao Phraya River near the floating vegetable market in the heart of Bangkok. It had screened floor-to-ceiling doors and windows and balconies overlooking the river on three sides, and bamboo ceiling fans turning lazily. Outside, barges and the famous "long-tail" water taxis churned the broad, brown river. A golden-domed Buddhist temple shimmered in the hazy heat across the way. Farmers would bring their produce down the river in long, narrow wooden skiffs and tie up beneath the house at night, waiting for the market to open at dawn. They would cook their meals over charcoal in braziers beneath the house, and wonderful aromas would drift upward. When Ann and Elizabeth arrived, we hired three Thai women as a live-in team to care for the house—a cook, a maid, and a baby amah, all for less than a hundred dollars a month, plus room and board—and settled in to live like colonials. All in all, it seemed about as exotic and as far from New York as I could imagine.

7

Southeast Asia

I wasn't covering the Vietnam War, but I couldn't escape it, either. Thailand, I quickly realized, was a vast staging area. US pilots were flying everything from giant B-52s to F-4 Phantom fighter-bombers to smaller reconnaissance planes and rescue helicopters out of six huge American-built air bases throughout the country from Udon Thani to the north to U-Tapao to the south. They were striking targets in North Vietnam and along the Ho Chi Minh supply trail, which wound south through Laos and Cambodia and into South Vietnam. When President Lyndon B. Johnson announced a preelection halt in the bombing of North Vietnam on November 1, 1968, the planes simply concentrated their air strikes on the trail.

In Vientiane, in Laos, just across the Mekong River from Thailand, the crew-cut young Americans drinking at the hotel bar were pilots for Air America, the ostensibly private airline sponsored by the Central Intelligence Agency, which ferried pilots and gold and, allegedly, drugs in and out of the war zone. Sitting at the bar one day, I could hardly fail to notice the enormous, clunky gold Rolex on the wrist of the pilot on the next stool. "What's that for?" I asked. "Surely there are easier, lighter ways to tell time." The pilot laughed and agreed. "Of course," he said. "We wear these to bribe our way out of a jam if we get shot down in Pathet Lao country."

Bangkok itself was the favored haunt for GIs on R & R—rest and recuperation tours from Vietnam. They usually got a week or more away from the battlefield in the course of a yearlong tour. Planeloads of soldiers would arrive every week, pause briefly for a largely ignored lecture on avoiding sexually transmitted diseases, and pour into the bars and hotels and massage parlors sprinkled throughout downtown. For most, it was a weeklong, nonstop party—although some maintained that a hot shower was equally high on their list of vacation priorities. If the blatant sexuality and sidewalk drunkenness offended Thai sensibilities, it did not stop them from raking in the cash the soldiers spent every week.

Exploring my new beat, I made reporting trips to Malaysia and to Singapore, which was newly independent and still adjusting to the reality of a British withdrawal that was to be complete by 1971. After 150 years of colonial rule, the Singaporeans were almost wistful about the prospect of the impending British pullout.

"It's really rather sad, like the end of a romance," a Singaporean doctor told me over a drink in his comfortable home. "Singapore right now is like a man who has just learned that his occasionally domineering but generally agreeable mistress is about to walk out on him. All he can remember are the good moments."

Singapore itself certainly hadn't lost its Britishness. I checked into the wedding cake that was the Raffles Hotel, where afternoon tea was served on the patio, and found that an hour after my arrival freshly printed stationary had materialized in the room that read "Terence Smith, Suite 10, Raffles." Classy. Not far away, prosperous businessmen were drinking their gin and bitters without ice in the paneled lounge of the Cricket Club, and outside, Austin taxis were whirling clockwise around the roundabouts. The Empire may have been evaporating, but it was not quite gone yet.

Nonetheless, the Singapore government was wasting no time in transforming the island nation into the hugely successful commercial entrepôt that it would quickly become. While I was there, the vast British naval base, once home of Britain's fearsome Far East Fleet, was being converted into a major new port, industrial center, and repair facility. The sense of industry was everywhere. Glass skyscrapers were being built in the center, and scores of new companies were being chartered every week. Singapore, festooned with construction cranes, was in a hurry and clearly knew where it was going. Crazy Rich Asians-in-the-making.

Indonesia, on the other hand, seemed sleepy by comparison. It was verdant, lush, beguiling in its slow-paced charm, but hardly moving. President Suharto was firmly in control, having beaten back an at-

tempted Communist coup three years earlier. He had his more flamboyant predecessor, Sukarno, safely under house arrest in Bogor, a mountain resort thirty-five miles south of Jakarta, and a coterie of former
generals comfortably established in many of the ministries. Suharto was
running a tight, profitably corrupt ship.

The "news" in the region, such as it was, was next door, in the Malaysian state of Sabah, former British North Borneo. Sabah had been incorporated into Malaysia upon independence five years before, but the
Philippines disputed this, arguing that Sabah had originally been part of
the Sulu Sultanate, most of which was in the southern Philippines, just
across the Sulu Sea, and properly belonged to them. The two countries
were tussling over the territory, sending warships and planes around
the northern Sabah coast, even forcing the Malaysian prime minister to
cancel a scheduled trip by frigate through the disputed waters. I flew
from Jakarta to Kota Kinabalu, the Sabah capital, to have a look.

What I found was an attractive, neat town clustered around a scenic
harbor that everyone still called Jesselton, commemorating Sir Charles
Jessel, the British colonial governor who had administered affairs in
Sabah for the North Borneo Chartered Company in the late 1800s. The
new Malay name, Kota Kinabalu, was a bit of a puzzle. *Kota* is the
Malay word for "fortified town" and *Kinabalu*, the name of the high-
est mountain, translates as "Chinese widower." So, as of the previous
January 1, the former Jesselton had become The Fortified Town of the
Chinese Widower.

While the Brits doubtlessly had plundered the riches of the mountain-
ous Sabah state for 150 years, they were nonetheless fondly remem-
bered. The streets were still named Prince Philip Drive and Middlesex
Road, the horses ran the wrong way (clockwise) around the track at the
Royal Sabah Turf Club, traffic moved on the left, and the red, white,
yellow, and blue state flag was known affectionately as the Sabah Jack.

As in Singapore, the British had left behind in Sabah a smoothly efficient civil service and the trappings of a modern state, most of which
was being run by British expats as contract employees of the Malaysian government. It was a delightful place with a soft, tropical climate,
and the residents seemed untroubled by the rumblings of war between
Malaysia and the Philippines. They were more concerned with hanging
flags on every lamppost to celebrate the upcoming birthday of their
chief minister. The only Americans I encountered were a few Peace

Corps volunteers who seemed to think they had ended up in paradise. The Vietnam War—being fought across the water to the northwest— could have been a million miles away.

Cambodia, another country in my new beat, had been largely closed to western reporters in recent years. Prince Norodom Sihanouk, the mercurial head of state, had kept his little nation intact up to that point by balancing his disputatious neighbors—Thailand, Laos, and Vietnam— off against each other and keeping his country's borders mostly closed. But in November 1968 he suddenly switched tactics and announced that the Western press was welcome to breach the Khmer Curtain. The ostensible occasion was the celebration of Cambodia's fifteenth independence day and the annual Water and Moon Festival, which is a major holiday in Phnom Penh, but the real reason was that the prince, who loved publicity, was anxious for a little attention. Specifically, he wanted to display eleven captured American sailors who had blundered into Cambodian waters on the Mekong River from South Vietnam the previous July and been seized by a Cambodian naval patrol boat.

Dozens of Western reporters poured into the country on thirty-day visas. I took the short flight from Bangkok and checked into the delightful, antiquated Hotel Le Royal in Phnom Penh. With its French colonial architecture, lovely garden, and pool, the Royal reeked of Graham Greene and intrigue and clandestine encounters. The people-watching over a kir royale in the garden was first-rate.

Cambodia was a pocket-sized, technically neutral country that occupied some crucial real estate. The North Vietnamese were using its eastern provinces for the Ho Chi Minh Trail, and the United States was bombing targets along the Vietnamese border to disrupt the flow of Vietcong supplies into South Vietnam. Sihanouk was powerless to stop either intrusion into his territory, but he saw the captured US servicemen as leverage.

At forty-six, the energetic, diminutive Sihanouk was putting his playboy past behind him—he told me he'd once had five "wives" but was now down to a more manageable and economical one—and relishing his emerging role as statesman. But he retained great flair. He took the visiting press on bus and plane trips around his beautiful country, making himself continuously available for interviews or small talk, holding forth near the magnificent Khmer ruins of Angkor Wat or in the garden of the Royale in Phnom Penh. It was one long, running news conference, with the prince giggling at his own jokes and exhorting us all to see his five feature films, the most recent of which, *Shadow over Angkor*, starred—you guessed it—Sihanouk and his wife Monique.

The eleven captured servicemen became cast members in a Sihanouk-produced theatrical extravaganza on November 15, Cambodia's independence day. The prince dressed them in specially tailored white suits, dress shirts, and red ties and lined them up next to the diplomatic corps while he lit a flame at a morning ceremony at the Independence Monument. Later, the men, who hadn't been out of their prison barracks in 116 days, were taken on a bus tour of the capital, treated to lunch at a French restaurant, and welcomed at one of Phnom Penh's better brothels. Needless to say, they reported to the visiting press that they had been very well treated.

Sihanouk repeatedly offered at his nonstop press conferences with the Western media to release the soldiers if the United States would pledge to not bomb Cambodian villages along the Vietnamese border, where he maintained two hundred innocent Cambodians had been killed. Finally, after Washington issued a diplomatic note promising to do everything possible to avoid Cambodian civilian casualties, and after 156 days of relatively comfortable captivity and one more visit to the fleshpots of Phnom Penh, the men were allowed to fly home just before Christmas. It was a vintage Sihanouk performance.

During one long, rambling interview that I did with the prince, he turned dead serious and gave me this prescient forecast for the outcome of American involvement in Vietnam: "You will be forced to take your troops and leave Vietnam. You cannot block the majority will. You cannot stop the reunification and, yes, the communization of Vietnam. The majority of the people want to be with Ho Chi Minh, and there is nothing you can do about it. You would be wise to withdraw and let the Vietnamese settle their own problems themselves." I published this word-for-word in the *New York Times* on Sunday, November 17, 1968, seven years before Sihanouk's prediction came true with the Fall of Saigon and the complete takeover by the North. Doubtless it was read in the White House and Pentagon. But it was not what they wanted to hear.

It took seven more years, billions of US dollars, and countless American and Vietnamese lives, but every word Sihanouk said proved true.

The next day, November 18, 1968, was my thirtieth birthday. I didn't know it yet, but I was headed for Vietnam myself.

8

Out of the Frying Pan . . .

It was Seymour Topping, the *Times'* foreign editor, again. This time, he was proposing that I move to Saigon, as bureau chief. He wanted me to succeed Eugene Roberts, who was being summoned back to New York to become national editor. (Gene would later go on to win a basketful of Pulitzers as the redoubtable editor of the *Philadelphia Inquirer*.) Saigon, at that point, was the largest and unquestionably most import *Times* overseas bureau, with five correspondents, several of them older and more experienced than I.

I didn't really want to go to Vietnam. For one thing, after just six months I had barely gotten around to the four corners of my beat as Southeast Asian correspondent. For another, the war was in its most divisive and depressing stage. Richard Nixon had been elected president with an empty promise to end the war but with no more idea how to do it than Lyndon Johnson had. His famous "secret plan" to end the war remained just that—secret. The best formula Nixon could come up with in his first term was "Vietnamization," the illusory notion that the United States could equip and train South Vietnamese forces to take over the defense of their own country while the American and allied forces carried out an orderly withdrawal. A "modified, limited bugout," in the lingo of the period. It was a fig leaf of the first order.

At the same time, there was no escaping the fact that if you were an American correspondent overseas in December 1968, Vietnam was the center of the news universe. In fact, much of what I was covering in Southeast Asia was in reality a sideshow to the main act. That, essentially, was the argument that Gene Roberts made to me when I discussed the prospect with him over a long dinner and even longer session of drinks afterward at his apartment in Mid-Levels in Hong Kong. At Topping's suggestion, I had flown over from Bangkok to talk over the pros and cons of the idea with Gene, who had been in Saigon for a year and is famously one of the most quietly and powerfully persuasive people in American journalism. As he talked, the lights of Victoria Harbour glowed brightly.

"If you want to get anywhere in this business," Gene said repeatedly as he poured one drink after another in his living room, "you've got to do it." He was right, of course, but frankly, all I remember from that night is Gene telling war stories, refilling our drinks, and slowly sliding down in his chair until he and I were both slumped on the carpeted floor, still talking, with dawn creeping over Victoria Harbour. I assume I got back to my hotel; I don't recall. But by the next morning, along with a roaring hangover, I was on my way to Vietnam.

All this while I was exchanging long, funny letters with my father. Normally, fine writer or no, he was a lousy correspondent. Just too busy. But now, separated by half the globe, he and I both made the effort to stay in long-distance touch. I was relieved that he sounded upbeat, was traveling and following the sports calendar, was seeing friends, and even occasionally was taking a woman to dinner in New York.

When I got to Saigon, I found a city accustomed to living with war. The airport, Tan Son Nhut, doubled as the city's civilian terminal and a huge military air base, with passenger planes and jet fighters peeling off the same runways. Driving into the city center, there were sandbags and concertina rolls of barbed wire outside many buildings, but the markets were full and the sidewalks busy. The magnificent trees along the broad boulevard leading in from the airport, planted by the French decades before, were mostly lopped off at the trunk, apparently to improve visibility from above. But the streets were clogged with traffic, civilian and military—a great smoking, cacophonous jumble of cars, trucks, jeeps, cyclos, and motorbikes. Wherever you looked, you saw the two faces of Vietnam, war and peace, side-by-side, progressing simultaneously downward.

Traveling around Southeast Asia, I was often the only American or Western correspondent on the scene. In Saigon, I was suddenly part of an army of some five hundred accredited journalists. All three of the US broadcast television networks had large bureaus staffed by producers, correspondents, editors, and multiple camera crews; every major

US and European newspaper and wire service was represented; *Time* and *Newsweek* and *U.S. News* all had offices, as did the major Australian, Japanese, and Korean news organizations. The *Times* bureau was staffed by five American correspondents, a Vietnamese reporter, an office manager, and a driver. All of them, obviously, knew more about Vietnam than I did.

I arrived in Saigon thinking, like many Americans at that point, that the war was a lost cause. It had never seemed to me worth the price in blood and treasure, and now, after just a few months in Southeast Asia, I was convinced that the much-advertised domino theory was an illusion. Thailand and the other neighboring nations were fiercely independent. They were not going to fall to communism even if South Vietnam did. The war between North and South Vietnam was fundamentally a struggle over nationalism and control. The danger that Vietnam would fall into the Communist Chinese orbit if the United States pulled out was laughable. The Vietnamese had been fighting off the Chinese for five hundred years and were not about to roll over now. All of which raised a troubling question: if the fruitlessness of the US effort in Vietnam was obvious to me, why was it not acknowledged inside the Washington Beltway? And what, as a reporter for the *Times*, could I do about it?

Nevertheless, in my first months in Vietnam, I was determined to keep my skepticism out of my reporting. This was the largest, most sustained, and costly US involvement overseas since World War II. It had splintered the nation at home. My job was to report the reality on the ground in Vietnam as best as I could determine it—not what I privately believed but what I could find out. I hoped and believed the case against the war would make itself.

The challenge of separating fact from fiction was obvious from the first day, when I attended the infamous "Five O'clock Follies," the daily war briefing staged by MACV, the US military command. An officer, usually an Army major or lieutenant colonel, would report the enemy body count and allied casualties from the engagements of the previous twenty-four hours, the number of air sorties flown against enemy targets, and the like. The numbers provided might be accurate, or close to it, but in no way did this barebones, enumerated, sanitized account actually convey what was going on in the war. The truth was far more elusive. I immediately decided that we, as a bureau, would follow up the official account of any significant battle with a visit to the field. The reconstruction we reported always shed a different, more revealing light on the official account.

The fighting was in something of a lull when I arrived, but a few weeks later, on February 24, 1969, roughly a year after the Tet Offensive, the relative calm ended with a vengeance. North Vietnamese and Vietcong troops launched simultaneous attacks on Saigon and 115 other towns and military targets around the country. The enemy showered rockets into the heart of Saigon and fought pitched battles on the fringes of the capital. By the end of the first week of the offensive, 453 American soldiers had been killed, the highest weekly casualty rate in nearly a year. By the end of a month, 1,140 Americans and an estimated 15,000 North Vietnamese and Vietcong were dead, South Vietnamese president Nguyễn Văn Thiệu was offering to negotiate terms, and the antiwar movement in the US was in an uproar. It was a classic example of Hanoi's "fight-talk" strategy, where the real, immediate target was American public opinion and the US negotiators at the Paris peace talks, not territory. Just as they had after Tet, the US command in Saigon declared victory in the offensive—which became known as "Mini-Tet"—refusing to acknowledge that Hanoi's achievement had been political, not military.

Then, just as quickly as it had escalated, the fighting subsided again, and the Nixon administration began to announce further US troop reductions. The drawdown was depicted as justification of the "Vietnamization" strategy, but to those of us in Saigon, the pattern was clear: the US was pulling out of this war, slowly but surely, tacitly acknowledging that, despite all its advantages in firepower, a purely military victory in this endless quagmire was beyond its grasp.

Up to this point in the war, most US correspondents had left their families back home or stationed them in Hong Kong or Bangkok or Singapore and themselves lived in hotels or apartments in Saigon. But I concluded that the security situation in the capital had stabilized to the point where I could bring Ann and Elizabeth in safely. I found a house to rent on a street that ran the length of the sprawling, walled Presidential Palace compound in the heart of Saigon. There were guards just inside the walls and a small military contingent stationed in barracks near the palace itself.

Good idea, right?

Wrong.

It turned out that the Vietcong gunners who set up their rockets most nights in the rice paddies across the Saigon River used the palace communication tower and the twin towers of the nearby Notre-Dame Cathedral Basilica of Saigon as aiming brackets. They could only get off a few rounds before the AC-130 gunships circling the capital overhead would lay down suppressive fire, but the rockets they did get off would land with a crash inside the compound just across the street. Baby Elizabeth, sleeping in the bedroom next to ours, would wake with wide eyes and say, "Boom!" It may have been her first word. Ann and I would gather her up and head downstairs for cover beneath the concrete staircase. By the time we got there, the shelling would be over. Our house was never hit, but some nights we could smell the smoke from the nearby explosions.

In addition to covering the war and the endless political infighting among the South Vietnamese leadership, I had a bureau to run. The correspondents included Charles Mohr, arguably the finest combat correspondent of his generation; B. Drummond Ayres Jr., a fine writer who had graduated from Virginia Military Institute and understood the military mindset; Joseph Treaster, a versatile correspondent who could cover any story from a mob murder to a battlefield; and Iver Peterson, a young reporter who had come to Vietnam as a volunteer, learned Vietnamese, and joined the bureau as an intern. In addition, Le Kim Dinh doubled as the bureau's local reporter and translator, and Mai Thanh Loan, daughter of a senior South Vietnamese army officer, served as office manager. Later we were joined by James Sterba, a gifted writer and reporter, and in 1970 by Gloria Emerson, a career foreign correspondent who had covered Northern Ireland and the Nigerian Civil War for the *Times* as well as high fashion in the Paris and London bureaus. Gloria had lived in Saigon in the 1950s under French rule and wanted to see what the war had done to a country she loved. I could not have asked for a more talented team. Missing, of course, from our ranks was an African American reporter who could communicate best with the many Blacks in the US units scattered across a surprisingly vast country. In truth, there were precious few Black reporters at the *Times* in those days.

That year, 1969, was agony in Vietnam. The war ground on, the casualties on both sides mounted, the so-called peace talks in Paris were locked in stalemate, the rural population in South Vietnam was caught in a continuous crossfire, the beautiful countryside was being incinerated by US napalm and poisoned by Agent Orange, and the North Vietnamese, accurately sensing the erosion of support for the war among the US public, had dug in for the long haul. They realized that they could never defeat the US forces militarily, but they knew they could and would outlast them.

In Saigon forty-six-year-old President Nguyễn Văn Thiệu was dancing as fast as he could. He was scrambling to assemble a workable coalition among the constantly warring political factions in South Vietnam, fending off potential mutinies among his generals, meeting with a near-constant stream of visiting senior US officials and members of Congress, telling them all what he thought they wanted to hear, and, all the while, watching his back lest his clever, conniving vice president, Nguyễn Cao Kỳ, pull off a coup. It was a spectacle.

About once a month, Thiệu would have a dozen or so of the bureau chiefs from the major US news organizations over to the presidential palace for dinner. There would be drinks on the terrace of the modern glass-and-marble residence, exquisite Vietnamese food served on china in the high-ceilinged dining room, and a long monologue from Thiệu about the crisis of the moment. The dinners were revealing not in terms of scoops but as a gauge of US-Vietnamese relations and Thiệu's byzantine thinking. He was clever and shrewd but hardly the rock upon which the United States was going to be able to build a postwar democratic movement in Southeast Asia. You realized this when he acknowledged during one of the dinners that he checked the timing of his army's offensives and even the scheduling of his overseas trips with the palace astrologer.

While President Thiệu held his press dinners in the palace, the American ambassador, Ellsworth Bunker, would have periodic background sessions with the US bureau chiefs at his sprawling, white-walled compound just down the avenue. Here, over drinks and dinner beneath spinning ceiling fans, the food was bland and the atmosphere and message relentlessly upbeat. The fighting was invariably going well, in Bunker's telling, the pacification program in the countryside was winning hearts and minds, the South Korean and Thai allies were steadfast, the enemy was crumbling. You came away wondering why, given all this progress, the US didn't simply declare victory and quit. Bunker himself, a tall, slim, elegantly tailored New Englander, was always calm and confident. I would come home from these dinners wondering if Bunker was peddling the same, rosy reports in his cables to Washington, and hoping that the CIA station, at least, was providing a more realistic account in its back-channel communications.

I certainly got a better, more hard-headed sense of the battlefield and the halting, checkered progress of Vietnamization from occasional background dinners with the US commander, General Creighton Abrams, a short, stocky, blunt-spoken former World War II tank commander. Every six weeks or so he would entertain a small group of US reporters in a handsome French Colonial villa on one of Saigon's broad avenues. If US or South Vietnamese forces had suffered a setback, he said so. If the Thiệu government was undercutting his strategy, he minced no words. The corruption of the Thai and South Korean contingents was a favorite topic. Once, when talking about his plans to dismantle a decommissioned allied base, General Abrams said it would be easy.

"I'll let a South Korean battalion in there, and they'll rip out the air conditioners and appliances and dump them on the black market. The place will be bare by nightfall."

General Abrams entertained in the villa, which was doubtlessly bugged by the South Vietnamese, and probably the CIA, but his private quarters were in an air-conditioned trailer at MACV headquarters. "I keep one book by my bedside," he said. It was *The Peter Principle*, a best seller at the time about how mediocrity rises to the top in corporate America. "Tells you all you need to know about the US Army," he said dryly.

To check up on CORDS—the vast US-managed pacification program to gain the allegiance of the Vietnamese countryside population—I would head out to visit the province advisers, the young US foreign service and CIA officers posted in each of South Vietnam's provinces to advise the Vietnamese province chiefs. The advisers, who lived and worked in the countryside, were closer to the ground in every sense and rarely had any illusions about the tasks before them. I would visit them on my own or, on occasion, make a flying trip to a distant provincial capital with William Colby, the long-time CIA official who ran CORDS and its component, the much-maligned Phoenix Program, which often seemed little more than an assassination campaign targeting local officials whose loyalties were suspect.

I liked Colby and had known him in the United States through my wife's family. Bill had been a young intelligence officer in Rome when Clare Luce had been ambassador to Italy and my wife's aunt, Dorothy Farmer, had been her aide. Like General Abrams, I believed Colby was straight in what he told me. Either man might withhold sensitive information, but neither, in my experience, lied to me.

A province visit with Colby could be an adventure. We would meet at Tan Son Nhut around 5 p.m. Typically, a helicopter would be warming up on the tarmac and huge afternoon thunderstorm clouds would be rising in the darkened western sky. On one occasion, the normally fearless pilot told me it would be "crazy" to take off into the gathering storm. But when Colby's car pulled up, he bounded out of the back seat and straight into the chopper, loosened his tie, rolled up the sleeves of his white dress shirt and said, "Let's go."

"Not a good idea," said the pilot, shouting over the roar of the engine, gesturing at the towering bank of clouds.

"Let's go!" called Colby, impatiently.

The chopper took off, banked toward a black cloud, got rocked a bit by the downdrafts, rose above the clouds just as the rain began coming down in sheets, and headed off to the south. We got away from the center of the storm and raced toward the Mekong Delta. The pilot looked relieved, and I started to breathe again. Colby, cool as could be, never looked up from the memo he was reading.

Once we got to the province advisers' compound, a modest collection of huts and tents, we sat down at a hard, wooden table in their kitchen with a few cold beers and listened. Their report was bleak and unvarnished. The province chief was on the take, his family was cleaning up on contracts with the US military, the chief was targeting his rivals as suspects in the Phoenix Program, the people in the villages—mostly rice farmers—were ready to go over to whatever side, Vietcong or government, that would let them live in peace. The South Vietnamese army unit in the area patrolled during the day and stayed in their barracks at night. The Vietcong owned the countryside after dark. Colby had heard it all before, and so had I. His commitment to his job wouldn't allow him to despair or give up, but I came away wondering how the hell this huge, costly, deadly "pacification" effort in the countryside was ever going to make much difference, much less succeed.

Another question: did Ambassador Bunker ever hear this kind of a report? If he did, did he just ignore it because it didn't fit with his larger picture of inexorable progress against "the enemy"? And who was the enemy? The Vietcong or the North Vietnamese? Both, of course. But what about the crooked province chief or the South Vietnamese commander who saw no percentage in sending his patrols out at night? Were they allies or enemies?

Mostly I went into the field by myself to get the answers. I'd hitch a ride with military transport, hook up with a US unit, and learn, in short order, how it was going.

One morning, May 6, 1969, I got a lift out to Camp Carolyn, an artillery position twelve miles from the Cambodian border, northwest of Saigon. It blocked a traditional North Vietnamese supply and infiltration route into the Saigon River valley. After weeks of relative calm, some eight hundred soldiers from a North Vietnamese regiment, the Ninety-Fifth, had attacked earlier that morning, charging out of the bamboo forest and blasting through the barbed-wire defense line, seizing two bunkers and hurling satchel charges of explosives.

"It was a blitzkrieg assault," Captain Harry Taylor recounted to me later, squinting into the morning sun. "It was the damndest, bloodiest thing I ever saw."

After six hours of hand-to-hand fighting, the assault had been driven off. The bodies of 101 North Vietnamese soldiers were found on or just inside the perimeter. Thirty-three others were taken prisoner and were being interrogated when I got there before 9 a.m. Nine Americans died defending the camp, and sixty-two were wounded. The camp, what was left of it, looked like an auto junkyard after a bad rain, with twisted bits of steel atop mounds of black mud thrown up by the explosions. After several hours interviewing soldiers and officers, I flew back to Saigon in an Army chopper. The door was left open for the door gunner, and the floor was covered with dead soldiers in body bags.

What had been accomplished by either side? The Americans, who were still dragging North Vietnamese bodies off for burial, had proven that they couldn't be driven away from sensitive territory. The North Vietnamese had demonstrated with incredible courage that, despite their losses, they still could mount a devastating assault. They weren't going away, either. But when the American casualties had been flown back to the States in flag-draped coffins, and the North Vietnamese had begun to rot in their mud graves, would anything have really changed?

The battle would be reported that evening at the Five O'Clock Follies in dry, statistical terms. The body count would mount. I would write about the battle of Camp Carolyn in the next day's *New York Times*, illustrated by a grisly picture I took and wired from Saigon. And the war would go on.

What about me? What had I accomplished by writing about the battle? I suppose the *Times'* readers would be reminded, once again, that the war was still grinding on, that soldiers on both sides were still dying, that the North Vietnamese still were not giving up, that there was still no military end in sight. Would that further incite the antiwar public back in the States? Probably. Would the battle influence the policy makers in the administration? Would the negotiators at the Paris peace talks redouble their efforts? Would the generals in Hanoi draw any conclusions? Or, most likely, would the bloody, ultimately fruitless assault on Camp Carolyn be just another battle in a long, stubborn stalemate?

9

War Redux

Unlike Israel, and despite the war, there was no direct censorship in Vietnam. A correspondent was accredited by both the South Vietnamese government and the US military command. The latter credential was more important, and to get it a reporter was required to sign a pledge that he or she (there were a few) would not disclose in advance any troop movements or planned assaults or tactics. In exchange, accredited correspondents could get access to the Follies and other briefings, plus lifts on military transportation on a space-available basis. The military being the military, reporters were assigned simulated ranks: a bureau chief for a major organization would be the equivalent of a colonel, a senior correspondent the equivalent of a captain, a junior member of the bureau, a lieutenant, et cetera. Space-available transport was provided accordingly.

While there was no censorship, the government press office and the US command could and did read any copy that was filed through the telex system. The *Times* and the *Washington Post* and a dozen other organizations filed via Reuters, which had three or four telex lines to "the world." (Reporters in Saigon divided the globe into two spheres: "'Nam," the crazy place where we lived and worked and where nothing made sense; and "the world"—i.e., everywhere else.)

Not only did the authorities read the coverage that was going out, they reacted. On more than one occasion they jumped the gun, challenging or denying a report before it had even been published or broadcast. But compared to Israel, the US military oversight and interference was light and rarely invoked.

When reporters were thrown out—and a few were—it was usually for exchanging money on the black market, where the "unofficial" rate was two or three times the official rate. Most reporters changed money at "the bank of India," the Indian-run bookstores and money changers along Tu Do Street. It was profitable but risky: if the government didn't like what a correspondent was writing or broadcasting—usually about President Thiệu or his cronies—the authorities would charge the correspondent with illegal currency manipulation, take up their credentials and visas, and show them the door. That was censorship Vietnam-style. It didn't happen often, but it happened.

The Vietnamese telephone system was a haphazard, unreliable affair, largely left over from French rule, but the US Military Assistance Command, Vietnam had its own system, and when necessary a reporter could get a call through to the States. You could call MACV locally, ask the operator to put you through to the Pentagon, and then ask the Pentagon operator to call a local D.C. number—in my case, The *Times'* Washington bureau—which would then pass along a message to New York or even patch you through. The twelve-hour time difference complicated the process, and the military system was frequently overloaded, so telex was the preferred line of communication, even if you knew that the government and the US command were reading your messages.

So, too, on occasion, was the competition. The *New York Times* and *Washington Post* bureaus were housed in adjacent offices in a modest building a few doors down from Hotel Continental, a fine rococo remnant of the French Colonial era, opposite the National Assembly and just a block from the US military's press and briefing center. The Continental's spacious, open terrace was gossip central, a gathering place and watering hole for a constant stream of reporters, officers, diplomats, spies, and hookers. The terrace—aka "The Continental Shelf"—was also safe, immune somehow from the satchel charges that VC agents would occasionally toss from a passing motorbike into other open-air cafes. The assumption was that the Continental paid off the VC and the "white mice," as the white-shirted Saigon police were called, to keep the terrace safe.

Anyway, the central location was all the office had going for it. It was one large room off an open-air hallway that we shared with the *Post*. It had five metal desks for the reporters, two more for the office manager and Dinh—the Vietnamese reporter—a fridge, and a groaning window air-conditioner with two settings: freezing or stuffy. Charlie Mohr frequently kept a weapon behind his desk, and I found a loaded pistol in the locked drawer of the bureau chief's desk when I arrived, which some of my predecessor bureau chiefs had taken into the field on occasion. I kept it, loaded, in the drawer to deal with any unfriendly visitors. During the Tet Offensive, Vietcong infiltrators had made their way into some downtown Saigon buildings, but we never had anything more threatening than the occasional drunk or nutcase who might wander in during the night.

The office was almost always open, and one or more of us could be found writing at midnight or later, taking advantage of the time difference. With a 7 p.m. deadline in New York for the first edition of the paper, we could file as late as 5 or 6 a.m. and still make that day's paper. We would type our copy, drop a carbon in a common basket so the others in the bureau knew what we were filing, and then walk the hard copy up to Reuters, a few blocks away, to be telexed to New York.

One night after dinner in a nearby restaurant, I came back to the office around 11 p.m. to find Robert Kaiser, a relatively new and ambitious young reporter for the *Post*, rifling through the copy basket, reading the pieces that had been filed earlier that evening. If he found anything exclusive and worth matching, he still had plenty of time to produce a piece for the *Post*.

I told him that snooping was incredibly bush-league and to get the hell out of the office. I caught him in the office a second time a few nights later and a third time reading our copy at Reuters after it had been telexed and tossed in the outgoing basket there. Finally, I had to tell him to stay out of our office altogether. Up to that point, the reporters from the *Times* and the *Post* had been colleagues and friends as well as competitors, and that was typical of the Saigon press corps as a whole. We were in and out of each other's offices all the time, but reading each other's copy crossed the line, and Kaiser, of course, knew it. I'm sure he was under pressure from his editors to be competitive, but so were we all. To his credit, he went on to become a first-rate correspondent and editor for the *Post*, rising to managing editor, where he distinguished himself as one of the best. We remain friends to this day.

For broadcasters, reporting from Vietnam was still in the technological dark ages. The networks had full-scale operations in Saigon, with correspondents, producers, multiple camera crews, and editors, many of them among the best in the business. Network careers were made and, on occasion, unmade there. But the process of getting material on air was incredibly cumbersome and slow compared to today's instantaneous satellite capability, where any breaking story anywhere can be broadcast live.

News footage was shot on film, which had to be developed and edited and carried by courier back to a feed point in "the world" or shipped straight to New York, a process that could take twenty-four hours. And yet this was the first genuine "living room war," where the American viewer could sit in a Barcalounger and watch Morley Safer reporting on troops igniting thatched-roof huts with their Zippos or US jets dousing the countryside with napalm or Vietnamese children fleeing a bombing strike on Highway 1 or hear—as Walter Cronkite concluded after Tet—that the war had become a stalemate at best and the only realistic outcome for the US was withdrawal. The impact on the US public psyche and the antiwar movement was huge.

No amount of spin from US Army briefers at the Follies or "clarifications" in the Pentagon pressroom could sanitize what Americans could see with their own eyes. In the wake of the war, a whole generation of officers—those who would be the commanders in Iraq and Afghanistan years later—would conclude that they had "lost" Vietnam through the camera lens. It was a simplification, of course, but those captains and majors in Vietnam emerged determined never to let the media have such unfettered access to the battlefield again. This led decades later to the practice of "embedding" reporters with military units in the field in Iraq and Afghanistan, an arrangement that gave the media some semblance of the access they had experienced in Vietnam, while giving the military greater control over what was covered. For news organizations, it was half a loaf, but better than a blackout, especially in settings where unilateral coverage of a battlefield was either impractical or too dangerous.

Vietnam was plenty dangerous. It was a war without defined front lines, where the enemy was difficult to identify from allies, where an assault or a sniper's bullet could catch a reporter anywhere, anytime. Sixty-three American reporters died covering Vietnam. But even so, the wars the United States fights these days—in Iraq and Afghanistan and in brushfire engagements in half a dozen countries in the region and Africa—seem vastly more dangerous for the media. Reporters have become actual targets in conflicts today, while in Vietnam they were generally accorded a neutral status; they might well get caught in a crossfire, but they were not typically singled out by either side.

Many of the bravest and most committed war correspondents today are women. In conflicts like Libya and Syria and Yemen, women are providing frontline coverage in countries where they frequently need to be veiled just to conduct an interview. And yet they are there, convinced that the world needs to know what is going on in shadowy conflicts where, as usual, the civilian populations pay the biggest price.

10

Green Beret Murder

In early August 1969, I was writing a Sunday piece in my office in Saigon when I got a message from the foreign desk in New York with a tip that had come in over the transom to Scotty Reston's office in Washington. A country lawyer from South Carolina had cold-called the *Times'* columnist to say that several top officers in the Green Beret unit based at Nha Trang, including the commander, Colonel Robert B. Rheault, two majors, three captains, and others had been arrested and charged with murdering a suspected North Vietnamese agent. The lawyer, George Gregory, said he was representing one of the majors, Thomas C. Middleton, and that the Pentagon was stonewalling him, refusing even to acknowledge that the men had been arrested and were being held in the stockade at Long Binh, a huge base twenty miles outside Saigon.

Murder? A suspected North Vietnamese agent? It sounded fanciful. North Vietnamese agents, suspected and real, got bumped off all the time in the Phoenix Program. Nobody considered that murder. Why this case? This was a war, after all. A commanding officer in jail? Two majors? Three captains?

I couldn't believe it, but I called the US military spokesman and asked him about the case.

"Nothing to it," was the immediate reply. He had nothing about intelligence officers arrested in a murder case. I passed that response along to New York and went back to writing my News of the Week in Review piece about President Nixon's trip to Guam, where he had announced the first set of US troop withdrawals.

Unbeknownst to me, the tip was entirely correct, and MACV and the Pentagon had clamped a top-secret lid on the case, which would become one of the most celebrated and controversial in the course of the war. It laid open the tensions between the regular US Army and the Special Forces and threatened to lift the lid on the secret bombing of Cambodia, an ostensibly neutral nation. The spokesman, who probably knew none of the details himself, had been instructed to lie and deny even the existence of such a case.

It couldn't hold, of course. Middleton and the other jailed officers were writing letters back to their families and friends and members of Congress asking for help. As it turned out, my inquiry to the military press office convinced the command that the story was about to come out. They issued a brief release of the bare facts of the case, which became known as the Green Beret Murder Case. An Associated Press dispatch moved on the wires reporting that the Green Beret commander and seven of his staff, including three intelligence officers, had been charged with murder and conspiracy in the death of a Vietnamese man near Nha Trang on June 20.

I was furious at being lied to so baldly, although it was neither the first or last time that happened. The paper felt stupid having blown a valuable tip. Instead of our exclusive, the story was "out there" on the wires. After roasting the spokesman for lying, I dispatched Jim Sterba to Nha Trang to see what he could learn there and made plans to meet the attorney, George Gregory, as soon as he landed in Saigon. The army continued to keep the lid on anything but the barest facts, citing "sensitive national security" considerations.

To my surprise, James Greenfield, the new foreign editor, cabled to say that he had struck a deal with Gregory to keep us ahead of the competition as the story unfolded. I was to meet the lawyer at the airport, spirit him away from other reporters if possible, and—this startled me—book and pay for his hotel room. The plan sounded impractical, and smacked of tabloid checkbook journalism, but Greenfield was emphatic, so I reserved a suite for Gregory at the Caravelle, the fanciest hotel in Saigon. If the *Times* were going to pick up the tab, Gregory might as well be comfortable.

The publicity-seeking lawyer had made no secret of his travel plans, so I wasn't the only one waiting for him when he arrived at Tan Son Nhut after the long flight from the States. A knot of reporters and network television cameramen clustered around Gregory as soon as he cleared customs, showering him with questions. The small-town lawyer from Cheraw, South Carolina, was loving the limelight. "Don't worry, boys," he said with a chuckle to the reporters pressed around him, "I'm big enough for all of you."

It quickly became clear that Gregory knew no more about the case than we did. I pulled him through the terminal, got him into my car, and drove him to my house, shaking the other reporters along the way. Gregory told me a little about himself. He was the classic Good Ole Boy, overweight and sloppy, but smart, funny, and irreverent. He had served as a lawyer in the US Army himself, so he was familiar with, and unimpressed by, the byzantine ways of the military justice system. I decided Middleton had made a good choice.

Sitting in my second-floor living room, I used my access to the MACV phone system to get Major Middleton on the line from Long Binh for his attorney. They talked for twenty minutes, but Middleton made it clear that he was not going to say much over a phone that was surely tapped. They agreed to meet the next morning at Long Binh.

I drove Gregory the few blocks to the Caravelle, where he was greeted by another group of reporters in the lobby. "Come on up, boys," he said grandly, ushering the crowd up to his fourth-floor suite. "Drinks are on me!" Right. On Jim Greenfield, I thought sourly.

With the reporters in his suite, Gregory repeated much of what he had told me at home, spiced with a few colorful country-boy quotes. His client was a patriotic, honorable citizen who was surely innocent, he said. "We are not going to let the army sacrifice one of our good South Carolina boys!" There wasn't much substance in what he had to say, but he was the first figure in the case to talk at all, so George Gregory made all the front pages the next day. So much for our high-priced exclusive.

It took a while for the facts of the case to come out.

The victim was Thai Khac Chuyen, a pleasant, chubby-faced young Vietnamese interpreter with almost perfect colloquial English, who worked for the Special Forces units that were sending agents into Cambodia to spy on North Vietnamese movements on a section of the Ho Chi Minh Trail. Chuyen's Green Beret handlers began to suspect his loyalty when a captured enemy photograph showed a man who looked like him posing with some North Vietnamese soldiers inside Cambodia. It was impossible to say from the grainy photo that it was Chuyen, who denied it, but the Special Forces had their doubts, so they subjected him to days of relentless questioning, sleep deprivation, truth-serum drugs, and a polygraph test in a holding cell in Nha Trang.

Chuyen never cracked, but his answers only aggravated the doubts of his interrogators. Finally, two of the Green Beret officers took their suspicions to officials from the Central Intelligence Agency who were attached to the Saigon embassy. The CIA officers, who were running agents all over the country, said that they didn't know Chuyen and couldn't say whether or not he was a North Vietnamese agent, but that if the Green Berets were worried about him, perhaps the best thing to do—certainly the easiest—was to eliminate him.

On the moonless night of June 20, 1969, three Green Berets, believing they had the approval of their superior officers and at least the tacit support of the CIA, drugged Chuyen, bundled him into a poncho, wrapped the package in heavy chains weighed down with tire rims, and took him out to sea off Nha Trang in an open boat. They shot Chuyen in the head and rolled him overboard into the dark water.

Chuyen was finished, but the Green Berets' problems were just beginning.

Colonel Bob Rheault—a handsome, forty-three-year-old, Hollywood-perfect picture of a Green Beret officer—had just assumed command of the Fifth Special Forces Group days earlier. A member of a distinguished New England family and graduate of Phillips Exeter Academy and West Point, Bob Rheault was on the fast track to a general's star. When he heard that his men had gone ahead and killed Chuyen, he decided to cover it up with a story that the suspected agent had been sent on a mission inside Cambodia—a mission from which he was not expected to return. This, in Rheault's view, was the way to handle a messy case like Chuyen: don't bother your superior officers with it; bury it and move on.

When reports of the killing reached MACV in Saigon, General Abrams was furious. As an army traditionalist, he was no fan of the Special Forces. As far as Creighton Abrams was concerned, there were no "special" forces; all his forces were special. He summoned Colonel Rheault to Saigon and listened impassively as the Green Beret officer rolled out the cover story as gospel. Abrams didn't believe it for a minute and promptly ordered an investigation by the CID, the Army's Criminal Investigation Division.

The cover story unraveled in short order, and Colonel Rheault and his men were charged and jailed. I covered the story as it went along, filing more than a dozen pieces, but our supposed inside track with George Gregory was never worth the price of his hotel room. He gave us one side of the story—his client's—but never the whole picture, which he never fully understood himself. As the full story began to emerge in the Article 32 preliminary hearing in a sealed courtroom in Long Binh, the US Army and, more importantly, the Nixon administration, realized where it was leading and panicked. Finally, the secretary of the army, Stanley Resor, on orders from the Nixon White House, stepped in and shut down the court martial process. The murder and conspiracy charges were dropped, the men were released, and the case was over.

The ostensible justification was that the CIA would not allow its officers to testify on the grounds of national security and that the defendants therefore could not get a fair trial. The real reason was that the trial, had it gone forward, not only would have revealed how the CIA routinely assassinated real and suspected enemy agents but also would have blown the cover on the increasing military operations and extensive bombing underway across the border in Cambodia—a theater of the war that President Nixon was determined to keep secret as long as he could. The stakes were simply too high.

The Green Beret Affair, as it became known, crippled the independence and reputation of the Special Forces and severely embarrassed the US Army and the CIA. It effectively ended the military careers of Colonel Rheault and his men and apparently contributed to Daniel Ellsberg's decision to leak the secret history of the war, known as the Pentagon Papers. That, in turn, led to the White House–inspired break-in at Ellsberg's psychiatrist's office, which added to the scandals that eventually brought down Richard Nixon. Altogether, it was a chain of events that no one could have anticipated when a few low-level officers began to question the loyalty of one of their interpreters.

Was Chuyen in fact a double agent? It was never definitively established. But if he was, his death would hardly have been unusual. In 1973, Bill Colby, at his Senate confirmation hearings to become CIA director, testified that some twenty-one thousand Vietnamese had died as a result of Phoenix Program operations.

For me, the Green Beret case was an object lesson in the futility of checkbook journalism. It violates every principal of honest reporting.

It's not that sources and information can't be bought; they can. Supermarket tabloids do it all the time. But you can't buy the whole story, not one as complicated as this, with as many players and motives, and you end up with a bad case of buyer's remorse and a distinct feeling that you brought it on yourself.

11

Life in Saigon

Despite the war, Ann and I built a life in Saigon in 1969 and 1970. It was hardly "normal," given the rockets landing across the street, the periodic offensives throughout the country, and my forays into the field every week or so, but it was a life. We entertained, went to occasional cocktail and dinner parties, and joined the Cercle Sportif, the sprawling French Colonial tennis and swimming club adjacent to the Presidential Palace. We sipped limón pressés beneath lazy ceiling fans on the shaded veranda and waited for Graham Greene to come around the corner. I played some tennis on the red-clay courts and took Baby Elizabeth to splash in the kiddie pool. It was a good way to forget about the war for a few hours.

Mostly, I worked, seven days a week, often late into the night. My arrangement with the *Times*, similar to those of other correspondents at other papers, was to work full time while you were in Saigon and then take a weeklong R & R break every six or eight weeks out of the country, usually in Hong Kong, Bangkok, or Singapore. We celebrated Elizabeth's first birthday with a party in the Repulse Bay Hotel in Hong Kong. I think the first phrase she learned was "room service."

We lived in a three-story, white-stucco villa—every house in Saigon was a "villa"—set in a walled, two-house compound on Nguyen Du Street. Our neighbors to the rear were hard-partying civilians attached to the Australian contingent. There were only five of them, but they had great parties, and at the end of a weekend they would drag tall trash bins full of empty Foster's Beer cans to the curb.

"Got to chase away the miseries," one of the five would explain with a cheerful wave.

I covered two of President Thiệu's overseas trips—one to Seoul, South Korea, an ally of sorts in the war, and a second to Midway Atoll, where he met with President Nixon, who made it clear that the American troop withdrawals were going to accelerate.

"Vietnamization" was underway, but at the same time Nixon and Henry Kissinger had secretly decided to put more pressure on Hanoi by expanding the air and ground war into ostensibly neutral Cambodia. The president didn't discuss it publicly for fear of inflaming the antiwar movement at home, but in Saigon we could see it coming.

In March 1970, fighting intensified along the South Vietnamese border with Cambodia. Then a military coup led by Lieutenant General Lon Nol ousted Prince Sihanouk as Cambodian head of state. The new, openly anticommunist military government in Phnom Penh immediately announced an offensive against North Vietnamese and Vietcong troops in the Cambodian provinces along the border. The South Vietnamese, delighted to see their old rival Sihanouk gone, pitched in with artillery, ground troops, and coordinated air strikes. The border region was clearly heating up.

The American bombing of enemy supply routes inside Cambodia had been an open secret for some time, but now it intensified, and American spotter planes started flying frequent missions across the border. The stage was set, and on April 30, 1970, President Nixon announced the invasion of Cambodia in a televised speech to the nation. I listened to the speech on Armed Forces Radio at home in Saigon, where it was already the morning of May 1. I was scheduled to wrap up my fifteen-month tour in early May, but this was not the time to leave. Instead of winding down, this war was expanding.

The moment Nixon stopped speaking, I rushed out to Tan Son Nhut and boarded a US Army helicopter that lifted up and swept over the treetops toward the so-called Fishhook section of Cambodia that protrudes into South Vietnam, about seventy-five miles north and west of Saigon. The sky around me was filled with helicopters ferrying an initial invasion force of ten thousand US and South Vietnamese troops. Their mission was to find and destroy the Communist base known as COSVN, or Central Office for South Vietnam, from which the enemy commanded and coordinated its assaults throughout the southern sections of South Vietnam. It was thought to be dug in and hidden in a bamboo forest a few miles inside Cambodia.

Hundreds of helicopters, planes, tanks, and armored vehicles descended on the Fishhook in the largest allied operation of the last two years of the war. From the window of the helicopter, it looked like what I imagined a World War II offensive must have been like.

At dawn, a fifteen thousand–pound bomb had been dropped four miles inside Cambodia, creating a huge crater that became an instant forward artillery base. Heavy guns were flown in by Chinook helicopters and put into action immediately.

I was in a Huey, sitting next to several soldiers in full combat gear. As we descended to a site designated as Landing Zone X-Ray, the pilot radioed that the zone was "hot." With that, the door gunner opened up with his fifty-caliber machine gun, spraying the trees that bordered the ragged clearing. Helicopters to either side of us did the same, sending bullets everywhere. It was ear-splitting pandemonium. The chopper hovered a few feet above the ground, and we jumped out, ducking low and running for the tree line. Breathing hard, we got under the canopy of a stand of rubber trees and took stock.

Troops had been dug in here. There were trenches and trash and discarded gear but no enemy. The only people we rounded up were fifteen frightened Cambodians, including several small children. They reported that a substantial force of North Vietnamese soldiers had been dug in among the rubber trees but had pulled out that morning after the heaving bombing began. As the Americans continued to search the area, I found myself next to Sergeant Carl Holzschub. "I never thought I'd be in Cambodia," he said with a sense of wonder as he moved through the underbrush. "I suppose we're making history, but as far as can see, Cambodia is no different from Vietnam."

The troops pushed out north and west from the landing zone on the heels of the retreating North Vietnamese. There were brief firefights but no sustained contact. As the light faded in the afternoon, I hitched a ride back to Saigon and filed my piece, which ran on page one, along with an AP photo of US troops leading their first prisoners, blindfolded and bound, into custody.

The allied forces continued to flood into Cambodia. It was a huge operation that, I learned later, had been in secret preparation for weeks before Nixon's speech. Remarkably, it had not leaked, not even around the bar at the Officer's Club in Saigon. After seventy-two hours, there were twenty-five thousand US and South Vietnamese troops in the Fishhook searching for COSVN. There were skirmishes; 476 enemy were reported killed versus eight Americans and 32 wounded in the first three days.

But the pattern inside Cambodia was the same as it had been over and over again in Vietnam: the North Vietnamese simply slipped away into the jungle. COSVN was never found. It supposedly had included a temporary hospital, sleeping and working quarters for top commanders, and a communications center, but it was all movable, and it had been moved. The Fishhook operation was a metaphor for the Vietnam War: an overwhelming air and land force blasted its way into dense forest only to find that the principal target had melted away to reestablish itself elsewhere.

I began to think this would never end. It reminded me of what Sihanouk had told me in Phnom Penh in November of 1968: in essence, that the United States would ultimately lose because the North Vietnamese would never give up. The US forces could go home at some point. The Vietnamese *were* home.

I stayed another month, covering the invasion and its aftermath. But I was ready to go. On June 1, I filed a long, deeply pessimistic news analysis wrapping up my time in Vietnam. Yes, enormous progress had been made in securing portions of the countryside. Yes, Vietnamization was underway, with 110,000 Americans withdrawn, leaving 429,000 still to go. Yes, the South Vietnamese army was more capable and certainly better equipped than before. But the fundamental problems were the same: corruption, lack of political will, and disunity in the south versus steely determination in the north.

I wrote then that the only possible solution was a negotiated one—that neither side could win militarily, that a political settlement had to be found. Of course, it would take another five years and tens of thousands of additional casualties, but in the wake of the phased American and allied withdrawal and the signing of a hollow "peace" agreement that had been negotiated in Paris and had never had a chance, the North Vietnamese rolled through the south in 1975, the last helicopters lifted off the US Embassy roof, and, presto, Vietnam was unified at the point of a gun. It was a resolution, and it certainly was military, not negotiated.

No dominos fell, incidentally. A communist tide did not sweep over Southeast Asia. The United States did not lose its standing in the world. The US lost its first war and suffered some fifty-eight thousand casualties. It endured wounds to its sense of self and its psyche, and divisions were opened at home that have yet to heal, but the world continued to turn on its axis.

12

At Home at Home

After three years abroad and two wars, I needed a break. Instead of heading home, I flew to Dublin. Ann, who had taken Elizabeth home a month earlier, left our daughter with her grandmother in Washington and joined me in Ireland. We took a vacation in the green and gorgeous west country, staying in a charming inn near Galway, where we drank Jameson's and played silly, tipsy croquet with the other guests until the light finally faded after 10 p.m. We wanted a place that was on the opposite end of the earth from Vietnam. Ireland, despite its continuing "Troubles," was just that.

I had left Vietnam, but the war had not left me as an assignment. From Dublin, I flew to France to interview Nguyen Thanh Le, spokesman for the North Vietnamese delegation at the Paris Peace Talks, which had long since taken on a life of their own. A slight, bespectacled man, he had represented Hanoi in Paris for two years. We talked for more than two hours in the comfortable living room of the delegation's villa in Choisy-le-Roi, a suburb of Paris.

Le, smoking French cigarettes and sipping a small glass of vermouth, pumped me about President Thiệu and Vice President Kỳ and the Saigon leadership, which seemed to fascinate him. I pressed him about Hanoi's negotiating position, what they might and might not agree to, trying to learn their bottom line.

Le seemed content to counter every new proposal that came out of Washington with one of his own. When I asked him about a new offer from U Thant, secretary-general of the United Nations, to convene an expanded international peace conference that would include Saigon and the new Cambodian government, Le laughed and dismissed it as

"sheer hypocrisy." Working out of the *Times*' Paris bureau, just around
the corner from the Paris Opera, I filed a piece leading with Le's "sheer
hypocrisy" response to U Thant's proposal. It was the first authorita-
tive North Vietnamese response and foreshadowed Hanoi's position.
Another peace proposal promptly met its predetermined fate.

Clearly the talks were going nowhere, and neither, I could see, was
Mr. Le, whose quarters were quite comfortable, thank you, especially
compared to those of his countrymen, who were dug into the jungles of
eastern Cambodia, eating rations, and dodging American B-52s.

Coming home was something of a culture shock. I'd only been away
three years, but it had been an intense three years, and I looked at the
US with different eyes. We flew into Washington, D.C., where I had
accepted the assignment as the *Times*' diplomatic correspondent, covering the State Department and national security out of the White House.
Driving in from Dulles Airport, I marveled at the Dulles Toll Road. It is
an ordinary stretch of divided highway, restricted to traffic to and from
the airport, and no different from other highways around the country.
But to me, after Southeast Asia, it was amazing. I hadn't seen a road
like it in three years of travel. My first trip to a supermarket for groceri-
es was another eye-opener. So much food, so many choices! The US
suddenly seemed an incredibly rich country, full of people who took it
all for granted. Obviously it wasn't all that different from the place I'd
left three years before, but I marveled at the abundance, nonetheless.

Ann and Elizabeth and I house-sat for a month in the home of Jack
Rosenthal, a *Times* correspondent away on vacation, and looked for a
place of our own. We saw a couple dozen places on the market and
ended up buying one of the first we'd seen, a recently renovated 1920s
four-bedroom four-square in Chevy Chase Village, a leafy suburb a bus
ride away from the *Times*' Washington bureau. It cost $59,500, which
seemed like a fortune to me at the time, but I had saved a good chunk
of my largely tax-free salary overseas, and with a loan from my father I
could swing it. It was the first house I'd ever owned and my first mort-
gage, at age thirty-two.

Working in the *Times*' Washington bureau was another shock to the
system.

Overseas I had gotten used to setting my own schedule, selecting my
own stories, and deciding what to cover when. I learned to vary the pace
and style of the coverage, mixing breaking news with analyses, profiles,

features, "talk" pieces, and the like. I decided most of this on my own, with only the occasional long-distance guidance or reaction from New York. The freedom and independence was liberating—and stimulating.

In the forty-five-member *Times* Washington bureau, then housed in one large floor of an office building ten minutes from the White House, it was journalism-by-committee. I was reminded once again that the *Times* was—and is—an editor's paper, with the direction coming from New York through layers of editors there and in Washington, which was by far the largest bureau outside the home office. This, presumably, gave some coherence to the paper's overall coverage, but it was very much a top-down operation. You'd submit a story idea to the Washington bureau chief or news editor, who would pitch it to New York in the morning story conference. Your copy would be edited first by the desk in Washington, then again by the national or foreign desk in New York, and finally by the news editor in New York. By the time a piece ran through this gauntlet, many hands had massaged the copy. Any semblance of spontaneity or spark was ironed out of it.

I learned only later, years later, as an editor myself, that there was one failsafe measure to protect a particularly bright piece from the flattening effect of the *Times'* editorial process. If the foreign or national editor, say, saw a piece he particularly liked come across his desk, he could send it over to the copy desk with an acronym scrawled across the top: TTMFAYNTAA. The copy editors knew it meant, "Touch This, Mother Fucker, And You'll Never Touch Anything Again." Very un-*Times*ian, but effective.

The *Times'* Washington bureau, then headed by Max Frankel, was in fact the personal fiefdom of former bureau chief and Pulitzer Prize–winning columnist James "Scotty" Reston, who had hired many of the best writers and reporters and still guided coverage of big events.

A press conference by the secretary of state, believe it or not, was a big event in those days. Today the SecState—as the nation's chief diplomat was known in bureaucratese—would have to fight his or her way into the paper, but then it was the oracular voice from Delphi pronouncing policy, which the Paper of Record treated as Big News.

If it was, say, a 2 p.m. press conference in the auditorium at the State Department, roughly ten minutes from the bureau, Scotty would hire a stretch limousine and pile three or four reporters into the back. On the way over, Scotty would stress the questions he wanted to hear asked, if not by others then by us.

The "gentlemen from the *Times*," would tumble out, march into the auditorium, and take seats in the front rows. In the limo on the way back to the bureau, Scotty would review his notes and hand out assignments: "Smith, you take his comments on Vietnam; Ben Welles, the Middle East; Tad Szulc, Europe; Ed Dale, the economic stuff; and I'll do a news analysis over the top."

That would produce five separate stand-alone pieces for the Paper of Record by 7 p.m. Today, unless the secretary's comments were earth-shaking and a real departure in policy, they'd likely be no more than a few paragraphs inside another piece from the White House, which has totally overshadowed State and Defense in foreign policy.

Today, in the world of the constant, twenty-four-hour, nonstop, mobile news cycle, remarks made at a 2 p.m. news conference could well be ancient history by midnight. The major points would move online, be tweeted and shared and very possibly be overtaken by a reaction abroad or on the Hill or subsequent developments before the print paper hit the streets. In the Age of Trump, where The Donald commanded the news agenda, the SecState's view might get lost altogether.

The insights in Scotty's news analysis might hold up, but the four "breaking news" pieces would be broken into bits of action and reaction. This is not a bad thing in and of itself, but in today's scenario the secretary's carefully crafted remarks become little more than a few notes in a continuous news cacophony.

Today, in the unlikely event that a secretary of state has made genuine news, very few of the *Times*' subscribers who still get the paper on their doorstep will not have read or heard of them by the time they pick up the paper the next morning. Indeed, Stephen Colbert might well have lampooned them the night before. The world will have moved on.

But in 1970 and 1971, foreign policy was a huge story for the *Times* and other "serious" news organizations. It was an incredibly active period for the United States internationally. Washington was trying to extricate itself from the war in Vietnam, stabilize Indochina, open relations with mainland China, calm the frictions between India and Pakistan, deal with the Soviet Union, encourage integration in Europe, and, oh yes, broker peace between Israel and her Arab neighbors. The first step in that process was to get Israel and Egypt to agree on terms under which the Suez Canal, which had been closed since 1967, could be cleared and reopened to international shipping.

From my perch as State Department correspondent, I wrote about all this. There was some overseas travel, but instead of creating my own itinerary I was part of the entourage accompanying the secretary of state, William Pierce Rogers, a courtly, genial, soft-spoken corporate lawyer whom President Nixon had lured from his lucrative legal practice to Foggy Bottom.

On one eighteen thousand–mile jaunt, Rogers visited Saudi Arabia, Jordan, Lebanon, Egypt, and Israel after stops in London, Paris, and Ankara. On his way home, he stopped in Rome to chat with the pope. I was one of perhaps a dozen journalists who traveled with him aboard a presidential jet. On the last leg, when the 707 stopped to refuel at Shannon, Rogers bounded into the duty-free shop and emerged with a honey-colored Scottish cashmere sweater that he proudly announced he had gotten for sixteen dollars.

"Great for golf," he said with a grin.

Walking and Talking: As City Hall Bureau Chief, interviewing then NYC Mayor John V. Lindsay in 1966 after his weekly cabinet meeting at The Arsenal, Central Park. Courtesy of Neal Boenzi, *The New York Times*, Redux.

Interviewing Senator Robert F. Kennedy (D, NY) on a television panel in 1966. Author photo collection.

Father and son tourists, at Masada, overlooking the Dead Sea, 1967. Author photo collection.

Desert Reporting: In the Sinai, after the 1973 Yom Kippur War, with a local expert. Author photo collection.

Interviewing President Jimmy Carter at the foot of the steps to Air Force One, with Sam Donaldson of ABC News horning in over my shoulder. Official White House Photo.

Airborne to Asia: With Vice President Walter Mondale aboard Air Force II, 1979. Official White House Photo.

The Wordsmith at work. Walter Wellesley "Red" Smith, on deadline. Note the crumpled first try on the floor. Author photo collection.

From print to broadcast: newly minted CBS News White House Correspondent reporting in front of the West Wing of The White House, 1986. Official White House Photo.

Christmastime at the White House, with President Ronald Reagan December 11, 1986. Official White House Photo.

CBS Sunday Morning senior correspondent. Author photo collection.

In the control room at *The NewsHour with Jim Lehrer,* now *The PBS NewsHour.* Author photo collection.

Three generations of Smiths in the owners' box, watching the then Washington Redskins at RFK Stadium, 1980. From left, Terence, Chris, and Red. Author photo collection.

13

Diplomatic Dissonance

As the *Times'* diplomatic correspondent, I occasionally found myself in the middle of the prime navel-gazing conflict within the Beltway: the ongoing battle of egos between Secretary of State William P. Rogers, polite but prideful, and Henry Kissinger, the brilliant, mercurial, vain, witty, and explosively temperamental national security advisor. Three years into Nixon's first term, Kissinger was on a determined campaign to capture foreign policy as his own personal preserve. In his own mind, anyway, he was uniquely qualified: a modern-day Disraeli, the single figure equipped to guide the projection of US power abroad in the latter half of the American Century. He saw Rogers as an obstacle that had to be undercut and brushed aside.

It was in no way a fair fight. Kissinger was a compulsive, take-no-prisoners bureaucratic infighter, while Rogers mostly sat back, relying on his personal friendship with Nixon to protect his status as the senior foreign policy player in the administration. The two men pushed back and forth in testy, incredibly petty conflicts that frequently had to be resolved by H. R. Haldeman, Nixon's top aide, or Nixon himself.

I managed to annoy both Rogers and Kissinger in January 1971 when I wrote the lead piece in a ponderous seven-part series about the making of foreign policy in the Nixon administration. My opening sentence was less than kind but unarguably true: "The Department of State, once the proud and undisputed steward of foreign policy, has finally acknowledged what others have long been saying: that it is no longer in charge of the United States' foreign affairs and that it cannot reasonably expect to be so again."

The piece went on to describe how foreign policymaking had shifted during the Nixon presidency from Foggy Bottom to the White House and how Kissinger had usurped many of the secretary of state's prerogatives. Needless to say, Rogers was not happy about being portrayed as an incidental player, even though the piece quoted numerous State Department officials conceding the central thrust. He never complained to me directly, but his aides told me that the whole series gave the secretary indigestion.

Kissinger, instead of being privately pleased by the piece, threw one of his patented tantrums and summoned William Safire—then a Nixon speechwriter, later a *Times* columnist—to his office and ranted about how the whole series was a clever State Department plant and ploy to get the president to publicly endorse Rogers as the man in charge of foreign policy.

"Remember, Bill," Safire quotes Kissinger as telling him in *High Adventure*, his White House memoir, "I had nothing to do with this *Times* story, nor did any of my people talk to Terence Smith." (Not true.) "This is just State's way of getting the president to come out and say the secretary of state is the principal adviser on foreign policy. If Rogers doesn't knuckle under, I go!"

Such were the wondrous workings of Kissinger's mind. Even a piece trumpeting his ascendance in the making and execution of foreign policy appeared to Kissinger a plot to take him down.

He promptly called me in to complain about the piece, insisting that I say or write that it had not come from him or his staff. I smiled and reminded him, not for the first time, that I wasn't going to talk about my sources for this or any article. In fact, I had interviewed some of his aides on background in reporting the piece, and I assumed he knew that. But mostly I had talked with current and former State Department officials and foreign diplomats who dealt with them and the White House.

Kissinger grudgingly accepted that and switched tactics, complaining about a passage in the piece in which I wrote that he had privately undercut the State Department's public endorsement of West Germany's diplomatic openings to the Soviet-dominated nations of Eastern Europe. This was undeniably true, but Kissinger nonetheless had called the *Times*' Washington bureau chief, Max Frankel, with whom he had close relations, to object. He wanted Max to come over to his office to see the cable traffic on the issue, but Max, to his credit, said he would only come with me, since I had written the piece.

When we got to the national security advisor's large, sun-splashed office in the northwestern corner of the White House, Kissinger was the gracious host. But after a little small talk, he effectively cut me out of the conversation by addressing Max in German, which is native to both of them. Max and I both immediately objected, and Henry, not the least embarrassed, switched back to English and briskly made his case that he had not undercut State's position. Then, as I left the office, Max stayed behind, and they both lapsed back into German, laughing at some shared joke.

Another piece that riled Henry was a Washington Notes column on June 27, 1971, in which I reported that at least five senior ambassadorial posts were expected to change hands in the fall. This was entirely accurate, but Kissinger was upset when I mentioned speculation that President Nixon was angling for an invitation to Beijing (then Peking) and might send his national security advisor ahead as a personal envoy. This was sensitive because it was true and because Kissinger, who had already made secret trips to China via Pakistan, was trying to keep the lid on until he and the president could announce Nixon's upcoming trip, which would finally take place the following summer.

Again, Kissinger read this piece as a Rogers plant, designed to steal his thunder. He blew up in this recorded exchange in the Oval Office, according to the famous Nixon Oval Office tapes, released years later.

At 11:39 a.m., Haldeman addresses the president:

HALDEMAN: There is a *New York Times* story that speculates about five ambassadorial transfers soon, written by Terence Smith, the State Department guy. No real problem on the ambassadorial transfers, but one of the four pictures they run is Henry Kissinger. The caption under says, "Presumably the man for the Peking tour." Then it says, "The White House has refused to confirm—and pointedly declined to deny—repeated reports that Mr. Nixon asked some months ago that he or a representative be invited to China in early 1972. The representative would presumably be Henry A. Kissinger, his special assistant for national security affairs." That's all it says. One little paragraph in a long story.

NIXON: [Annoyed] Yeah, yeah.

HALDEMAN: Henry is convinced that this is Rogers's next move in the "Battle on Kissinger" tour. And this, of course, has him practically paranoid, and he has been rattling all over the walls in my office. My problem is, what do you want me to do about it?

NIXON: Rogers put this out?

HALDEMAN: Yes.

NIXON: [Shouting] Well, how the hell? Rogers doesn't know anything about China!

This goes on for several pages in the transcript until Kissinger comes into the Oval Office and joins the conversation:

KISSINGER: In my judgement, Mr. President, what happened was this: When Rogers was told— First of all, Terence Smith never calls my staff. He has never done it in all the years that we've been here. [Not true.] Secondly, my staff is on additional instructions not to return any *New York Times* calls here. [True, but largely ignored by staff.]

NIXON: That's right.

KISSINGER: So, that's out of the question . . .

The conversation goes on for two hours, until 1:40 p.m., with Kissinger blaming Rogers for a report that was potentially embarrassing. Nixon, probably wanting his lunch and apparently trying to calm Kissinger down, comes up with another theory: that the Chinese had put out the report for their own tactical reasons. (Not true.)

None of this mattered in the end, since Kissinger's secret trips were revealed and the president got his invitation and, historically, visited China the following year, opening up relations for the first time in decades. But it illustrates Kissinger's obsession with his press coverage and with Rogers and his relentless campaign to convince President Nixon that his old friend Rogers was not to be trusted—and in the process, promote himself. It was a classic example of what Safire called Kissinger's "bombastic triviality."

Later, when I kidded Kissinger about his chronic obsession with Rogers, he famously growled, "Just because I'm paranoid doesn't mean I don't have enemies."

The tapes also illustrate how much time the Nixon White House spent fretting about the coverage it got, especially in the *Times*. You would think that most of the reporting would roll off their backs, that they would be too busy running the country to worry about such small matters. But no, not at all.

I had no idea about these conversations until the tapes came out years later. It is actually just one of several instances in which the tapes reveal that Nixon was angry about something I had written from Saigon or Washington. I never made his official "enemies list" that I know of, but I didn't get any Christmas cards, either.

14

A New and Different Israel

Our family expanded on September 7, 1971, with the birth of our second child, Christopher Wellesley Smith, at the Columbia Hospital for Women just off Pennsylvania Avenue in Washington, D.C. I was in the delivery room when Chris arrived on the Tuesday morning after Labor Day, literally pissing and moaning, but otherwise happy and healthy. As was Ann. We took Chris home to our house on West Irving Street in Chevy Chase Village, just across the Maryland line, now a family of four.

My father had remarried by this time. His bride was Phyllis Warner Weiss, a widow with five children whose first husband had died in a plane crash. Ann and I had first met her while we were still in Israel, on a weekend getaway to Rome for a rendezvous with Pop and Phyllis, who were traveling together through Europe. I can't say it was love at first sight. Phyllis, a slight, shy, quiet artist and intellectual, was as different from my mother as two people could be. Where my mother had been outgoing, funny, warm, and open to the world and most of the people in it, Phyllis was far more reserved and self-contained. Phyllis and I got along well enough over the next years, but a warm relationship it was not. Did I resent her for taking my mother's place? Maybe, but not consciously. In any event, she and my father were good to each other and for each other, and I was delighted that he had found companionship. Selfishly, it relieved me of some of the guilt I felt for being so far away when he was alone at home.

I continued on the diplomatic beat, covering the State Department and, for a few weeks in the fall, the United Nations General Assembly session in New York. I was writing across the board on foreign policy:

the US moves to extricate itself from Vietnam, the equally fruitless efforts to negotiate peace in the Middle East and a resolution between India and Pakistan, the politization of the Peace Corps, which accelerated during Nixon's second term, and, in 1972, the explosive release of the huge, secret history of the Vietnam War that became known as the Pentagon Papers.

The beat was varied and full and certainly kept me busy, but increasingly I missed the freedom and adventure of an overseas assignment. My wanderlust gene was reasserting itself. Ann was game, and the kids were too small to have an opinion in the matter, so I began to talk with the *Times* management about taking another posting abroad. Paris, I reminded them, would be fine.

Instead, it turned out to be Jerusalem. Back to the future! That was more than fine with me. I had spent barely a year there between 1967 and 1968, knew firsthand what a riveting story it was, had covered US Middle East policymaking in Washington for the last two years, and was delighted to go back, this time as bureau chief for a full four-year assignment. We packed up our household, rented out the house in Chevy Chase, and headed off, two small children in tow, and arrived in Jerusalem and checked in to a handsome suite overlooking the courtyard of the American Colony Hotel in the first days of September 1972.

It felt like home. Horatio and Valentine Vester, the delightful Victorian couple who owned and ran the American Colony, were still in residence, still serving cocktails in the lush garden behind their quarters, still sardonic about both Israel and Jordan. Father Jerry Murphy-O'Connor—the Irish-born biblical scholar at the École Biblique, the French archeological school in East Jerusalem—was still leading small groups of friends on Sunday morning walks in the Judaean Hills, and on the Israeli side of town dozens of friends we had met five years earlier were still there to welcome us back. Some had risen to more important positions in the government and were ready-made sources waiting to be tapped.

In short order, we moved into the sprawling, high-ceilinged flat on the ground floor of a big stone house at 21 Hovevei Zion ("lovers of Zion") Street in the Talbiya section, not far from the King David Hotel, where a succession of *Times* correspondents had lived before us. It was a grand place, with a garden in front and a balcony overlooking another garden in the rear, an octagonal living room with an intricate tiled floor and four bedrooms, one of which served as my office. We also inherited Fayeh, a houseman who took care of the place, and promptly hired Georgette, a young woman from the Old City, as a nanny for the baby.

Much seemed the same, but Israel in 1972 was a different place.

Five years of occupying the West Bank and Gaza had hardened attitudes on both sides of the cease-fire line. Israelis who had originally thought of themselves as enlightened, even beneficent occupiers had now spent five years subduing and policing an increasingly restive Palestinian population using ever-more-harsh tactics. By 1972, a new generation of Israeli soldiers had spent their army service firing rubber bullets and tear gas at stone-throwing protesters in the occupied West Bank and Gaza. The mood throughout the occupied territories had turned ugly.

A Labor-led coalition government was in charge, with Golda Meir as prime minister. Despite her grandmotherly image, Golda was tough, especially on the Palestinians, whose identity she had famously denied, once arguing, "There is no such thing as a Palestinian people."

Moshe Dayan was still defense minister, but now, in addition to overseeing the occasional firefight on the Egyptian and Syrian frontiers, he was in charge of administering the occupied territories, where new Jewish settlements had begun to take root in the West Bank. Hopes and prospects for a negotiated peace had ebbed to the point where another war seemed the more likely outcome. Bitterness, on both sides, had replaced the optimism that had followed the Six-Day War. Israel was a different place, indeed.

I didn't have a lot of time to ruminate on the changes. A couple of days after I arrived in Jerusalem, Arab gunmen broke into the Olympic Village in Munich and seized eleven Israeli athletes as hostages. All the Israelis and five of the gunmen died in the ensuing firefight with German commandos. The next day, under a broiling sun, I was at Lod Airport outside Tel Aviv covering the somber state occasion as the athletes' coffins were unloaded slowly and carefully from an El Al airliner and placed aboard a cortege of army command cars. The crowd wept as Israeli leaders mourned their dead and vowed revenge. It was a grim, angry scene that accurately reflected the bitter relations between Israel and the Palestinians, occupier and occupied.

As a side note, that day was the first time my father and I covered the same story in the same edition of the same paper. I filed from Israel, and he wrote his column for the *Times* about the aftermath in Munich, where he had been covering the Olympics.

The reprisal for the massacre didn't take long in coming. The next day, scores of Israeli Air Force planes struck simultaneously at ten targets deep in Syria and Lebanon, targets that military authorities described as training camps and headquarters of Black September, the Palestinian group that had taken responsibility for the Munich blood-bath. It was a huge, coordinated attack, the biggest in scope and depth of penetration since the opening hours of the Six-Day War, and striking evidence that Israel had had Black September in its crosshairs even before Munich.

Suddenly I was back in the midst of it, attending military briefings at the defense headquarters in Tel Aviv, filing furiously, trying to anticipate the next outbreak on the next frontier. It came fast enough: a massive Israeli ground invasion of Lebanon, a three-pronged assault with tanks and armored personnel carriers driving a dozen miles into Lebanese territory, dynamiting houses, shattering villages, killing scores whom the military identified as Palestinian guerrillas who had established bases inside Lebanon. I say *whom the military identified* because, of course, there was as usual no way to independently confirm who had been killed and by whom. There was neither access to the battlefield itself nor time to get there. I had to rely on the accounts provided by the military. A statement issued by the Lebanese described the victims as civilians, the Israelis as terrorists. The only thing the two sides agreed upon was that people had been killed. Welcome back to the Middle East.

Reporting all of this was similar to 1967, but accelerated. From action to reprisal to renewed action, everything moved faster. The Israeli forces, resupplied by the United States, were larger and more capable: the sweeping air raid in the wake of the Munich killings had taken only seventeen minutes; the ground action had penetrated Lebanon in a matter of hours. The Palestinians, too, were better organized and more powerful than they had been. Both sides had ramped up in the years that I had been gone from the region.

I still had to clear what I wrote through military censorship and file it via telex or telephone, but even that was faster and more efficient. I now had a telex machine installed in my office in Jerusalem, so that was faster as well. For me, this latest outbreak was reminiscent of covering the Six-Day War, but at warp speed.

Once again, as had happened on the eve of the 1967 war and when I arrived in Saigon just before the countrywide offensive known as Mini-Tet, the story had erupted as soon as I got there. Why? A nose for news? Some sixth sense? Keen journalistic timing? None of the above. Mostly dumb luck and coincidence. I obviously had no premonition about either North Vietnamese battle plans or Black September operations. For a reporter, it was simply a matter of being in the right place at the right time. That's easier, of course, when history helps by repeating itself. So I wasn't totally surprised when I found myself up to my ears in a fast-breaking story once again.

But in 1972 I had an assistant, Moshe Brilliant—an American-born Israeli and longtime *Times* stringer—helping in Tel Aviv, and I quickly hired Marsha Pomerantz—an American journalist living in Jerusalem who was smart, funny, and fluent in Hebrew—as an office assistant and interpreter. Micha Bar-Am, a superb photographer, eventually came on board as well. The *Times* operation in Israel was expanding, and soon enough it became clear that my home office in Jerusalem was impractical, especially with two small children underfoot. Eventually, I opened the paper's first real office in Israel, renting a three-room suite in a handsome old building in the center of Jerusalem near the government press office. We got telephone and telex lines installed and had a sign painted and mounted outside the ground floor entrance that read,

THE NEW YORK TIMES
Jerusalem Bureau
2nd Floor

Before long, we got a succinct editorial critique of our work when someone smeared the sign with a blotch of black paint. I decided to leave it there as a badge of honor, and when I left in 1976, I pried it off and took it with me. It decorated my study at home for years.

The Israeli invasion into Lebanon targeting Fatah guerrilla camps continued for two days. The tanks and artillery ultimately pulled back, but every few weeks for the rest of 1972 a Palestinian hijacking somewhere would bring another round of Israeli air strikes into Syria and Lebanon.

It was neither peace nor war, but inside Israel life went on more or less normally. Once again, I covered the fighting and when I could wrote pieces about everyday life. I was trying to describe Israel and Israelis as a place and people, not just a running, endless war story. It was a country in which people were pursuing their hopes and ambitions despite the firefights that erupted along their borders and the bombs that occasionally went off in the central marketplace. For Israel, this was the new normal.

I wanted to convey a fuller picture of the country. So I wrote features about an exuberant and drunken wedding that joined the children of two of the leading Israeli families in the Galilee that took place within range of Syrian artillery on the Golan, the conversion of the rubble-strewn former no-man's-land in Jerusalem into parks and a public space, the creation of an artist's colony in refurbished buildings overlooking the Old City walls, the thriving theater scene in Tel Aviv that was trying to throw off outdated government censorship. One day I went to the location where a Hollywood crew was shooting the musical film *Jesus Christ Superstar* atop a Nabataean ruin in the Negev. I loved the musical score and still know all the lyrics.

In the Araba, a rocky plain just north of the southern port city of Elath, I wrote about Hai-Bar, an ambitious conservation experiment in which the Nature and Parks Authority was trying to revive the herds of long-horned antelope, gazelle, and ibex that roamed the land in biblical times.

When the hard news flow slowed, I could write about the wildcat labor strikes in which everyone from customs clerks to doctors walked off their jobs, and the economic conditions that were making it hard for new immigrants, especially, to make ends meet in a land that was, of course, not all milk and honey. My goal was a fuller, rounder picture of Israel as it approached its twenty-fifth anniversary as an independent nation.

I was trying to follow the advice I had received from editors when I had first gone abroad for the *Times*: think of yourself as writing a letter home. Describe what people are talking about, what they worry about, how they have fun, what it is like at a wedding, or a funeral. And, as my father had always told me about covering a sports event, give the reader a sense of what it was like to be there—or, as famous sports editor Stanley Woodward put it more graphically, describe the smell of the cabbage in the hallways.

There were news stories that seemed small at the time but foreshadowed something much more significant. In February 1973, for example, I heard unofficial reports of heavy construction along a north-south line about ten miles west of the Jordan River in the occupied West Bank. The Israeli military spokesman said he knew nothing of it, but when I drove out to see for myself, the project was obvious: Israel was building a six-lane highway from the Beisan Valley in the north to the Jerusalem-Jericho road in the south, connecting two new Israeli settlements and carving out the portion of the West Bank that Israel hoped eventually to annex under the terms of the Allon Plan.

This was the brainchild of Yigal Allon, the deputy prime minister, who conceived of the road as the eastern frontier of a Greater Israel, at the expense of Jordan and the Palestinians. Under the Allon Plan, Israel would absorb most of the high ground on the West Bank, with strategic military positions overlooking the Jordan Valley below. The plan was never adopted as official Israeli government policy, but it was being implemented by road construction and new settlements anyway. The Israelis called it "creating facts." Today, decades later, the West Bank is laced with Israeli roads, some of them closed to Palestinians, and a huge security wall has been built to stop Palestinian infiltration into Israel proper. The Allon Plan clearly lives, in spirit if not in letter. The Trump administration, and Jared Kushner, would embrace Allon's idea of annexing the Jordan Valley in the "peace plan" they would produce in 2020.

There were also stories in February 1973 that served as a reminder of the state of virtual war that existed between Israel and her Arab neighbors.

On the 21st, a Libyan Airliner carrying more than one hundred civilian passengers bound for Cairo strayed over the Israeli-occupied Sinai. As the pilots tried to correct their navigation error and bank back toward Cairo, Israeli fighters intercepted the Boeing 727 and ordered it to land. When the pilots failed to respond, the Israeli Phantom jets shot it down, killing 106 passengers and crew, leaving seven survivors.

Black smoke was still rising from the wreckage in sand dunes about twelve miles east of the Suez Canal when I and other correspondents reached the scene. From the charred remains of the plane and the wide, fire-blackened furrow in the sand, it appeared that the plane had been headed west, toward Cairo. I picked up a business card half-buried in the sand that read "Commandant Jacques Bourges, Pilote de Ligne, Air France." Captain Bourges and the crew, on loan to Libyan Airlines, were all killed.

At first Defense Minister Dayan blamed Libya for the downing, arguing at a news conference that the pilots had ignored repeated instructions to land. But later, after Israel returned one hundred charred bodies across the Suez Canal, Dayan conceded that Israel had erred in shooting down a civilian airliner that had lost its way. Israel subsequently paid compensation to the families of the victims. The whole incident illustrated how tense the situation remained along the cease-fire lines and the hair-trigger response time of the Israeli Air Force operating out of bases in the Sinai.

As the months passed, Israel continued building new settlements in the occupied West Bank. More than fifty were planted in the Palestinian territory by the summer of 1973. Others were started on the fringes of the Gaza Strip, and Dayan announced plans to build an Israeli city of 250,000 persons, to be called Yamit, at the southern end of the Strip. The Israeli government's official position was that it was ready to negotiate the return of at least portions of the occupied territories in exchange for peace, but everything it did day-to-day suggested otherwise. When I asked Dayan at a news conference what he envisioned for the settlements and the settlers in the event that Israel withdrew to or near the 1967 lines, he dismissed the question. "If we can make peace with the Arabs," he said, "the settlers will be no problem." I didn't believe it then, and I doubt he did either. Today, the hundreds of thousands of settlers occupying government-subsidized apartments and homes in East Jerusalem and the West Bank constitute a major pressure point in contemporary Israeli politics. I wonder if Dayan could see it coming before he died in 1981—or whether, privately, it was what he had hoped and planned for all along.

Meanwhile, the Israeli economy was booming, assisted in part by major infusions of aid from the United States and other Western countries. The demand for farmhands and day laborers grew, so Israel started importing Palestinians from the territories. By the summer of 1973, some fifty- to sixty thousand Palestinians were crossing into Israel every day, creating a dependency on both sides. The workers were supposed to go home every night, but thousands would sleep three or four nights a week inside Israel. Soon the Israelis became the overlords and the Palestinians the hired hands.

This was so contrary to the Labor-Zionist principles of many Israelis that a national debate erupted in the newspapers. One woman resident of a moshav wrote a widely circulated letter to Moshe Dayan in which she said that her farmer husband had become a labor contractor, providing Arab workers for other farms.

"We don't lift a finger on the farm," she wrote. "My son refuses to even mow the lawn—'Mohamed will mow it.' We have become the effendis . . . If the situation is this appalling after five years, what will happen after ten or fifteen years?"

Dayan was unmoved. To him the stream of workers crossing the lines was a sign that Israelis and Arabs could work together. He saw it as one of the major bonuses of the 1967 war and a huge boost to the Israeli economy. His glass was half-full and filling further.

At age twenty-five, as a nation Israel was certainly losing its egalitarian edge. The founders had been determined to establish a socialist utopia in Mandatory Palestine. The early Israelis were meant to work the land and build industries themselves under this construct. Tipping, neckties, saying please and thank you—these were bourgeois affectations that had no place in their Israel. The communal kibbutz was the ideal model. Socialism and cradle-to-grave social programs were the goal.

By 1973, however, there were two hundred private-enterprise millionaires in Israel, many of whom lived in mansions in Herzliya and Caesarea. Two marinas were under construction along the Tel Aviv waterfront to cater, as the advertising put it, "to the needs of the Israeli yachtsman." The economy was overheating; major technological, aircraft, and armament industries were abuilding; important universities were expanding. It was a happening place.

To celebrate its twenty-fifth anniversary, the nation threw itself a three-day party. Some 450 international guests nibbled stuffed vine leaves under the stars, watched Rudolf Nureyev dance in the Herodian Ampitheatre in Caesarea, and sang "Hello, Golda / Well, hello, Golda . . ." to the premier at a separate torchlit party in the two thousand-year-old Herodian Citadel in Jerusalem.

A dozen of the US guests—including actors Arlene Dahl, Susan Strasberg, and Hugh O'Brian and the opera star Patrice Munsel—arrived aboard *La Belle Simone*, the 234-foot yacht of developer William J. Levitt and his wife, Simone. This was heady stuff for Israel.

The planned high point of the weekend—a glamorous, all-star gala at an outdoor stage in the ancient citadel, taped by ABC for broadcast in the States—turned out to be a windblown mess. As the evening breeze came up, skirts flew, sheet music took off, and the best efforts of the Israel Philharmonic and baritone Robert Merrill floated unheard into the dark night. Comedian Alan King, the master of ceremonies, said he had never worked in such conditions: "Here we are in surroundings built by Herod," he told the audience, "and never swept since the Crusaders." The redoubtable Josephine Baker saved the night during a break in the breeze by singing a sultry version of "My Bill."

It was a great party. Herod would have loved it.

But the euphoria couldn't last. Six years had passed since the Six-Day War, and Israel continued to occupy virtually all the territory it had seized during the fighting. Negotiations on a peace agreement were stalled, despite episodic US efforts to restart them. On the West Bank and in the Gaza Strip, Palestinians were increasingly restive. Egypt and Syria were rearming, courtesy of the Soviet Union, and the Israeli military was upgrading, thanks largely to the United States. The stage was being set for the next chapter.

15

Anguish in Austria

In the fall, I headed to Vienna, Austria, to do a feature about the Jewish Agency's transit camp for Soviet Jews emigrating to Israel and elsewhere. It was located at Schönau Castle, a slightly tired old Hapsburg hunting lodge in the Vienna woods just south of the Austrian capital. I timed my trip to be there for Rosh Hashanah, the Jewish New Year, with no idea of what was about to unfold in Vienna—or, for that matter, on the banks of the Suez Canal.

For reasons known only to Moscow, the Russians had opened the gates to Jewish emigration from the Soviet Union. Some sixty thousand Jews had exited over the previous two years, almost all of them via Vienna and the Schönau transit camp. All but a few hundred went on from there to Israel. It was a hugely important flow of new citizens to Israel, because the Russian immigrants were educated, skilled, and motivated to start a new life. They included doctors and scientists and engineers and musicians, most of whom were fiercely anticommunist, relieved to get out from under Soviet rule and ready to begin afresh.

The morning after I arrived in Vienna, I met the famous Chopin Express as it pulled into Wien Südbahnhof, carrying more than a hundred Jews. They were weary from the twenty-four-hour journey from Moscow and clearly apprehensive. When the train bumped to a halt, Israel Wilshinski, the Jewish Agency's greeter, met the new arrivals on the platform with a handshake and "Shalom aleichem," or peace to you, one of the few Hebrew phrases they knew. I followed the Russians to Schönau and wrote a feature about their adventure that the *Times* displayed under the headline "FOR JEWS FROM SOVIET, FEAR AND JOY IN VIENNA."

After the piece ran, I had a day to kill before going on to Strasbourg, France, to cover a speech Prime Minister Golda Meir was scheduled to deliver to the Consultative Assembly of the Council of Europe. So I played tourist, spending the sunny, warm day wandering around the magnificent Schönbrunn Palace and making plans to attend a George Shearing jazz concert that night. But when I got back to Hotel Sacher in the afternoon, looking forward to a slice of Sacher torte, there was a stack of pink "while you were out" message slips waiting for me. "I think you'll want to look at these," the concierge said. They were all from the London bureau. "Please call," said the first and second, then "Please call immediately," said the third and fourth, and finally, "Assume you will be filing on the hostage-taking ASAP."

I looked up stupidly at the urbane, slightly amused concierge. "Hostage-taking?" I asked"

Yes, he said, two Arab gunmen had raided the Chopin Express earlier that day, seized three Soviet Jews and an Austrian customs official, and had them at gunpoint at the Vienna Airport. They were demanding that the Austrian government close Schönau immediately. Hadn't I heard? It was all over the news.

"Shit!" I cried, and raced up to my room.

Today, in the digital age, I would not have been so blindsided. The headline would have chirped on my cell phone while I was wandering around the Schönbrunn gardens, and the office would have called moments later. The drama would have played out live on CNN International, and I would have headed straight for the airport. As it was, by the time I caught up with the news, the airport was totally surrounded and cut off by Austrian commandos, and there was no way to get anywhere near it. Instead, I grabbed my gear and headed across the street to the United Press International office, where I could follow the standoff as it unfolded on Austrian television.

It took hours to play out, but finally, around 2:15 a.m., with the gunmen still threatening the hostages at the airport and an Israeli commando team en route to Vienna, the Austrians capitulated. They struck a deal in which the government agreed to close the Schönau camp if the two gunmen released their hostages unharmed. The Arabs were given a small plane and allowed to fly out of the country.

The Israelis, whose SWAT team was still en route to Vienna, were furious. Prime Minister Meir flew directly to Vienna from Strasbourg to confront the Austrian chancellor Bruno Kreisky about his decision. It was a classic collision between two strong-willed politicians. They had an angry, tense meeting behind closed doors in which Meir demanded that Austria reverse its concession to the gunmen and Kreisky refused. He said Schönau would be closed but that individual Soviet Jews could still pass through Vienna if they had valid visas. Enraged, Meir skipped a scheduled press conference and left immediately for Israel. She gathered the ninety Soviet Jews waiting at Schönau and took them to Tel Aviv aboard her commandeered El Al airliner. I hitchhiked a ride back to Israel with her party.

In the end, no lives were lost. But the Palestinians claimed a victory, and Israel felt that the principle of no negotiations with terrorists had been compromised.

16

War-Redux Redux

It had been an exhausting, deflating trip for the seventy-five-year-old prime minister, but real trouble was waiting for her at home.

Defense Minister Dayan, Deputy Prime Minister Yigal Allon, Army Chief of Staff Lieutenant General David Elazar, and a colonel from army intelligence were waiting at her Jerusalem residence when Golda—everyone called her Golda—arrived from Vienna close to midnight. They laid out the latest intelligence: under the guise of military exercises, large-scale buildups were underway on the Egyptian and Syrian fronts. The Egyptians had brought up to the Suez Canal tens of thousands of troops, tanks, armored personnel carriers, artillery, and engineering units with mobile pontoon bridges capable of crossing the waterway. The entire Second and Third Egyptian armies were deployed along the west bank of the canal across from the thinly stretched Israeli units dug into the Bar Lev Line, the Israeli fortifications on the eastern bank.

To the north, Syria had mobilized its reserves and moved troops, artillery, and equipment up to the cease-fire line on the Golan Heights. The Syrian Air Force was on high alert.

Despite the ominous signs, Dayan and the other advisers were skeptical that war was imminent. They had been burned earlier in the year when similar Egyptian and Syrian maneuvers had prompted Israel to mobilize its reserves at a cost of $45 million, only to stand down when it proved to be a false alarm. The current situation could be another feint designed to fool the Israelis into another costly and disruptive mobilization.

In hindsight, Dayan's skepticism seems almost cavalier, given the stakes. But several considerations accounted for the cocky Israeli calculation: after their stunning victory over the combined Arab armies in 1967, the Israelis had grown complacent about their military might versus the Arab armies'. Second, Israeli intelligence services had concluded that Syria would never attack without Egypt and that Egypt would not dare to try to retake the Sinai until they received updated MiG-23 fighters and Scud missiles from the Soviets. Put together, this conventional wisdom was known among Israeli intelligence circles as "the concept." Israel's military and intelligence chiefs believed it and stuck to it religiously when assessing the threat from their neighbors.

The Israelis had reasons to believe that the Egyptians would not attack without the new materiel from Moscow. Unbeknownst to me, and the public, the Israelis had a secret weapon in Ashraf Marwan, the late President Nasser's son-in-law, who had been functioning since 1970 as a senior Mossad agent, feeding Israel a steady stream of intelligence about the Egyptian order of battle and war plans. Marwan, who was an adviser to Sadat, was considered by Israeli intelligence to be "a miraculous source" and "a superspy." Not all of Marwan's information had been perfect—his warnings had prompted the earlier, costly mobilization—but the Israelis had been able to verify enough of it often enough to take him seriously. Meeting his Mossad handlers clandestinely in Europe, Marwan endorsed the thinking behind "the concept," especially about Egypt's need for advanced Soviet fighters and missiles. He said repeatedly that the equipment was essential and that Egypt would not attack without it.

Given all this, Golda agreed with her advisers in Jerusalem that the prospect of war was remote despite the menacing maneuvers. The meeting broke up that night, October 3, with no new orders to the military.

The picture changed partially the next day when it was learned that the families and dependents of Soviet advisers stationed in Egypt and Syria were being airlifted out of the region. This was a flashing "red light." Israel's military chiefs put the regular army on alert but still stopped short of a full-scale, nationwide mobilization.

The next day—Friday, October 5—the eve of Yom Kippur, the Jewish holy day when the entire nation grinds to a halt, Israeli intelligence learned that heavy Soviet transports were arriving in Cairo and Damascus, apparently loaded with weapons. It appeared that the essential missing ingredient—advanced Soviet weaponry—was being added to the mix.

Even more urgently, Ashraf Marwan signaled to his Mossad handlers that he had urgent information to impart. Zvi Zamir, the Mossad chief, flew immediately to London to meet with Marwan at midnight. Marwan reported that Egypt and Syria definitely would launch full-scale attacks the next day at 6 p.m., October 6, Yom Kippur. (This tip was off by four hours; the Egyptian and Syrian assaults actually launched at 2 p.m., leading to subsequent speculation that Marwan may have been a double agent, deliberately misleading his Israeli contacts. Or had he simply been wrong? It is not clear to this day. Marwan himself never admitted his role publicly and died semimysteriously in a fall from the balcony of his home in London's Mayfair district in June 2007. Such are the perils of playing both sides against each other.)

At the time, Marwan's information seemed irrefutable. But, astonishingly, Moshe Dayan remained doubtful that war was about to break out. He was still confident of the concept, especially the belief that Egypt would not attack without more advanced weaponry, when he and General Elazar met with Golda Meir at 8:05 a.m. on Yom Kippur, six hours before the actual assault would begin. General Elazar, citing the Soviet airlift, urged a preemptive air strike against Syria's air force and army, beginning at noon, in the hope that Israel could knock Syria's planes on the ground, just as it had done against Egypt six years before. The prime minister demurred and then, after more discussion, decided definitively against a preemptive strike. Her considerations were diplomatic, not military.

Israel by this stage was almost entirely dependent on the United States for military support and equipment, and Henry Kissinger was urging her to hold back. "Don't preempt," was his urgent message. If Israel struck first, he famously said in a cable to the prime minister, she would not receive "so much as a nail" in resupplies nor any political backing from Washington. It may have been a hollow threat, but Meir decided she couldn't risk it—that Israel couldn't risk it. "If we strike first," she has been quoted as saying, "we won't get help from anybody."

Elazar then proposed a massive mobilization of the entire Israeli Air Force and four armored divisions, about 120,000 men. Again, Dayan objected, urging only a partial mobilization. This time Meir gave Elazar the go-ahead. Israel was about to undergo its fourth full-scale war against its Arab neighbors in little more than a generation.

As usual, I was oblivious to all the drama going on behind closed doors. True, I knew and had written about the reports of the Egyptian and Syrian buildups. I knew that the regular Israeli army was on alert—and would expect no less, given the circumstances. I had read the reports of Anwar Sadat's bellicose threats over the recent months. But all that had happened before and not led to war. In fact, Sadat had declared the year before, 1972, to be "The Year of Decision" in which Egypt was going to regain the Sinai. The year had passed with occasional shooting incidents but no war, no "decision."

I had just returned from Vienna and written a Sunday News of the Week in Review piece about the implications of Golda Meir's failure to reverse the Austrian decision to close the transit camp at Schönau. Like the Israeli population and the expats living in the country, I was winding down in Jerusalem on October 4 and 5 for a quiet holiday weekend. In fact, for secular Israelis, who were the majority, and for non-Jews, Yom Kippur, the Day of Atonement, Judaism's holiest day, was a holiday, an excuse for a party, and there had a been a good one the night before at the home of David Rubinger, an Israeli friend and photographer for Time Life. While the observant were in synagogues, we had been partying. No doubt we should all have been atoning for our sins on the morning of October 6, but we were sleeping late instead.

So, for the second time, my first word of war came from a phone call. No hangover this time but surprise, when the Government Press Office called late morning with word of the countrywide mobilization in response to the Egyptian and Syrian threats. The streets of Jerusalem, which had been deserted and silent in the early morning, were suddenly busy with soldiers hurrying to join their units. Heavy trucks and olive-drab military buses rolled toward assembly points all over the country. Kol Israel, the state radio, broke its holiday silence to broadcast word of the mobilization. The Yom Kippur observances were interrupted and, for the soldiers at least, forgotten. If the Egyptian military planners thought that Israel would be slow to mobilize on Yom Kippur, the opposite was true; the streets were clear of traffic, and so the called-up reserves could head out that much faster.

But when massive, coordinated assaults were launched on both fronts at 2 p.m., the shock to the Israeli public was genuine.

The Egyptians, who had deployed some 100,000 soldiers, 1,350 tanks, and 2,000 guns and heavy mortars along the western bank of the

Suez Canal, poured thousands of troops across the water on pontoon bridges under cover of a punishing artillery barrage. In their six years of occupation, the Israelis had constructed sixty-foot-high mounds of sand to reinforce the Bar Lev Line. The Egyptians punched holes in these with high-pressure water cannons and rushed through. On the eastern bank, 450 Israeli soldiers of the Jerusalem Brigade dug into sixteen forts along the Bar Lev Line fought back as best they could but were quickly overwhelmed. The Egyptians established several bridgeheads on the eastern bank that first day and night. By 8:30 p.m., the first Egyptian tanks crossed the canal and pushed several miles into the Sinai. There was jubilation in the streets of Cairo and on the radio. In the Egyptian mind, the stinging humiliation of the Six-Day War had been salved. The October 6, 1973, crossing has been a national day of celebration every year since.

On the Golan Heights, Syria opened with an airstrike by one hundred aircraft and a fifty-minute artillery barrage. Thousands of Syrian troops backed by tanks and artillery quickly bypassed the UN observer posts and pushed into Israeli-held territory. By nightfall, they were in position to threaten the northern Israeli cities of Tiberias and Safed on the western side of the Sea of Galilee.

Israel was stunned by the ferocious attacks, her sense of invincibility badly shaken. The whole nation awoke suddenly from a deep, complacent sleep to confront a stunning pair of devastating attacks on two fronts. But at a news conference in Tel Aviv on the evening of October 6, an oddly buoyant Moshe Dayan put the best possible face on the day's fighting. He conceded that Israel was engaged in "an all-out war" and had suffered setbacks on both fronts and substantial losses but insisted that Israeli forces would regain everything that was lost and inflict "very heavy casualties" on both Egypt and Syria. Dayan was confident, almost jaunty, as he spoke about what had clearly been the darkest day of fighting in Israel's short history. It was a bravura, theatrical performance by a man who had insisted privately up until that morning that the Arabs were bluffing and that war was unlikely. Doubtless he knew already that the balance of forces had changed and that Israel was being sorely tested. But he did not let on. Watching from the front row in the briefing, I could not help but be struck by his curiously upbeat manner. Frankly, I assumed it was mostly an act, designed to cover his own grievous errors of the preceding seventy-two hours.

The Egyptians and Syrians pressed their advantage on both fronts
for the first two or three days of the war, inflicting heavy casualties on
undermanned Israeli units. But the Israeli Air Force went into action
quickly, striking Egyptian units in the Sinai, knocking out some of the
pontoon bridges across the canal and hitting military airfields deep
inside Egypt.

Some of the heaviest fighting was on the Syrian front. Israeli tanks
and troops rushed to confront the advancing Syrian units, launching
fierce, set-piece tank battles across the Golan Heights. Scrambling,
Israeli fighters knocked out the Syrian air defenses and bombed Syrian
airfields near Damascus.

Now that I had been jolted into action, I covered the first two days
of the war from Jerusalem, monitoring the Israeli military briefings and
watching the eastern front to see if Jordan would join the battle. King
Hussein, having lost half his kingdom to the Israelis in the space of a
few days in 1967, wisely held back in response to US urgings.

But by the third day of fighting, it was apparent that, while the Israelis might eventually prevail, this would be no cakewalk and would
take weeks, if not more, to resolve. I moved my operation to Tel Aviv,
where the Ministry of Defense is headquartered and where the military
spokespeople were briefing several times a day.

This was a huge, sprawling story that no one person could cover
alone. The *Times* flew in two veteran war correspondents as backup:
Charles Mohr, who had been in my bureau in Saigon and covered more
war than many generals ever see, and Henry Kamm, a widely experienced, resourceful foreign correspondent based in Paris. Locally I
added Cornell Capa, a superb Magnum photographer who was a friend
and happened to be in the country when the fighting had erupted. He
immediately started filing pictures from the front lines and around the
country. Among us, we filed three to six pieces a day to the *Times*, rang-
ing from a daily overall lead war story depicting the fighting to news
analyses about the ebb and flow of the war and the diplomatic maneu-
vering to features and notebooks from the front lines and neighborhoods
around the country to interviews with key military and political leaders,
when we could get them. I handed out the daily assignments, rotating
them so that we all got to see and do all of it during the course of the
next three weeks.

The wire services and other major news organizations beefed up their ranks as well. The daily evening military briefings at the government press office in Tel Aviv, which had attracted a smattering of foreign correspondents before the war, now became jam-packed affairs with some six hundred reporters, photographers, camera operators, and television anchors from the United States and Europe jostling for space and attention. Harry Reasoner, then senior anchor for ABC News, parachuted in, as did other famous faces. It got to be such a crowd of bold-face media names that Nora Ephron jetted in for *Esquire* to do a piece about "the war lovers," most of which she researched in the crowded bar at the Hilton Tel Aviv.

That bar would fill up beginning around 10 p.m. with correspondents dusty from a day in the Sinai or on the Golan Heights, trading stories about their adventures. Some of the tales were actually true. Often the most exaggerated accounts came from Charlie Wilson, an engaging, swashbuckling US representative from the State of Texas, who had come to see the fighting for himself. The Israeli army cleverly assigned him a gorgeous escort who looked trim and glamorous in her short khaki uniform skirt and high heels as she headed up to his room with him each night around midnight. In her case, anyway, an escort's work was never done.

My *Times* colleagues and I basically commuted to the war on a daily basis. To get to front lines in the Sinai and meet with commanders in the field, one of us would leave Tel Aviv around 4 a.m. and drive six or more hours with a military escort officer to catch up with one of the Israeli units. We talked with tank commanders who were engaging the Egyptians in one of the great tank battles of all time and at the Sinai airfields, with pilots returning from sorties over the Egyptian lines and Egypt itself. Almost always we got a better, more candid account of the battle in the field than at the canned military briefings in Tel Aviv. But there was no way to file from the field, so we would drive all the way back to Tel Aviv and write and file from there. Often it was close to midnight Israel time (6 p.m. Eastern Standard Time) before the material was cleared by the military censors and on its way to New York.

Today, of course, with sat phones and instant communication from the field, most of that driving and commuting would be unnecessary. The television networks would have mobile units with satellite uplinks capable of transmitting directly and staying in the field indefinitely.

Reporters would even "embed" with units willing to have them along, with all the pluses and minuses that come with that. The coverage today would be more immediate, and doubtless dramatic, but not necessarily more comprehensive or even more accurate.

Battlefield reporting, especially from fast-moving front lines, is famously like viewing the entire war through a soda straw. You get a sharply focused look at the fighting in front and around you but struggle to fit it into the larger picture. Even the field commanders we talked to could only explain what their units had or had not accomplished up to that point. How was the overall battle going? Who was winning or losing? Most commanders could not tell you beyond their immediate theater.

One who could—or at least thought he could—was the flamboyant Ariel "Arik" Sharon, later Israel's prime minister. On more than one occasion the press-conscious Sharon had a major on his staff round up key reporters in Tel Aviv and escort them to his command trailer as his armored units gradually reversed the Egyptian advances, recrossed the canal, and ultimately surrounded the Egyptian Third Army on the western bank.

With a bloodied bandage wrapped dramatically around his forehead (caused not by a bullet but by a friendly tank turret that had turned at the wrong moment), Sharon played host in his command trailer, serving brandy and tins of smoked oysters while he regaled the corralled reporters with his and his soldiers' triumphs. I joined him in his trailer one morning on the western bank of the canal to hear him describe how he had closed the vise around the Third Army, cutting off their last avenues of escape. He was funny, irreverent, and openly unhappy with his superiors at GHQ. He was ready to move toward Cairo, he said, if he could just get the go-ahead from the reluctant chiefs back in Tel Aviv. He didn't use the word "wimps," but that was the message. Sharon's bravado made irresistible copy and, of course, fed his considerable ego and built his tattered political reputation at home. He loved to get out ahead of the briefers back in Tel Aviv and paint a picture of a battle that was, in fact, turning dramatically and decisively in Israel's favor. At headquarters, in the presence of superior officers, Sharon had to restrain himself, but at the front, surrounded by his own troops and tanks, he was in his element and loving it. He had no doubt that his theater was the decisive stage on which the war would be won or lost.

Of course, not everything went as smoothly and successfully as Sharon would have had us believe. In fact, for two days, when the Israeli counteroffensive in the Sinai stalled, the military in Tel Aviv barred reporters from the front and effectively closed the Sinai; there was no point in advertising the fact that, at that stage, the counterattack was frozen. But as the tide gradually turned and Egyptian units began retreating back to and across the canal, the Israeli command wanted the world to know about it. The Sinai was reopened to general coverage, and I and two other US reporters were flown from Tel Aviv to the Sinai front in a small plane that hugged the terrain as we skimmed above the dunes and landed about four miles east of the canal. Hooking up with an Israeli battery of 155-millimeter howitzers, we found ourselves too close to the Egyptian artillery, which pinned us down in the hot, dry sand. Their shells came whistling over our heads in batches of four, landing with a deafening thump behind us. They did little damage, but an Israeli officer lying next to me pointed to a convoy of ammunition trucks halted on the side of the road just ahead.

"Let's hope they miss that," he said. Suddenly the shelling stopped. The officer sat up, brushing himself off. "See how stupid they are?" he said. "They could have scored a big hit, and now they've stopped." A moment later, the shelling resumed in the same four-shell patterns, and the officer and the rest of us burrowed ourselves into the sand again. But this time the Egyptian shells landed about half a mile to the south, crashing loudly but harmlessly. The Egyptian gunners may have missed a juicy target, but the battle for the Sinai wasn't over yet.

Nonetheless, as the situation on the Egyptian front stabilized after the first three days of the war, the Israeli high command turned its attention to the Golan Heights, where the Syrian Army and Air Force, backed by Iraqi armored, artillery, and infantry units, had pushed westward and sent artillery shells and Soviet-supplied FROG missiles into Israel proper. Many of the residents of the towns and villages in northern Israel were spending day and night in underground shelters. Syrian commandos even flew in helicopters to the ten thousand–foot summit of Mount Hermon and retook the strategic overlook that Israel had captured in 1967. But Israeli Air Force fighters struck back, pummeling the forward tank units and halting the Syrian advance. Over Damascus, Israeli jets sent a signal to the regime by bombing the headquarters of the Syrian Air Force, the Syrian general staff, and the Syrian Ministry of Defense.

On the fifth day of the war, October 10, I got up onto the Golan Heights, driving east behind the Israeli forces that by then had pushed the Syrians back in heavy fighting beyond the 1967 armistice line. The rocky, exposed Golan was a graveyard, with burned-out wrecks of Syrian tanks, armored personnel carriers, and trucks littering both sides of the highway. The fields on either side were burning or blackened from artillery shells, and the houses in the few scattered settlements had been pounded into rubble. Cornell Capa was with me, capturing the scene with his wonderful photos as we drove east in my car in pursuit of the advancing Israeli units. At one forward point, I stopped the car long enough for Cornell to photograph a roadside marker that read "Damascus, 55 kilometers." Beyond, Israeli units were sending up a column of dust as they raced east. Cornell's vivid picture told the day's story.

The Israelis were advancing, but the battle was far from over. We stopped repeatedly as Syrian long-range artillery shells whistled overhead and landed behind us. Facedown in a roadside ditch, we waited out an artillery duel and watched a dogfight overhead between a Syrian MiG and two Israeli Skyhawks. The MiG pitched into a steep dive and leveled off just a few hundred feet above the rocky terrain. With the Skyhawks screaming in pursuit, the Syrian plane broke off and headed east, disappearing inside Syria.

Not all the MiGs escaped, however. We saw one that was hit over the Golan, forcing the pilot to eject behind Israeli lines. Later, when I talked to the Israeli doctor who treated the pilot in a makeshift field hospital, he said the Syrian had lost an eye but would live. "He was very afraid," the doctor said, "and kept repeating over and over that he had no weapons on him."

Cornell and I covered the Golan battle for the next three days, returning each night to file our copy and pictures from the resort town of Safed, above the Sea of Galilee, which was the headquarters of the Israeli Northern Command. There I was able to interview Major General Mordechai Hod, who had retired as Air Force chief of staff five months earlier but had been hastily recalled to direct the northern air operations against Syria. The Israeli pilots' biggest problem, he said, came from batteries of sophisticated SAM-6 antiaircraft missiles the Syrians had installed along the front.

"These are the latest and best missiles the Russians have," he said. "Better than anything the Americans have encountered in North Vietnam." But, he said, each day his pilots were confronting fewer SAM-6s as they flew over the Golan.

"Maybe they are running out of them," he said with a smile. "I hope so."

Unlike the Sinai, where reporters were required to have an Israeli military escort to approach the front, the Syrian front was so chaotic and fast-moving that, after the first couple of days, Cornell and I could simply drive ourselves across the Golan to follow the fighting first-hand. It was hairy at times, and by the third night Cornell had had enough. He came to my room in our hotel in Safed around midnight with two beers and sat down on the opposite bed to talk. "I've got to stop this," he said softly. "I am the last surviving male in my family."

His famous photographer brother, Robert Capa, had been killed when he'd stepped on a land mine covering the French-Indochina war in 1954. And Cornell had covered wars all over the world. Cornell told me he was going to break off his contract with the *Times* and return home to New York the next morning. He said he was going to pursue his dream to create a center for concerned photography that would exhibit and honor the work of photographers like his brother who had risked their lives to cover important stories around the world, stories that made a difference.

"I want to do it, for my brother and the rest of my family" he said, "but I have got to be alive to do it."

Cornell was twenty years my senior, and that night, sitting in a dimly lit hotel room, he looked old and tired. I didn't want him to leave while the war was still underway, but I could see that he had made up his mind. As a thoroughgoing professional, Cornell was not about to desert the *Times* without a photographer in the middle of a major story. He told me that he had arranged with Shlomo Arad, a top Israeli photographer, to relieve him in the morning. Cornell headed home the next day and over the next couple years, with the help of Jackie Onassis and other prominent New Yorkers, went on to raise the funds to found what is today the renowned International Center of Photography in Manhattan. In fact, I had hired Cornell for the duration not only because he was so good but because the *Times*' regular contract photographer in Israel, Micha Bar-Am, another splendid Magnum professional, had been called up to active duty on the first day of the war to shoot pictures for *BaMahane*, the Israeli army's magazine. Micha had been born in Berlin, emigrated with his family to Palestine as a boy, and grown up on a kibbutz, where he had developed his skills as a photographer. He had fought and taken pictures in Israel's previous wars and now was with frontline units as they moved through Gaza and across the Sinai. His remarkable pictures of the Sinai campaign were published in *BaMahane* and today hang as art in museums around the world.

He was—and is—great company as well. Micha and I had become close friends as well as colleagues in the year before the 1973 war. We traveled everywhere together in pursuit of stories throughout Israel, the occupied West Bank of the Jordan, and across the Sinai. Micha speaks English, French, German, and some Arabic in addition to Hebrew and seemed at times to know everyone in the country. If we were stopped at an army checkpoint, as we often were, half the time Micha would know one of the soldiers or they would know him from his work at *BaMahane*. Their frowns as they approached the car would turn to smiles as they recognized Micha behind his bushy beard. "Micha!" they would shout and, more often than not, wave us through. I would keep my mouth shut. It was a great collaboration.

Micha had his own adventures during the October War, including one marvelous moment when he and an Israeli photographer colleague approached a bombed-out Egyptian surface-to-air missile base in the northern Sinai that they were sure was deserted. As a gag, they pointed their cameras into the entrance and shouted in fractured Arabic, "Come out with your hands up! Move quickly!" Sure enough, a column of dazed, bedraggled Egyptian soldiers emerged, one-by-one, with hands over their heads. There were eighteen of them, left behind by the retreating Egyptian units, exhausted, hungry, and crazy from lack of water. Micha and the other photographer "captured" them and marched them single file back to the nearest Israeli unit, which took them into custody. The incident made a famous story for *BaMahane*, and I retold the tale in a reporter's notebook in the *Times* composed of other wacky wartime incidents.

I spent the closing days of the three-week war writing broader-picture and news analysis pieces from Tel Aviv and following Israeli units as they crossed the Suez Canal and encircled the Egyptian Third Army and the city of Suez. Sharon's forces had cut the Egyptian supply lines and were ready to annihilate the Third Army and push further west toward Cairo, but a United Nations–brokered cease-fire held them back. The initial cease-fire on October 22 quickly unraveled, with each side blaming the other for violations, but was reimposed by the Security Council on October 25. This time it held. When the guns finally fell silent, Israeli forces were 101 kilometers, or 63 miles, from Cairo. On the Syrian front, they were forty kilometers, or about twenty-five miles, from Damascus. They had withstood the initial Arab onslaught and finally, at great cost, gained more territory. But they were no closer to peace.

The October 1973 war, which the Israelis call the Yom Kippur War and the Arabs call the Ramadan War, was a watershed event militarily, diplomatically, and psychologically. In many ways, it created the standoff and realities that still afflict the Middle East almost five decades later. Negotiations after the war returned the Sinai to Egypt and led to the 1979 Camp David Accords and a peace treaty between Israel and Egypt that is still frosty but remains in place. The armistice and separation of forces along the Golan Heights that was negotiated after the cease-fire remains largely intact, despite the ghastly civil war in Syria. Israel ultimately signed a peace treaty with Jordan, and that frontier remains quiet. But peace with the Palestinians is as elusive as ever. Trust is arguably more elusive than ever, on both sides.

In fact, the 1973 war hardened attitudes on all sides. Over the five decades since the war, Israelis have grown progressively more skeptical, if not cynical, about ever achieving a lasting peace with their neighbors. Israeli settlers have become more determined to dig in. Today, as this is written, the Israeli political right challenges the validity of a two-state solution. The Israeli left is much diminished. Three generations of Israelis have grown up with the 1973 war as an object lesson that, despite their triumph in 1967, they are not invulnerable. Militarily, they are supreme in the region; David has become Goliath. But the existence of the democratic Jewish Israeli state and the success of the Zionist experiment are far from secure.

On the Arab side, the Ramadan War restored a sense of pride in themselves as warriors. Despite ultimate setbacks on the battlefield, Sadat eventually achieved his principal goal: breaking the diplomatic deadlock with Israel and forcing internationally supervised negotiations for the return of the Sinai. Syria's Hafez al-Assad emerged from the war battered but still in power and ultimately able to hand over power to his son, who has ravaged his own country almost beyond recognition.

Significantly, the 1973 war convinced many Egyptians of the futility of defeating Israel on the battlefield. Although they believe 1973 restored the honor they had lost in 1967, the Egyptian officer corps seems to have accepted that they will not prevail militarily. The Egyptian Army has grown wealthy and powerful since, but they haven't fought Israel in almost fifty years and are not likely to in the next fifty. Their problems are at home, in the Sinai and Tahrir Square, with the Muslim Brotherhood, with corruption and terrorism, and with their crippled economy. The Palestinians emerged from the war as the recognized authority of any future independent, sovereign Palestinian state, should such a state ever come to be, but their own divisions have only multiplied, and their leadership seems weaker than ever.

There were major international repercussions from the war as well: the newly established détente between the Soviet Union and United States survived its first major challenge, Europe felt the sting of the first organized Arab oil embargo, and the United States emerged as the indispensible negotiator of any future agreements in the Middle East. What the war didn't produce any more than the wars before it was peace.

The full consequences of the war were far from clear in its immediate aftermath. I spent the next months writing about the impact on Israeli society and the national psyche. The Israelis are a resourceful, resilient people under most circumstances, but they had been shaken to the core. I wrote about how on Kol Israel, the state radio, psychologists were advising people to keep busy and get a lot of physical exercise to deal with depression. Counseling services were opened at universities and hospitals. The continuing tension was reflected in everyday events: the way people would jump when sonic booms from high-flying jet fighters rattled windows in Tel Aviv or Jerusalem, the instant silence in a restaurant or shop when the hourly news came on the radio, the searching looks between friends meeting for the first time after the war, each unsure whether there had been a casualty in the other's family.

Even the famously mordant Israeli humor reflected the atmosphere. When the nationwide blackout was lifted and motorists were allowed to scrape the blue paint off their headlights, one joke went, you could tell the difference between the optimists and pessimists: the pessimists left the paint on while the optimists cleaned off one headlight. I wrote about all this, and in many respects it made more interesting and more revealing copy than the war itself. This is the great advantage of the resident foreign correspondent over the war lovers and news anchors who parachuted in at the start of the war. Once the fighting was over, they were gone, on to the next conflict or back to their studios in New York or London. Even the bar in the Hilton Tel Aviv emptied out. But those of us who were assigned to Israel on a continuing basis stayed on, covering a more-nuanced and multidimensional story. Having lived and worked in Israel before the war, we could appreciate just how different it was after.

17

Postwar Blues

Israel and the West Bank changed in the wake of the war, economically, politically, and, most strikingly, psychologically. The big story now was not the front lines of a shooting war but the attitudes of one people who had undergone the shock of their lives and of another whose plight deepened into near despair. The change for the first group, the sense that things now were deeply different for them, was underscored by the death in early December of David Ben-Gurion, Israel's first premier and, arguably, the father of his country, at eighty-seven. A short, stocky bundle of explosive energy given to public rages and moody, contemplative periods, Ben-Gurion had headed the powerful Jewish Agency in prestate days, the dominant Labor Party, and the Histadrut, the giant labor federation that organized and represented most of the workers in Israel. He was the man who, in May of 1948, had read out Israel's declaration of independence, guided it through the war of independence, and fathered its secret entry into the family of nuclear-weapon nations. At five-foot-seven, he was the towering figure of the founding generation, and now, just weeks after the nation had endured its costliest war, he was gone.

Israel mourned Ben-Gurion's passing with simple dignity. His body lay in state in front of the Knesset, or parliament, atop a windy, exposed hilltop in Jerusalem while two hundred thousand people slowly passed by his flag-draped bier. I spent most of the early December day there watching the procession of faces that made up modern Israel: soldiers in fatigues and combat boots, fresh-faced sabras in school uniforms, short, stumpy women immigrants from eastern Europe in babushkas, Oriental Jews from North Africa and Asian countries, rabbis in black homburgs, political and military leaders, and, as a reminder of the recent fighting, wounded veterans hobbling on crutches and canes.

"That was a man," one mourner said with a nod toward the simple wooden coffin. "We needed him then, and we need him now even more."

In fact, over his final ten years, Ben-Gurion had largely withdrawn from public life. He had retired to his modest home in Sde Boker, a desert kibbutz in the Negev, where he read and wrote in the library of the university he had founded there and occasionally received Moshe Dayan and other leaders seeking advice, which he dispensed in increasingly dark and apocalyptic terms.

After a full-dress state funeral in Jerusalem in the morning, David Ben-Gurion was laid to rest in a starkly simple forty-five-minute religious service on a breathtaking promontory outside Sde Boker. The gravesite overlooked the rugged canyons and deep desert valley known in the bible as the Wilderness of Zin. I stood off to one side among three hundred mourners who included the nation's top political leaders, led by Premier Golda Meir—stolid and somber in a black suit and carrying a black handbag—representatives of foreign governments, former associates, and neighbors from the kibbutz. At Ben-Gurion's insistence, there were no eulogies, only a few psalms. "The Lord giveth," the rabbi intoned, "and the lord taketh away."

At the end of the ceremony, Amos Ben-Gurion, the former premier's only son, led the Ben-Gurion family away from the gravesite. Among the grandchildren was Yariv Ben Gurion, a soldier in the army who was limping slightly from a wound suffered in the October War. That said it all about the passing of the generations and how deeply the Yom Kippur War had penetrated the ranks of Israeli society.

It didn't take long for the finger-pointing to begin in Israel over who was to blame for the nation having been caught flat-footed by the war. Two formal commissions of inquiry, one judicial, one military, began taking testimony about what had happened and why. Meanwhile, the mutual accusations among political leaders started flying.

Golda Meir and Moshe Dayan defended their actions as best they could under withering criticism from the opposition and veterans of the fighting, but both ultimately had to tender their resignations in April 1974, after the Labor Party lost seats in the Knesset elections in

December. Yitzhak Rabin, the former chief of staff and ambassador to Washington who had spent the war as an informal adviser to Chief of Staff Elazar, replaced Meir as premier. Nor did the military escape responsibility. General Elazar and several of his top officers were recommended for dismissal. Given the sour public mood, they were lucky they weren't strung up.

Talks toward an Egyptian-Israeli disengagement began almost immediately after the ceasefire at Kilometer 101 alongside the Suez-Cairo highway. It was a bizarre scene, with senior Arab and Israeli military officers arriving and departing in swirls of dust by helicopter at the barren spot where the fighting had halted in place. The talks took place at wooden tables set beneath a huge camouflage canopy strung among four Israeli tanks. The negotiations were ticklish, because Israeli and Egyptian units were thoroughly entangled on both sides of the canal; but both sides were motivated to reach a deal quickly. Egypt needed Israel's cooperation to get supplies through to relieve Suez and the encircled Third Army; Israel needed Egypt's cooperation to return captured prisoners of war and the remains of their fallen and to consolidate their lines.

I covered the talks at Kilometer 101 along with a small army of foreign journalists who came to the remote site separately from Cairo and Tel Aviv. As luck would have it, the senior Israeli negotiator was General Aharon Yariv, whom I had interviewed and gotten to know when he had been head of Israeli intelligence. He didn't give away any state secrets, but he was an invaluable source about how the talks were going. Yariv and his Egyptian counterpart, General Mohamed el-Gamasy, hammered out and actually signed a detailed six-point disengagement plan over several days of negotiation. But little of it was announced at Kilometer 101, because Henry Kissinger wanted to save the big news for a multiparty peace conference he was stage-managing under UN auspices in Geneva just before Christmas. Kissinger was determined to demonstrate to the Soviet Union and the rest of the world that the United States was in the diplomatic driver's seat, with Henry at the wheel.

I flew to Geneva to cover the conference, which turned out to be a largely theatrical event conducted mostly behind closed doors and punctuated each afternoon by dueling news conferences by spokespersons from the different parties. In the end, the diplomats emerged

with essentially the same disengagement and prisoner-exchange deal
that Yariv had hammered out and leaked to me at Kilometer 101. The
efforts to reach a broader political settlement at Geneva were mostly a
bust, because Syria ultimately refused to attend. But it was not a total
loss: I managed to get in several outstanding meals in Geneva and a
weekend of skiing in the French Alps before flying back to Jerusalem
on Christmas Eve.

By this time, I had my priorities in order.

Henry Kissinger remained the key and indefatigable player in the political negotiations that took place over the next months and ultimately
led to disengagement and separation of forces agreements on both the
Egyptian and Syrian fronts. He made repeated trips to all the capitals
in the region and eventually undertook his famous shuttle diplomacy
between Jerusalem and Damascus that led to the armistice agreement
and creation of a UN-supervised buffer zone on the Golan Heights. But
early 1974 was hardly peaceful in the region. Israel and Syria clashed
repeatedly over the Golan and fought a pitched battle in which the Israelis retook the strategic outpost atop Mount Hermon. At the same time,
Palestinian gunmen began assaults of their own, repeatedly crossing the
border from Lebanon and Jordan to attack civilian targets in northern
Israel.

The most horrific of these occurred on May 15—the twenty-sixth anniversary of Israel's independence—when three Arab guerrillas snuck
across the border from southern Lebanon just after midnight and shot
their way into the town of Ma'alot, just five miles inside Israel. Not
coincidentally, Ma'alot and its sister Arab village of Tarshiha had been
held up as a showcase example of Arab-Jewish cooperation. The two
settlements had a common town council, with a Jewish mayor and an
Arab deputy mayor, and the two communities had managed a peaceful,
if strained, coexistence. Until now.

Dressed in khaki fatigues and heavily armed with automatic weapons and explosives, the Arab gunmen had shot a family in an apartment building and descended upon the school, where some eighty-five
teenage students on an outing from a religious school had camped in
sleeping bags overnight. It was never clear whether the guerillas knew
the students would be in the school that night or stumbled upon them.
In either case, they had at gunpoint an especially vulnerable band of
hostages to use as pawns in negotiations with the Israeli authorities. In

exchange for the lives of the students, the gunmen demanded the release of twenty Palestinian prisoners held by the Israelis. They wanted the prisoners delivered to Damascus or Cyprus by 6 p.m. I heard a radio report about the hostage-taking shortly after dawn and set off for Ma'alot, about a two-hour drive from Jerusalem. Micha Bar-Am started driving at the same time from his home near Tel Aviv. By midmorning, we were both lying in a grassy field outside the perimeter set up by Israeli soldiers around the school. We had a clear view of the scene and could hear the negotiations being conducted in Hebrew, Arabic, and English via bullhorns. In late morning, the gunmen released a young Israeli woman from the school and sent her out with a demand that the French and Romanian ambassadors to Israel be brought to the scene to serve as go-betweens. Through the long, hot day, we could hear the crackling back-and-forth between the two sides.

"We mean the ultimatum, every word of it," the guerrillas said at one point. "We warn you, 6 p.m. is the final deadline. You are playing with these children's lives."

"You have a guarantee of safe passage to any Arab country," an Israeli negotiator shouted back. "The French and Romanian ambassadors are on their way, I promise you."

Defense Minister Dayan arrived by helicopter from Jerusalem and took command of the rescue operation along with the Army Chief of Staff Mordechai Gur. At this point in the long struggle with Palestinian terrorism, the Israeli policy was supposedly ironclad: no negotiations, no concessions. But in this case, probably because of the presence of so many children among the hostages, negotiations were audibly underway. In the afternoon, the scene fell strangely quiet. Nothing moved. The Israeli soldiers crouched soundlessly in the grass around the school. I could hear birds chirping in the fields but no voices. At one point, Micha climbed the steel ladder to the top of a nearby water tower to get an overhead shot, stayed there for a while, and then came back to my side.

Inside the school, a boy came on the megaphone. "Give them what they demand," he shouted frantically in Hebrew. "Do it quickly, or they'll kill us all."

"Don't worry," an Israeli officer replied, at 5:25 p.m., thirty-five minutes before the deadline. "We'll give them what they want, and we'll be freeing you soon."

As if this were a signal, firing burst out, and the Israeli soldiers leaped up and rushed the school from all directions. In the pandemonium that followed, two of the three Arabs were apparently hit by the opening burst of fire. One was killed instantly, but the second had the strength to turn his automatic weapon on the crouching students, spraying the second-story classroom with bullets. The third tossed two grenades out the window to scatter the attacking soldiers and rushed downstairs to the entrance, where he had stashed enough explosives to blow up the entire school. He was shot and killed before he could detonate them. Micha and I rushed toward the school as the surviving students streamed out, some wounded, some carrying others who were bleeding profusely. The kids were shrieking and crying. It was absolute carnage. Suddenly, the firing stopped, and it was weirdly silent. The whole attack had taken less than ten minutes. In all, eighteen of the teenage hostages had been killed and seventy wounded, nine critically. The three gunmen were dead. From the nearby town of Safed, I dictated a long eye-witness account of the bloody day that the *Times* ran under a triple-decked headline five columns across page one, illustrated by Micha's up-close photos of the fleeing children.

The massacre at Ma'alot had a huge impact on me personally. The violence, the bloodshed, the brutality, and the utter senselessness of the whole thing made me wonder if anything was going to ever change in the region. The next day, I covered the funeral of sixteen of the teenage victims in nearby Safed. A huge, angry crowd of mostly Oriental Jews turned out, while the Israeli Arab residents cowered in their homes behind closed shutters. The crowd, shrieking "Revenge! Revenge!" turned on the Israeli president and deputy prime minister when they arrived from Jerusalem. Neither could deliver their prepared remarks. They were jostled and pushed inside a tight knot of police officers who struggled to get them back into their cars and away from the scene. The funerals were cut short, and the crowd scattered into the streets, looking for a fight. It was an ugly end to a horrific day.

The massacre—there was no other word for it—was one of the costliest terrorist incidents in Israel's twenty-six-year history. Ultimately, there were twenty-six fatalities in all, including the three gunmen. It underscored the new reality: Israel could win wars but couldn't secure the country or its people against determined infiltrators. It couldn't win the peace. For all its horror, the attack at Ma'alot interrupted

Henry Kissinger's shuttle diplomacy for just one day. He continued his relentless, exhausting trips between Jerusalem and Damascus, enduring endless hours of talks and heavy, postmidnight dinners with Syrian president Hafez al-Assad, until finally he produced a truce and separation-of-forces agreement enforced by a buffer zone on the Golan Heights and a UN truce-supervisory force that remains in place to this day. It was a remarkable achievement. I'm not sure anyone else could have accomplished it.

On the West Bank, the Palestinian residents resigned themselves to the prospect of an open-ended Israeli occupation. The Palestinians staged a general strike and several smaller stone-throwing protests, but privately they conceded that the war had made the creation of an independent Palestinian state even more remote. I traveled the length and breadth of the West Bank, interviewing Palestinians about their attitudes and writing about the new Israeli settlements that were being established, some with support of the Israeli government, some without.

I continued covering the fallout of the war through the spring and early summer of 1974 when suddenly, in July, a new crisis erupted on my beat: a ragtag group of Greek Cypriot National Guard officers overthrew the government of Archbishop Makarios and declared a shaggy-haired thirty-eight-year-old newspaper publisher, Nikos Giorgiades Sampson, the new president of Cyprus. I flew to Nicosia immediately and got there in time to cover Sampson's first news conference as president. It was a chaotic, almost comical event in which Sampson ranted about government corruption and abuse and, flanked by four green-bereted soldiers with submachine guns, pounded a table with a leather whip, billy club, and rubber hose that he claimed the Makarios regime had used to torture its political opponents. Two alleged victims of the torture were produced, including one man who told the assembled reporters that he had been paralyzed as a result of repeated beatings on his legs and feet over several weeks. The man had fresh casts on his legs.

"This whole thing is an act," a Greek Cypriot reporter whispered to me. "I know that man. He's a police sergeant. I saw him walking normally a couple of days ago."

Sampson himself seemed a clown, an ill-tailored nobody playing at president, but he had the backing, for the moment at least, of the newly installed Greek government in Athens. I wondered if they couldn't at least have found a more credible performer, perhaps a professional

actor, who could have been more convincing. But I didn't have to wonder for long. Along with dozens of other foreign correspondents who
had flown to the island, I had booked into the Ledra Palace, a handsome
four-story colonial-era hotel set in spacious, palmy gardens that abutted
the so-called Green Line that separated the Greek and Turkish sections
of Nicosia. I had stayed there before on reporting trips and once on
vacation with my family. Nicosia, like the rest of Cyprus, was strictly
divided along ethnic lines, with contingents of blue-bereted UN peacekeepers keeping Greeks and Turks apart.

A group of us had dinner that night on the Turkish side of Nicosia
and then recrossed the Green Line and regrouped at the Ledra Palace
bar, arguing past midnight over what, if anything, the Turkish government was going to do about the Athens-inspired coup. Dean Brelis,
a Greek-speaking American correspondent based in Athens for CBS
News, was convinced the Turks would seize the opportunity to attack
and capture more of the island. I was skeptical and bet him ten dollars
he was wrong. At dawn the next morning, I heard gunfire and rushed
up the stairs to the wide, flat Ledra Palace roof that commanded a
spectacular view of the Turkish section of the capital and the broad
Nicosia plain that stretched north to the Kyrenia mountain range. Suddenly, I could see what the commotion was all about. Dozens of heavy,
dark Turkish troop-transport planes crested the Kyrenia range and were
lumbering toward Nicosia. A few miles short of the capital, hundreds of
Turkish paratroopers came tumbling out of the huge planes. Greek Cypriot machine guns and antiaircraft fire opened up, to little discernible
effect. The waves of paratroopers kept coming, gliding gently to ground
at assembly points alongside the Nicosia-Kyrenia highway.

As I watched all this, Dean Brelis came up beside me and without a
word, put out his hand, palm up.

"Shit," I said, and put a ten-dollar bill in his hand.

"Never argue with a Greek about the Turks," he said confidingly as
he tucked the ten-spot into his pocket. I had learned a fundamental truth
about foreign correspondence: don't ever think you know more than the
local guy who speaks the language and knows the territory.

On the plain, out of range of the Greek Cypriot guns but clearly visible, the paratroopers assembled themselves smartly into units and were
quickly joined by trucks and armored personnel carriers that rumbled
up the highway from Kyrenia, where Turkish ships were landing thou-

sands of reinforcements. The battle for Nicosia that raged all that day and through the night was as close range and hairy as anything I had encountered in Vietnam and two Arab-Israeli wars. Greek Cypriot National Guard units—the army—set up heavy machine guns on the top floor of the Ledra Palace and mortars on the roof. Dean and I and other hotel guests took up vantage points inside the hotel. From the tall, curtained windows we could watch the lethal fighting firsthand.

Turkish units quickly penetrated Nicosia from the north, racing through the streets of the Turkish section to the cheers of their compatriots. They set up gun emplacements and targeted the Ledra Palace as a primary objective, pouring machine gun fire and rocket-propelled grenades into the hotel compound, splintering the lovely palm trees and shattering a terraced water fountain. Two young Greek Cypriot National Guardsmen raced past my room on the third floor and propped a machine gun on a tripod on the balcony outside a corner suite just down the hall. They started firing nonstop, pouring bullets into Turkish targets below, letting out a whoop and cheering when they scored a hit. After perhaps five minutes of this, a Turkish RPG shell sailed directly onto the balcony, killing one of the Greek Cypriots and savagely wounding the second, who staggered back into the hallway and collapsed by my open door. I had no dog in this fight, but I was not going to let this young national guardsman bleed to death at my door. Dean Brelis and another reporter helped me drag him down the stairs and into a white ambulance that had pulled into the hotel courtyard. The rear doors slammed shut, and the ambulance screeched out of the driveway, siren screaming. We learned later that the young soldier died at the hospital.

The fighting intensified around the hotel. Both sides considered it an important target. The UN troops, who had long regarded the hotel as neutral ground and their own private watering hole, were quickly losing control. A contingent of heavily armed Greek Cypriot National Guardsmen, with a senior officer at their head, flooded into the lobby and politely told everyone—several hundred UN personnel, journalists, hotel workers—that they were all the government's "guests."

"Hostages, you mean?" someone demanded loudly.

"I prefer 'guests,'" the officer said coolly in British-accented English. "But either way, you're not going anywhere." The lovely Ledra Palace, famous for its dry martinis and steak Diane, had become a hot, sweaty, crowded ground zero.

The siege of the Ledra Palace went on for thirty hours. Two separate UN-negotiated cease-fires were announced and promptly broke down. The 380 "guests," including nearly a hundred journalists, were squeezed into the high-ceilinged lobby and entrance halls, away from the tall windows. The once-glamorous and elegant hotel turned dark and dingy as the power and water failed, the food ran out, and nighttime approached. The civilian guests were scared and miserable, with the exception of a group of Australians who "liberated" the whiskey stocks from the hotel bar and had themselves a party in the hotel basement. The sole link to the outside world was the hotel phone. After a scramble, the journalists organized themselves into a semblance of a line outside the wood-paneled booth in the lobby. When I finally got my turn, I got through to the *Times* bureau in London to dictate a long description of the invasion and the standoff surrounding the hotel. Later that night the phone line was cut.

Fighting continued through the night, but relief came the next afternoon when a small contingent of Canadian troops wearing the blue berets of the UN peacekeeping force marched smartly into the hotel carrying a big UN flag. The officer in charge persuaded the Greek Cypriot commander that his hostages had outlived their usefulness, and all 380 of us made our separate ways out of the courtyard and into the streets of the Greek portion of the capital as the battle for Nicosia roared on. I went to the Hilton Nicosia, a modern hotel on higher ground on the edge of town. Turkish fighter jets were bombing targets in the Greek sector, sending up columns of black smoke. The Turks were clearly gaining the upper hand, and the outgunned, outmanned Greek Cypriots quickly agreed to a UN-proposed cease-fire. The international phone lines were down, so the only way to file news copy that day and the next was to drive south to a British Air Force base and use their overloaded telex to London.

The next day I set out with two other reporters, Holger Jensen of the Associated Press and Nicholas Proffitt of *Newsweek*, in a rented Volkswagen Beetle to test the latest UN-negotiated cease-fire, which was supposed to take full effect at 4 p.m. Racing east along the northern coast road west of Kyrenia, we inadvertently drove through the Greek Cypriot front lines and into the Turkish-controlled sector. The two sides were no more than two hundred yards apart and still firing wire-guided missiles at each other. The soldiers manning outposts on either side were as shocked to see a civilian car race through as we were to be doing it. Turkish jets were still striking targets on the hillside, setting off huge brush fires. We could see Turkish warships standing off the coast as wave after wave of Turkish jets roared overhead. I swung the car into the littered driveway of the Klearchos Hotel in the resort village of Karavas, a few miles west of Kyrenia. The hotel was deserted. It had taken several hits, and the lobby was covered with shattered glass. The guests had left in a hurry; their luggage was lined up near the front door, and no one answered our calls of "Hello?" Suddenly, a burst of heavy machine gun fire raked the front of the hotel, sending the three of us scrambling for cover behind a heavy wooden bar.

Miraculously, we found a working telephone behind the bar. I called the US Embassy in Nicosia. The political officer told me that the cease-fire was still scheduled to go into effect in about three hours, at 4 p.m., but that the Turks were still landing forces on either side of Kyrenia and the fighting was growing more intense.

Still huddled behind the bar, we got a second call through to the Associated Press office in Nicosia and dictated fragmentary stories about the scene around us. Just then, we heard the crunch of soldier's boots in the broken glass on the tiled lobby floor and froze. In an instant, four rifle muzzles swung over the top of the bar into our faces. The young Turkish soldiers holding them looked as startled as we.

"Don't shoot," we three shouted in a jumbled chorus. "We're Americans—press. Don't shoot."

Just then an English-speaking Turkish officer came up, inspected our passports and press credentials, and ordered two of the bewildered soldiers to march us—at gunpoint—down the road to his regimental headquarters in a private home a half-mile down the road. We were put in a room and held there as prisoners for the rest of the day and overnight.

The cease-fire took hold as scheduled, and that evening we had a long talk with an English-speaking reserve Turkish army officer who seemed at a loss as to what to do with us. A teacher at a university in Ankara in civilian life, he had visited the United States and wanted to go back. He seemed less than enthusiastic about his country's invasion of Cyprus, but no—accommodating and friendly as he was, he wouldn't let us leave. He had his orders. He let us get some food from the kitchen of a deserted, damaged resort hotel across the road and liberate a bottle of brandy from behind the bar, but that was it.

The next morning, we decided to test our young reservist friend. In fifteen minutes, we told him, forcefully, we're going to walk out of this house, down the road to our car, and head back to Nicosia. We suggested he tell the guards to look the other way. He said no, absolutely not, and then did just as we suggested. At the appointed time, we walked back to the car, pulled a spent wire-guided missile wire off the front hood, jumped in, and raced back across the Greek Cypriot lines. An hour later, we were poolside at the Hilton Nicosia.

The postscript to this semicomical misadventure came several days later. It proved that the diplomatic wheels grind exceedingly slowly but do grind. Bill Marmon, a *Time* magazine correspondent and friend, was walking along the harbor front at Kyrenia, by now securely in Turkish hands, when he came across a young political officer serving at the US Embassy. The diplomat told Bill that he had instructions to locate three American correspondents who had somehow managed to get themselves captured by the Turks.

"I'm supposed to do what I can to help them," the diplomat said. "Orders from Washington."

"You'll find them back at the pool at the Hilton Nicosia," Bill said. "They are just fine."

Unbeknown to me, when word of our capture reached Washington, Scotty Reston, the *Times'* distinguished columnist, had called his friend and contact Henry Kissinger and asked him to do what he could to free us. Kissinger, who had larger issues on his mind, had passed the word down through channels, and eventually, days later, it reached the harbor at Kyrenia.

I spent the rest of the month in Cyprus, covering a brief resumption of fighting and then negotiations for a new cease-fire, which finally took hold. The hapless President Sampson served only a few days and was quickly replaced by Glafcos Clerides, a fifty-five-year-old lawyer and veteran legislator who at least looked like a president. The Greeks and Turks have argued and negotiated over the disputed island ever since. Lovely Cyprus, with its gorgeous mountains and beautiful beaches, remains divided along much the same lines today as it was when the fighting stopped in the summer of '74.

Later that year, in October, I flew to Rabat, Morocco, to cover the first full-scale summit of Arab leaders since the 1973 war. One by one, the twenty presidents and premiers and princes and potentates of the

Arab League descended on Morocco's picturesque seaside capital and promptly disappeared behind an impenetrable wall of security. Yasser Arafat, head of the Palestine Liberation Organization, arrived with the full trappings of a head of state, driving through the streets in a black limousine with the PLO flag flapping on the fender behind a flying wedge of motorcycles. The pomp and circumstance that surrounded his arrival was a sign of things to come.

In addition to the official delegations, some six hundred international journalists arrived in Rabat, quickly overwhelming the capital's limited accommodations. With no room at the inn, I gratefully accepted the US Embassy's offer of a bed in the guest room of the large and comfortable residence of the chief information officer. It was a twin-bedded room, and my roommate turned out to be Peter Jennings, then the Beirut correspondent for ABC News and, later, anchor of the network's flagship *World News Tonight*.

Each day Peter and I would set out to cover the conference, which, beyond public opening and closing ceremonies, took place entirely behind closed doors. Security was so tight that frequently members of the same delegation couldn't find each other. Different credentials were required to move from one part of a hotel to another, and strategic information, like the phone number in any of the villas set aside for the leaders, was a state secret. Nonetheless, Peter and I managed to get a request for a joint interview through the security curtain to President Sadat, who invited us both to come out to his sprawling guesthouse on the edge of town the next morning for coffee.

Sadat was in high spirits when we arrived, graciously showing us into a sunny room and smiling as coffee was poured. He talked nonstop for an hour, telling some marvelously gossipy stories about the goings-on behind the scenes at the conference, poking fun at some of his fellow leaders. But, maddeningly, he insisted that it all had to be off-the-record or on background. No quotes, he said; no attribution to him. But had we heard what fools they had in the Syrian delegation?

Finally, on background—meaning we could use the material but not quote him—Sadat said he had just learned that the Saudis, who had brought much of Europe to its collective knees with the postwar oil embargo, had decided to cut the price of oil by 10 percent within the next week and freeze the price for a year. Sadat said he was sure the other OPEC countries would follow suit.

Peter and I were so focused on the political and military issues at the conference that neither of us recognized this tidbit for the market-moving bombshell it would prove to be. In fact, I mentioned it almost in passing to the news desk in the London bureau at the end of a phone call that evening. They jumped at the news and passed me immediately to the business editors in New York, who treated it like the second coming. "Holy cow!" the business editor said. "Stay on the line while I get a reporter who knows what he's talking about."

Still not realizing the significance of what I had, I dictated a straight-ahead news piece about the Saudi plans, quoting "a well-placed Arab source." After the business department confirmed the story with their sources and fleshed it out, the piece led the paper the next day (and probably *World News Tonight* as well), and, predictably, world stock markets soared on the tip. The gaps in my grasp of international economics and the oil market had never been more obvious.

After four days of closed-door discussion, the Arab leaders came out with a bombshell of their own. Representing the entire Arab world, and over Jordanian King Hussein's strenuous objections, the conferees declared the PLO "the sole legitimate representative of the Palestinian people" and therefore the responsible authority on the occupied West Bank and in any future independent Palestinian state. In so doing, they stripped away half of Hussein's kingdom and compromised his authority over the nine hundred thousand Palestinians living on the East Bank of the Jordan. The leaders also forced Israel to confront the fact that they would ultimately have to negotiate with the Palestinians directly.

From Rabat, I flew to Paris and on to Amman, Jordan, to discover what King Hussein really thought about the outcome he had been forced to accept at Rabat. After submitting a request for an interview with the palace, I cooled my heels for a few days in the comfortable quarters of the Jordan InterContinental Hotel. Finally, the request was granted, the palace sent a car, and I was ushered into the king's spacious office in the heavily guarded Basman Palace.

The PLK, or Plucky Little King, as reporters irreverently called Hussein after he survived innumerable assassination attempts, was his usual gracious, accommodating self. Dressed casually in slacks, a checkered shirt, and a beige sweater, he talked for fifty minutes about the fallout from Rabat.

"The situation has altered very basically," he said in his rumbling baritone. "A new reality exists, and we must adjust to it. The West Bank is no longer Jordan."

King Hussein went on to say that Jordan would rewrite its constitution, reorganize its cabinet and parliament to remove the Palestinians living in the Israeli-occupied West Bank, and play no role in any negotiations about its future status. The measures he described were decisive and forward-looking, but his voice was deep and sad. For Hussein, this was one more bitter pill from the Six-Day War. The Israelis had conquered half his kingdom in 1967, and now the Arab states were taking it from him for good. Rabat had been a watershed, he said; there would be no turning back.

Riding in the car from the palace back to the hotel, I thought about all the things that had happened to Hussein in the six years since I had started writing about him. The close brushes with death, the wars, the internal rebellions and palace coups, the rapprochement with the Israelis that would grow into a formal peace agreement. He was only thirty-eight, just two years older than me at the time, and he had already been on the Hashemite throne for a generation. He was still king, a semiabsolute monarch, living in a luxurious palace with a succession of beautiful wives, but I wasn't sure I envied him.

18

Wrapping Up the Holy Land

The next year, 1975, brought more of everything: more political squabbling among Israel's leaders, more high-wire shuttle diplomacy by the indefatigable Kissinger in pursuit of a second Sinai disengagement agreement, more Palestinian terror attacks on civilian targets in Israel, more counterattacks, more Israeli settlement construction—both rump and authorized—on the West Bank and in Gaza, and more travel for me. On a regularly scheduled home leave back to the States, I saw my father for the first time in three years. His wandering in the journalistic wilderness had ceased when Abe Rosenthal, now executive editor, had hired him to write the Sports of the *Times* column, and Pop had flourished. He was writing better than ever, at the top of his game. He and Phyllis had sold their respective houses and bought a lovely two hundred-year-old farmhouse in New Canaan, Connecticut, and built a summer home in Chilmark, on Martha's Vineyard. Life was good. I returned to Jerusalem thinking he had created a new life for himself.

In July, I flew with a small party of officials and journalists accompanying Yitzhak Rabin aboard an El Al Boeing 707 on an emotional and symbolically significant four-day official visit to Germany—the first by an Israeli prime minister in office. The trip was designed both to recognize the horrors of the Holocaust and to put Israeli-German relations on a better footing going forward.

As Israel's first native-born premier, Rabin had not suffered directly at the hands of the Nazis, but he was accompanied by his wife, Leah, who had been born in Germany, spoke German as her first language, and had fled with her family to Palestine in 1933 as the Third Reich came to power. I had come to know Leah Rabin, coincidentally, through a weekly tennis game. We were part of a rotating group that played Saturday mornings at the Holy Land Hotel courts just outside Jerusalem. She was a strong, competitive player who occasionally brought along her husband to make a fourth. He never looked very happy about it. Simply put, tennis was not his game.

On the flight to Germany, Leah Rabin told me she had never wanted to go back to Germany. "But if I had to do it," she said, "this is the way to do it, with my head up, as the wife of a prime minister of a Jewish state."

The Rabins' first stop was the former concentration camp at Bergen-Belsen, set in the flat, green farmlands of Lower Saxony. It looked more like a manicured park when we arrived than what one liberating British officer had described in 1945 as "an apocalyptic vision of a vast death camp." Rabin was stoic as he placed a wreath of blue and white carnations at a small stone monument. During the flight from Israel he had talked quietly about the significance of his trip. "Bergen-Belsen," said soberly, "belongs to the past."

But the past would not go away. Touring a small museum at the site, the Rabins stopped and stared at a plaque that marked one of the mass graves. It read, "Here rest 5,000 dead. April, 1945." Yitzhak Rabin, sabra, looked stunned. Leah Rabin, German native, stood just behind him, fighting back tears. "Terrible," she mumbled, "terrible," finally breaking down.

Undeterred and seemingly unaware of the impact he was having on the Rabins, a German official acting as guide prattled on briskly about how efficiently the camp had been run until January 1945. "But after that," he said, "there was bad overcrowding, and many prisoners died." He kept talking as he ushered the couple through a gallery of photographs of huge piles of twisted skeletons in mass graves that contained the remains of tens of thousands of Jews. Among the corpses found unburied on the day the camp was liberated, April 15, 1945, was the body of fifteen-year-old Anne Frank and her nineteen-year-old sister, Margot.

Finally, Rabin had had enough. "Just a minute," the prime minister said, cutting the guide off midsentence in front of the ghastly pictures. "I want to look at these a little longer." The room was totally silent as the Rabins stared at the pictures. Then they moved on without a word. The guide melted away.

The prime minister went on to stops in Berlin and Bonn. There was an extraordinary moment at a ceremony on the lawn of the Chancellery in Bonn when a German Army band played "Hatikvah," the Israeli anthem, and then "Deutschland über Alles," as the German anthem is known abroad. Later, Chancellor Helmut Schmidt, speaking extemporaneously as he proposed a toast at a formal dinner, said, "I want to thank you, Mr. Prime Minister, for the visit you made to Bergen-Belsen. It was not an easy thing for you to do, but it was necessary to do, and I'm grateful you did it."

The guests seated at the long, beautifully set dinner table were absolutely silent. Everyone looked at Rabin, including Leah. Rabin simply nodded, with that familiar, slightly crooked half-smile on his face, as if to say, "No, it was not easy."

While in Bonn, Rabin spent several hours conferring with Henry Kissinger in Gymnich Castle, an eight hundred-year-old, elegantly appointed guesthouse, complete with moat and drawbridge, just outside the capital. The irony of the United States' first Jewish secretary of state and an Israeli premier hammering out the final details of a Sinai disengagement agreement with Egypt in a schloss provided by the West German government in the midst of a state visit was not lost on anyone.

Back in Israel, the focus of my reporting turned more and more to the occupied territories, especially the increasingly restive West Bank, home to more than a million Palestinians. Demonstrations against the continued Israeli occupation erupted in most of the major cities and towns. Crackdowns by the Israeli army provoked riots, which led in turn to more crackdowns, and on and on, in a downward spiral. The government tried to break the cycle by authorizing municipal elections among the Palestinians throughout the West Bank. To no one's surprise, a new more militant, openly nationalist leadership emerged from the balloting. "Could the message be more clear?" Karim Khalaf, the newly elected mayor of Ramallah said in an interview the day after. "The vote shows the whole world that West Bankers are Palestinians who want to establish their own national entity and put an end to the Israeli occupation."

The message was clear enough, but the Israeli government didn't want to hear it. Instead, they authorized more Jewish settlements throughout the West Bank and continued the crackdown on the Arab population. There were more demonstrations, more riots, more deaths, and more bitterness on both sides.

In May, I got word that my father had won a Pulitzer Prize for his Sports of the *Times* column. He was the first sportswriter to win in the Distinguished Commentary category but not, to his annoyance, the first sports columnist to win a Pulitzer. That honor had gone to his predecessor at the *Times*, Arthur Daley, a few years before.

My father and Daley were colleagues on the sports beat and friends. But they were competitors as well. Privately, Pop thought Daley was an awkward, wooden writer with none of the style that he admired in others and strove for himself. My father was a generous, genuinely good-hearted person, but he was not above a little privately expressed sour grapes when it came to Daley and his Pulitzer. The prize, he would scoff within the family, had become nothing more than a sop the journalistic old-boy network gave to its favorites on the establishment papers. Not what it used to be.

So when I heard about *his* prize, I called from Jerusalem and reached him at the Pulitzer celebration party in the *Times* newsroom. I could hear laughter and champagne corks popping in the background.

I was all business when he came to the phone. "You'll refuse it, of course," I said, my voice deadpan. "After trashing the Pulitzers all these years, I'm sure you'll refuse it."

There was a pause, then he lowered his voice and growled into the phone, "Not on your life!"

We both laughed, and I congratulated him, and I could tell he was enormously pleased and gratified. He and his generation generally affected a studied diffidence about prizes, but this was high praise from his peers, and he was loving it.

"I'll just blush and dimple and say thank you," he whispered into the phone. "I'll be on my best behavior."

"Good," I said. "No smart remarks."

At the end of June, as I was preparing to wrap up my assignment in Israel, a huge story broke. A band of hijackers had seized an Air France jetliner with 257 persons aboard as it left Athens, forced it to refuel at Benghazi, Libya, and flew it to Entebbe International Airport in Uganda. There were nearly a hundred Israelis aboard the flight, which had originated in Tel Aviv, bound for Paris. The hijackers, who included German radicals from the Baader-Meinhof gang and Arab gunmen, held the hostages for nearly a week, demanding the release of forty Palestinian prisoners from Israeli jails. Stalling for time, Israel announced it would abandon its customary policy and negotiate with the hijackers for the release of the hostages. In fact, the Israeli army was assembling a commando team to carry out its famously daring night raid on the Entebbe airport in which it freed the hostages and flew them back to Israel.

It was an incredible operation, given the distances and the fact that Uganda's leader, Idi Amin, had been tacitly cooperating with the hijackers. Amin had even posted his palace guards around the airport. The commandos, who had secretly rehearsed the rescue down to the minute in Israel, flew 2,500 miles to Uganda in three C-130 aircraft loaded with vehicles and weapons. They also carried a black Mercedes limousine with a heavyset Israeli officer in blackface designed to impersonate Amin and two Land Rovers full of men dressed as the president's bodyguards. The impersonation briefly confused the Ugandan soldiers at the airport and gave the Israeli raiders enough time to reach the passenger terminal where the hostages were being held. Overhead, an Israeli military Boeing 707 circled, coordinating the assault. Another Israeli 707 carrying two surgical units and a thirty-three-doctor medical team flew to Nairobi's airport and set up a field hospital there to treat the anticipated injured. In the end, the only casualty among the Israeli commandos was Lieutenant Colonel Yonatan Netanyahu, whose brother, Benjamin, would later become Israel's longest-serving prime minister. Three of the hostages and about twenty Ugandan soldiers died in the gunfight at the airport.

It was a huge story that I covered every day for two weeks from Jerusalem, using every source I had developed over five years in the Israeli government, military, and intelligence services and the US and foreign embassies. The news of the actual rescue finally broke on July 4, 1976, the American bicentennial, when I had been planning to attend a party at the home of the US ambassador in Herzliya. Instead, first word of the rescue came at 3 a.m. with a terse announcement from the Israeli army's spokesperson, saying only that the hostages had been freed and were returning to Israel. Everything else had to be pieced together after that. Alvin Shuster, the *Times'* veteran Rome bureau chief, flew in that night, and together we reported and wrote an hour-by-hour reconstruction, or ticktock, of the week-long ordeal that filled an entire page of the paper a week later on July 11, 1976. It was a riveting tale, based on dozens of interviews with commandos and hostages, diaries, briefings by Israeli military commanders, and additional reporting from *Times* correspondents in Paris, Nairobi, and Athens.

We got portraits of the individual hijackers from an Israeli intelligence official who confided that the commandos had fingerprinted them to establish their identities before leaving Entebbe. We learned that four of the hijackers had boarded the flight in Athens and commandeered the plane with weapons hidden in their hand luggage, which, incredibly, had not been inspected by Athens security as they boarded. Two of these were German radicals who supported the Palestinian cause; the other two were Arab. They were joined by another group of Palestinian gunmen who were prepositioned at the airport in Entebbe. We got vivid, firsthand accounts of the hostage ordeal from several of the passengers, including Ilan Hartuv, a Jerusalem economist, and Moshe Peretz, a twenty-six-year-old Israeli who had taken copious notes in his diary throughout. When the plane landed in Benghazi to refuel, Peretz had written, "Arid landscape, four bored soldiers sitting on the runway, fire brigade trucks nearby."

"Must be Libya," Hartuv had recalled thinking to himself. Their recollections went on like that until the very end, when the rescue plane brought them back to Israel at the end of the week. The last line in Peretz's diary read simply, "11:20 a.m.—home." It was such a dramatic tale, I can't believe that Al Shuster and I didn't turn it into a book or screenplay. In truth, the idea never occurred to either of us. For better or worse, we were newspaper correspondents. Decades later, in 2018, a major film, *7 Days in Entebbe*, hit the big screen.

The Entebbe rescue was the last major story I covered as the *Times'* Israel bureau chief. I'd been there four years—five, if you include my first stint in 1967 and 1968—in an era when three years was the more-typical *Times* posting abroad. As I packed up and followed my family back to the United States in August, I wondered if I would ever have a comparable assignment abroad or at home. I had covered two wars—three, if you include the Turkish invasion of Cyprus—and the huge changes in attitude and society that they had wrought. I had made some of the closest friendships I would make anywhere. I had grown, I knew, as a reporter and writer. And throughout, I had enjoyed myself. I had been, as the title of Anthony Lewis's long-running column on foreign affairs suggested, been "At Home Abroad." I was leaving Israel convinced that there would never be another full-scale war with her Arab neighbors of the kind I had covered. There would be skirmishes, for sure, and even short-term campaigns, like the Israeli invasions of Lebanon and, later, Gaza, and intifadas that would cause casualties, but not the all-out battles that the Six-Day and Yom Kippur wars had been. Israel, with its nuclear arsenal, was simply too powerful for that, the Arab world too splintered, and the United States too dominant as Israel's patron.

But "never" is a long time, of course, and a risky bet about anything. I was certainly wrong back in 1967 in my belief that Israel and the Palestinians would reach an accommodation sooner rather than later. It had seemed like common sense in the wake of the Six-Day War—so clearly in the interests of both populations, whose futures are inextricably linked, like it or not. But common sense is frequently in scarce supply in the Middle East.

And I was heading home enthusiastic about opening a new chapter at the *Times*. I had been offered other foreign assignments; Paris wasn't available, but the never-a-dull-moment Beirut bureau was open. I had been abroad for most of the last nine years, though, and my children were starting school and needed to find out who they were; and Ann was anxious to use the master's degree in special education that she had acquired. She wanted to go home. Beyond that, I knew I was not a permanent ex-pat. The *Times* had a number of those correspondents, many of whom were born abroad and who chose to live their lives abroad, but that was not me. I was an American who was and would remain fascinated by the rest of the world, but it was time for me to go home. As it turned out, the *Times* had a promotion in mind: assistant foreign editor, a seat on the desk for which I had worked for nearly a decade and a chance to shape and direct the *Times*' staff of thirty-eight foreign correspondents. At thirty-seven, it sounded good to me.

19

At Home at Home Again

Foreign correspondents coming home in those days frequently talked—a bit melodramatically, it seemed to me—about a reentry crisis. It was no crisis for me, but the US certainly seemed different. I noticed, maybe for the first time, how incredibly rich it was. Everything seemed lavish: the homes, the highways, the cars, the endless choices in the supermarkets, the luxury stores. Americans seemed oblivious to their wealth, unaware and uninterested in how the rest of the world lived. After Jerusalem, Bangkok, and Saigon, it caught my notice. Of course, the country hadn't changed—I had. Arriving in New York, we jumped right into the excess ourselves, buying a car and renting a big old barn of a house in Fieldston, a leafy section of Riverdale, in the Bronx, and began our new life.

I commuted to work at the *Times* in a suit and tie. Rode the subway. Sat at the foreign desk in the cavernous, block-long newsroom. Went to meetings—the morning-story conference, the afternoon page-one meeting. Other meetings. Handled other people's copy. Lunch in the cafeteria or executive dining room. Drinks at Sardi's some evenings. Subway home at 7 p.m. Did it all again the next day. It was legitimate work, helping shape the daily and Sunday foreign report, but deskbound and bureaucratic compared to what I had been doing and, needless to say, a world away from Jerusalem or Bangkok or Saigon. I missed being my own boss in the field—or, at least, enjoying the illusion that I was.

Newsroom politics were a major preoccupation, especially when the mercurial Abe Rosenthal, by then executive editor, began shuffling editors. A new foreign editor was named months after I got there. Abe called me into his office and, with an excited smile on his face that indicated he'd had one of his brainstorms, offered me the job of sports editor, heading up the fifty-person sports staff, which included my father. I could see from his expression that Abe thought it was an inspired choice.

I didn't.

"You would be your father's boss," he said, grinning, pleased with himself.

"I know," I sputtered. "That's only one of several things wrong with it."

I explained that I had invested fifteen-plus years in news. I was interested in politics and foreign affairs. I told Abe that while I might have grown up around the sports world, and was a fan, I didn't really know it and certainly didn't want to live it twenty-four hours a day. Simply put, thanks but no thanks. Abe shook his head and shrugged, no doubt thinking, *People are strange*. Instead, determined to make an editor of me, he named me deputy metropolitan editor, second-in-command of the one hundred–person city staff, the largest on the paper. Suddenly I was immersed in local politics, city hall, crime—all the things I had first covered breaking into the business. Back to the future again.

Before long, I started looking for a way out. I missed writing and reporting, I missed covering the news in the field, and, vain and shallow as it was, I missed seeing my name on page one. I was making more money, had become officially part of management, was exempt from union rules and strikes, had started receiving stock options and a bonus, and was on the promotion track. The smart move would be to stick with it and see how far I could go. But I felt boxed in. It was just a year since I had come home; it seemed longer. The solution presented itself in the form of a plum job that opened up: national political correspondent, based in Washington, covering campaigns and politics around the country. I raised my hand and got it. Ann was delighted. Washington was her home; she'd grown up and gone to university, gotten her masters, and still had family there. Better yet, we still owned our home in Chevy Chase, which we had rented out for five years and now, as luck would have it, was about to be vacant at the end of a lease. The stars were aligned. We were bound for D.C.

The Washington bureau had relocated to new, more central quarters since I had worked in it between 1970 and 1972. Now it was just a few blocks from the White House. I moved into a spacious corner office that

I shared with John Herbers, the great national correspondent, and Leslie Gelb, the funny, irreverent foreign-policy specialist who, as a Defense Department official, had been one of the principal authors of the Pentagon Papers. Now a turn through Washington's famous revolving door had brought him into journalism. Later he would write an op-ed column for the *Times* and eventually head the Council on Foreign Relations. Our three-person office was down the hall and removed physically and psychologically from the bureau's sprawling main newsroom. We three exiles prided ourselves on trend stories, not breaking news. Fatuously, we indulged in our own private contest to see which of us could go the longest without writing "today" in the lead of our pieces.

I was traveling the country on the political beat and enjoying it. It was 1977, an off year politically, but there were plenty of stories and some interesting characters coming onto the national political scene, including a former governor of California named Reagan who was generating some excitement. That fall, I was covering a Republican Governors Association meeting, aptly set amid the cartoon characters and carnival rides at Disneyworld in Florida, when Anwar Sadat made his historic pilgrimage to Jerusalem to speak to the Israeli Knesset and set in motion the diplomatic process that would eventually produce the Egyptian-Israeli peace treaty. Watching it live on television in a hotel room in Disneyworld was disorienting, to say the least. I desperately wanted to be there, to write about it. Instead, Sadat was on the tube in my room in a Disney World hotel decorated with images of Mickey and Minnie Mouse.

Nineteen seventy-seven was the first full year of the Jimmy Carter administration. The "Georgians," as they were known, had taken over the town. The *Times'* team at the White House consisted of James Wooten, a fine writer and reporter who had covered Carter since his Georgia days, and my old colleague from Saigon, Charlie Mohr. Somehow the two of them had gotten crosswise with the Carter White House and, more importantly, out of sorts with the *Times'* power structure in New York. Management decided to replace the team and came to me with the proposal that I become chief White House correspondent with Martin Tolchin, an excellent congressional reporter, as number two. I was only a few months into the national political beat and would have been happy to continue with it, but the White House assignment was considered a major plum, so the offer was a no-brainer for me. "It'll monopolize your life," Scotty Reston warned, "but you have to take it. Just don't make any personal plans or think you can schedule any long vacations or have much of a private life for the next three years."

He was right, of course. The White House beat, especially for a paper that takes it (and itself) seriously, is a way of life. When the president travels, you travel; when the president pulls all-nighters, as Carter did throughout the Iran hostage crisis, you're on. When he vacations in Georgia, you're in Georgia. When he goes home to Plains to sweep the leaves off the front porch, you're in the Best Western (known among the traveling press as the "Worst Western") a few miles down the road in Americus, Georgia, a true garden spot. A travel pool, consisting of the wire services, television networks, news magazines, and major papers in rotation, is almost always with the president. The one exception is weekends at the presidential retreat at Camp David: privacy for the commander in chief, a respite for the press, save the bare-bones pool that camps in a motel down the road in Catoctin, Maryland.

You spend so much time with fellow reporters in the White House press corps that many become your friends, your on-and-off-the-job circle. Ditto with the staff—at least some of them, some of the time. Even when we were in Washington, staff and reporters hung out in the same bars. The Class Reunion, a dark but comfortable spot on H Street with great drinks and passable food a few blocks from the White House, was an after-hours favorite. The reporters from the *Boston Globe* spent so much time there that they installed a private phone line near the bar. A small sign instructed that, if it rang, you should answer, "The *Boston Globe*, Washington Bureau . . ." in your most business-like and professional voice.

Romances were inevitable in this small world, and some even lasted. I met my future wife, Susy Elfving, when she was part of the White House staff, although we didn't get together until years later, when I was separated from Ann and getting a divorce and Susy was long divorced from her first husband. But other relationships blossomed, broke up, got together again, and a few continue to this day.

The White House, and the traveling circus that surrounded it, was our world. It was a great beat. The work was nonstop demanding, but I dived into it and the life that came with it. Every major issue in Washington—which, in those days, included the slowing economy, a deepening energy crisis, soaring interest rates, the Panama Canal treaty, the Middle East, the strategic-arms-reduction talks, the Soviet invasion of Afghanistan—landed sooner or later at the White House for resolution. I found myself tackling a new subject every day, learning as fast as I could. The White House correspondent is the ultimate generalist, writing about the economy one day and foreign policy the next, "a mile wide and an inch deep," as the saying goes. But you were never bored.

There was domestic travel on Air Force One if you were on the rotating travel pool, or the accompanying chartered press plane if not. (A third chartered Boeing carried the photographers and television camera and sound crews and was known affectionately as the "Zoo Plane.") There was extensive international travel—to Europe, South America, Africa, and Asia. One trip, accompanying Vice President Mondale, took us twenty-eight thousand miles and two weeks through Southeast Asia, Australia, and New Zealand. It made precious little real news. All I remember about the endless flight home from Wellington, New Zealand, was that the whole planeload of us, vice president included, watched the movie *Saturday Night Fever*—twice.

In June 1979, the president and his entourage flew to Vienna for a three-day summit with Leonid Brezhnev, the ailing Soviet leader. It was my first trip back to the Austrian capital since the hostage-taking I had almost missed there in 1973, and six years later the lovely old imperial seat was bursting with thousands of officials, reporters, and security people, all competing for hotel rooms and restaurant tables with the army of tourists who annually converge on Vienna by the thousands for the spring opera season.

Soviet-American summits in those days were partly substance and partly theater, and the liveliest show in town that week was the nightly 8 p.m. joint news conferences in which White House Press Secretary Jody Powell and Soviet spokesperson Leonid Zamyatin offered their different takes on the day's discussions. The contrast could not have been greater: the shrewd, wisecracking Powell with his Georgian accent and good-old-boy manner, and Zamyatin, a tough-talking, unsmiling, unflappable veteran Soviet diplomat who never strayed from the approved Kremlin line on anything. It made for colorful copy, and at the end of the conference Carter and Brezhnev signed a Strategic Arms Limitation treaty beneath the crystal chandeliers in the ornate music room of the Hofburg palace. Carter then flew back to Washington and addressed a joint session on Congress that same night in a full-court press for ratification. No rest for the weary.

After a few days home, we were off again, this time on a twelve-day, 17,350-mile journey to Japan and South Korea for a multination economic summit, a visit with American troops along the DMZ in Korea, and a planned long July 4 weekend in Hawaii. After jetting through so many time zones in so few days, the presidential party, staff and press alike, was more than ready for a few days' break on the beach. But Hawaii was not to be. Instead, at the urging of his pollster, Pat Caddell, Carter scrapped his vacation plans and headed straight back to Washington to deal with a fast-escalating political crisis at home. The combination of the oil shortages brought on by the Iran-Iraq War, long lines at gasoline stations, soaring inflation, and a near-revolt among Democrats in Congress had put Carter in a precarious position. His answer was to clear his schedule and assemble a cross-section of counselors, staff, and the political and business leaders called the "wise men" for several days of closed-door brainstorming sessions at Camp David. A week later, he emerged from seclusion and made a nationally televised speech at 10 p.m. on a Sunday night in which he conceded that the nation was suffering a crisis of confidence and had stopped listening to him. There was actual substance in the speech—a six-point plan to address the energy crisis—but the headlines all dealt with the president's depiction of the foundering national morale. It became known universally as the "Malaise Speech," even though the president never used that word, and may well have persuaded Carter's chief nemesis, Senator Edward M. "Ted" Kennedy, to challenge him for the Democratic nomination the following year. For me, it meant nonstop run-and-gun coverage as the president reshuffled his cabinet and staff, appointed a new head of the Federal Reserve and three new cabinet secretaries, scrambled to rebalance the economy, and, despite his political problems, announced his intention to stand for reelection in 1980.

There was a memorable, funny moment in October when Carter flew to Boston to speak at the dedication of the new John F. Kennedy Presidential Library. It was a brilliant fall day, and President Carter was seated on an outdoor dais in front of the I. M. Pei–designed building with two rows of Kennedy family, children, and cousins, including Ted and his then-estranged wife, Joan. Behind them, white sailboats darted across the shimmering blue waters of Dorchester Bay as the Boston

Pops played selections from Aaron Copland. It was a classic American political scene, with a score of veterans from the New Frontier seated among the Georgians of the Carter administration, a mix of former and current Democratic royalty, plus the Prince and the Pretender, all poised for the campaign to come. Carter acknowledged the political irony of the moment when he recalled late President Kennedy's pointed advice to his brother Ted to wait awhile before running for president himself. "As you can see," Carter said with a grin and a sly glance at Senator Kennedy, "President Kennedy's wit and wisdom is as relevant today as it was then." Senator Kennedy roared with laughter and applauded along with the audience. The smiles would fade as the primary campaign picked up momentum and became personal and bitter, but for the moment the mood was upbeat.

All that changed on November 4, 1979, when Iranian protesters broke through the gates of the US Embassy compound in Tehran and seized fifty-two hostages. Effectively, the Carter presidency halted in its tracks. The president devoted most of his energy and time over the next fourteen months to winning the hostages' freedom. Nothing worked—not diplomacy, not bribery, not military threats, not a daring Delta Force attempt to extract the hostages by force. Politically, Carter adopted a Rose Garden strategy, canceling much of his scheduled travel and lowering his campaign profile. Even his formal reelection announcement, originally planned as a thirty-minute televised address, was reduced to a low-key nine-minute ceremony in the East Room. In his White House diary, written contemporaneously but published decades later, Carter acknowledged that he felt frustrated and trapped by the hostage crisis but could find no way out. Nonetheless, he beat back Kennedy's primary challenge and won renomination at the Democratic National Convention in New York in the summer of 1980. In the early going in the general election, both private and public polls showed Carter substantially ahead of Reagan. The likely voters clearly had doubts about this former movie actor who was approaching his seventieth birthday. But when the two candidates held their only debate in Cleveland ten days before the election, Reagan reassured the audience by coming across as genial, measured, and, most importantly, plausibly presidential. Carter, by contrast, provided the late-night comics some rich material by seeming to suggest that his daughter, Amy, was his chief adviser on nuclear strategy. The debate was a disaster. The election was slipping away, and everyone in the Carter camp knew it.

Carter finished the campaign with an exhausting cross-country barnstorming tour that started in Washington at dawn the day before the election and ended after midnight at a rally in a hangar at Seattle's SEATAC airport. Ironically, the president gave one of his best speeches of the campaign to an enthusiastic audience. I was standing in the back of the crowd, listening to the cheers, when Senator Henry "Scoop" Jackson, the neoconservative Washington Democrat, came up to me at the end of his own cross-country campaign swing on behalf of Democratic Senators. "It's gone," he whispered to me as we stood facing the stage. "The White House, the Senate—we're going to lose it all." Jackson was right, of course, and Reagan won resoundingly. An exhausted Carter made it worse by conceding on live television the next night before the polls had closed in California and in the Pacific Time Zone, probably costing a few Democratic West Coast congressional representatives their seats. He had lost, he was frustrated, and, clearly, he wanted to be done with it.

Carter continued to push hard for the hostages' release during the transition, sending Warren Christopher to negotiate terms with the Iranians in direct talks held in Algeria. They made progress on a deal, but it seemed obvious that Ayatollah Khomeini was not about to let his American pawns go so long as Carter was in the White House. In his White House diary, Carter writes of his suspicions that the Reagan camp had negotiated a back-channel deal with the Iranians to time the release to his inauguration, but such an arrangement has never been documented.

Nonetheless, that is the way it came down. I was in the press pool on January 20, 1981, and riding in Carter's motorcade to Andrews Air Force Base after the Reagan's inauguration ceremony when we finally received word that two planes carrying the hostages had cleared Iranian airspace. Deal or no deal, the ayatollah had succeeded in poking a final finger in Carter's eye. Reagan had given Carter the use of Air Force One for his trip home to Plains after the inauguration, and I was in that pool as well. Having covered three of his four years in the White House, with all the highs and lows, I wanted to see it through to the end. The mood on board the blue-and-white Boeing 707 was surprisingly buoyant. Jimmy and Rosalynn Carter and the tight circle of Georgians who had come to Washington with him four years earlier toasted the hostage release with champagne, kicked back, and relaxed. To a person, they looked relieved to be done with the White House and Washington.

The ex-president had one more official duty to perform. After a short night's sleep in Plains, he and aides and the press pool boarded the big SAM 26000 jetliner—no longer designated Air Force One, since Reagan was now president—for the eight-hour flight from Georgia to Wiesbaden, Germany, to meet the hostages, who were being treated at the US military hospital there. The emotional encounter took place behind closed doors, but Carter conceded afterward to the traveling press that the meeting had been tear-filled and at times tense. He said he had described everything he had done publicly and behind-the-scenes to try to win the hostages' release, including the abortive rescue attempt. But after 444 days in brutal Iranian captivity, the hostages were in no mood to be consoled. Several of them poured their frustration out on Carter, accusing him to his face of not doing enough to secure their freedom. Later, as we flew back to the US, one of Carter's aides described the session to me as "necessary and cathartic but far from easy." And, on that poignant note, the tumultuous Carter era was over.

So was my assignment at the White House. After three-plus years, I was more than ready to move on and regain some measure of control over my life. But I wasn't finished with the Iranian hostage crisis. Instead, I received an ambitious, challenging assignment to rereport the last days of the late shah of Iran for the *New York Times*' Sunday magazine. I spent the next three months reporting and writing a reconstruction of the protracted secret negotiations to free the hostages and, in particular, Carter's controversial and reluctant decision to admit the ailing shah into the US for medical treatment. Why had Carter, who had originally opposed admitting the shah, reversed himself? What I learned shocked me and made news.

To unravel the backstory, I traveled from Paris to Plains to Panama and questioned all the principal players. I interviewed the former president in the living room of his home in Plains; the shah's twin sister, Princess Ashraf Pahlavi, in her elegant Park Avenue triplex; the Shah's son and heir, Reza Pahlavi, at his home in exile, outside Paris; and key government officials in Panama. I talked with David Rockefeller in his fifty-sixth-floor office atop Rockefeller Center and Henry Kissinger and Dr. Benjamin Kean, the central figure in the shah's medical odyssey, in their Manhattan offices. Hamilton Jordan told me about his role in an interview in his apartment in Atlanta. The result of these and a dozen other interviews and document searches was a lengthy account of the last days of the shah and the hostage negotiations that filled the entire May 17, 1981, issue of the *New York Times Magazine*. With additional reporting on the experiences of the hostages themselves by Robert D. McFadden, Joseph Treaster, Maurice Carroll, and other *Times* reporters, it was published by Times Books under the title *No Hiding Place*. It made a riveting story that still reads like a thriller. I learned, for example, that Carter had been crucially misinformed about the urgency and seriousness of the shah's lymphoma; he had been led to believe that the shah, then living in exile in Panama, was at death's door and needed immediate treatment that could only be provided in the United States. Neither was true.

I learned that Carter, who had originally been determined to not allow the shah into the United States, ultimately gave in only after a relentless campaign was waged by the shah's influential old-boy network: David Rockefeller, whose Chase Manhattan Bank had handled Iran's billions; Henry Kissinger, who had carried out many missions for the Rockefellers; and John J. McCloy, the then-eighty-six-year-old lawyer-diplomat who had known the shah for years and whose law firm had represented the Pahlavi family. This high-powered trio hammered the Carter White House relentlessly and ultimately won permission for the shah to travel to New York for treatment. For Carter, it was a fateful decision that sparked the hostage crisis and, more than anything else, cost him a second term. In 2020 records came to light that revealed the lengths to which the Rockefeller-Kissinger-McCloy triumvirate went to persuade Carter to admit the shah for medical treatment. Their months-long campaign, which they dubbed "Project Eagle," included getting a dire medical report on the shah's medical condition in front of Carter. When I told the president in his living room in Plains that he had been misinformed, that Dr. Kean had told me in fact that the Shah's condition could have been dealt with by any number of medical facilities abroad, that it had not been crucial that he be treated in the United States, Carter became visibly upset. He insisted that he had been told that the shah was in imminent danger of death. I didn't doubt that this was what he had been told, but my reporting showed that it had not been an accurate depiction of the shah's condition.

After the fact, I was able to reconstruct the dozens of secret missions that Hamilton Jordan had taken to Europe to meet with Iranian contacts to get negotiations started. None of these had been made public at the time, nor the fact that Jordan had carried an almost-clownish disguise—a false mustache and glasses—that he had never had to use. We also got the details of the harrowing escape of six of the original hostages to the Canadian Embassy in Tehran and their subsequent flight out of the country. That tale later became the plot of the 2013 movie *Argo*, directed by Ben Affleck.

Rereporting the story that I had covered day-to-day in real time was fascinating. Once the shah was dead, the hostages released, and Carter no longer president, the need for secrecy dropped away, and the participants in the drama were willing to talk. Former President Carter, for example, was both candid and defensive about the decisions he had taken. Sitting in his modest living room in Plains, he insisted that he had been confronted with an impossible choice: let the shah come to the United States for urgent medical treatment that he could obtain nowhere else, or let him die. When I told Carter that Dr. Kean had told me that the choice had never been that clear-cut, that the shah could have received adequate treatment outside the country, the former president flushed with annoyance. Carter was emphatic about what he had been told and said that, ultimately, his aides were unanimous that he had been right to admit the shah, despite the risk to American personnel in Iran. Had the president been misled about a fateful decision? Was it the result of Project Eagle? Perhaps. Dr. Kean's medical evaluation had been turned over to the State Department's medical officer, who apparently had put his own spin on the evaluation and sent it up the chain of command to the president. Had the Rockefeller-Kissinger-McCloy team influenced the final product? Had they indirectly misled the president and forced his hand? It is not clear to this day.

It was a vivid illustration to me of how little we reporters actually know and understand in the moment during a huge, running story like the fourteen-month hostage crisis and how worthwhile it is to go back over the ground after it is over. The magazine project may only have been a second draft of history, but it was vastly better and more rewarding than the first, and it was nominated for a Pulitzer. Today, few news organizations have the resources, staff, and, most importantly, commitment to carry out such a project. But there is no shortage of stories that deserve a second look.

By this time—1981—my father's health had begun to slip. Defying all the odds, given his penchant for late nights at Shor's, lots of booze, and decades of unfiltered Camels, he had enjoyed excellent health for most of his seventy-five years. His energy level was extraordinary, his memory as sharp as ever, his enthusiasm for writing his column for the *Times* and even traveling the sports beat undiminished. The column was his contract with life; he was good at it, and he knew it. The eight hundred–word length and frequency suited him. At one point, he'd written seven-a-week, then six, then five, and, finally, at my urging, he cut back reluctantly to three. He hated the reduced schedule. Each new column is an opportunity to be good, he'd say. "If I write a stinker," he once told me, "I get a chance to do better with the next one."

Now that he and Phyllis were settled in their old colonial in New Canaan, Connecticut, he wrote most of his columns in a book-lined office in a barn on the property where months before his death he was interviewed by Morley Safer for a *60 Minutes* profile on CBS. He had won his Pulitzer at age seventy, and scores of other awards—so many, in fact, that he took to breaking the wooden backing off the plaques for fireplace kindling. One he treasured was the J. G. Taylor Spink Award that earned him a place in the Baseball Hall of Fame in Cooperstown, New York, for his contributions to the sport. He was inducted in a ceremony in Cooperstown that, in hindsight, I wish I had attended because it meant a lot to him and he would have appreciated my being there. But I was engrossed in my own work in Washington and, I suppose, unconsciously trying to separate my career from his to get a little professional breathing room from his increasing fame. Bummer; I should have been there. I belonged there. He deserved to have his son there.

Despite all his awards and accolades, Pop was far from confident that the *Times* would keep him on at his advanced age. His insecurity surfaced with each new contract renewal. Once, when he was near the end of a contract and had not yet heard from the paper about whether they intended to renew, he worried aloud to my sister, Kit, and me as we sat on a rocky beach overlooking Vineyard Sound. "They may want someone younger, someone new, and who could blame them?" he speculated. He mused that he and Phyllis would be okay financially—they had social security and their savings. But, seeing him sit there on the beach, at age seventy-five, it was painfully clear how much he wanted to continue. The column was his contract with life. He obviously had no idea what he would do without it. I had no doubt that he would be offered another turn at the wheel: The *Times* treasures its Pulitzer winners and does not discard them easily. Sure enough, the offer came through, and he signed up happily.

In his later years, Pop had battles with colon cancer, male breast cancer, and, later, congestive heart failure that made it difficult for him to take the long walks along New Canaan's back roads that he enjoyed so much or fish in the trout streams nearby. Not long before the end, I called him from California, where I was traveling, and asked him how he was feeling. Not great he said, adding that he was frustrated by a persistent shortness of breath. "I can hardly get down the road before I have to turn back," he said. I didn't like the sound of that or the discouraged tone in his voice. It was late afternoon Eastern Time, and he was finishing a column in his barn office. "I'll be fine after a couple of vodka tonics," he said. Amazingly, he kept writing until a few days before his death—and kept trying to be better with each column. I suppose he knew he didn't have much time left. One time when we were talking, he said he hoped to get better, hoped he could travel to the Super Bowl that was coming up. He wanted to see it for himself and write a column about it, a good column, and write a better one after that. Spring training, he said, was not that far away. But, if he didn't get better, he told me, he had no complaints.

"I've had a great run," he said.

And he had.

On January 13, 1982, I was skiing with friends in Sun Valley, Idaho, when I got a call from Phyllis. Pop, who had seemed to be improving in recent months, had taken a turn for the worse. The doctors said his organs were breaking down and he had been admitted to Stamford Hospital for what they said would be his last days. I raced back across the country the next day, flying from Hailey, Idaho, to Chicago, where many eastbound flights had been grounded because of an East Coast blizzard. Frantic, I caught a flight to LaGuardia that somehow landed in the snowstorm and took a van to Stamford that let me off in a downtown hotel about 10 p.m. There was a foot of snow on the ground by then, and nothing was moving. Finally, I saw a police officer getting coffee in the lobby, explained my predicament, and asked for help. "Come with me," he said. He drove me in his cruiser, which had chains, up the steep hill to the hospital. Pop was still alive but unconscious, breathing loudly through his mouth. I sat next to his bed, talking in his right ear, hoping that he could somehow understand me, telling him how much I loved him. "I'm proud to be your son," I told him repeatedly. "I always will be." I've read that people in a coma often hear what is being said to them, even if they can't respond. I hope he did that snowy night, because I meant every word and wanted him to know it. He died several hours later without regaining consciousness. Lying there in his hospital bed, propped up on pillows, he simply stopped breathing in the early hours of January 15, 1982.

We had a funeral for him in Saint Patrick's Cathedral on Fifth Avenue in Manhattan. Hundreds came. The great baseball pitcher Tom Seaver, whom Pop had admired when he had been with the New York Mets, was among the speakers, as was I, and Robert Merrill sang the "Ave Maria." As we came out of the cathedral, I told Merrill he had been wonderful. He smiled and whispered, "I sang the shit out of it, didn't I?" Afterward, we had a luncheon upstairs at the 21 Club. A bit rich for Pop's taste, but Shor's was gone by this time, and it seemed right. I think Pop would have approved. His death brought a major change to my life psychologically. I was no longer "the son of . . ." Now I was "the son of the late . . ." I was not only an orphan, fifteen years after the death of my mother, but head of our somewhat scattered family. It was the end of one chapter, the beginning of another.

Pop's ashes were interred in a grave next to my mother in a small country graveyard in North Stamford. After days of making arrangements, I went home to Chevy Chase and the rest of my life. Back at work in the *Times'* Washington bureau, I wrote several more long-form pieces for the magazine and was slipping comfortably into the role of staff writer when Abe Rosenthal came up with another of his brainstorms. By this time, Abe had essentially remade the *New York Times*, creating and launching freestanding sections Monday through Friday devoted to comprehensive coverage of sports, science, lifestyle, home, and the arts. The sections had attracted new readers and advertising and bailed the paper out of serious economic doldrums that were hurting all papers in the late seventies. Abe, with help from the business side, saved the paper from possible economic ruin and paved the way for its future growth and evolution into a prosperous, truly national newspaper. The key to modernizing the *Times*, he once told me, was simple: "I can do anything I like as long as I don't fuck with the basic product—the news."

Now Abe wanted to create a new feature that would take a fresh, offbeat approach to covering the politics and culture of Washington. It was to be a special page in the daily news section titled Washington Talk that would showcase the best writers in the bureau, with its own news budget, space, and designers. He wanted me to help conceive it and become its first editor. I was pleased to do it. It was new and different and a challenge. I could capitalize on my collective six years in Washington and create a fresh and occasionally irreverent look at the dynamics of the capital and the foibles of its boldface characters.

We launched Washington Talk, leading it with Briefing, a daily column, plus a Calendar feature that was meant to be breezy and up-to-the-minute. We ran pieces on everything from the president's politically calculated use of his box at the Kennedy Center to analyses of the inner dynamics of his cabinet. I could tap talented writers like Francis X. Clines and Bernard Weinraub to write the column and fast, gifted stylists like Lynn Rosellini, Phil Gailey, and David Shribman to crank out features that were entertaining and said something worthwhile about the way Washington worked. I got contributions as well from Howell Raines and Bill Keller, both of whom would later become the paper's executive editor. The page was immediately popular with readers. Even Abe Rosenthal, who was notoriously difficult to please, seemed satisfied with the page as we brought it along. This time, I enjoyed editing. The most creative part was patrolling the newsroom and talking to reporters about what they were covering and hearing around town. A five-minute conversation with a smart reporter who knew his or her beat almost always produced an original story idea. Among us, we came up with bright, readable pieces that often explained more about, say, how Congress or the State Department or the White House actually worked than anything that would appear on page one. And, to my surprise, I enjoyed editing the pieces, trying to make them brighter and better. Maybe I was actually growing up.

As Washington Talk editor, I was repeatedly invited on television as a panelist on the network Sunday talk shows and on *Washington Week in Review*, the perennial Friday night journalistic roundtable on PBS.

I felt comfortable on television and found, to my surprise and private embarrassment, that I could bloviate about the week's news as glibly as the next talking head. I didn't take it particularly seriously, but one television appearance led to another and, eventually, to a decision—surprising even to me—to leave the *Times* after nearly twenty years.

20

Goodbye, Print; Hello, Broadcast

By the mid-1980s, network television news had come into its own. Walter Cronkite, then anchor of the *CBS Evening News*, had been dubbed the "most trusted man in America," and more Americans were getting their news from television than newspapers or magazines. Presidential politics, especially, were playing out on the networks. The national political conventions were increasingly staged for television, and on election nights the American public gathered around the electronic hearth for the results. Politicians measured their standing by how much airtime they got, not how often they were quoted in the paper. The *Times* and other national newspapers were still the journals of record; they set the news agenda for the evening news broadcasts. But they were no longer the center of the action.

I was aware of all this when CBS News came calling in 1985 with an offer to come aboard as Washington correspondent. At this point, CBS was the undisputed leader in news, with the top-rated evening news broadcast and a slightly tarnished reputation as the Tiffany Network. Their producers and correspondents were recognized as the best in the business. The timing was perfect for me. My run at the *Times* had been great, and I had held many of the best jobs on the paper—as foreign correspondent, diplomatic and chief White House correspondent, and editor—but the next rungs up the *Times* ladder were filled, at least in Washington. I probably could have moved up to another editorial job, but that would have required a move to New York, and that posed another problem. Ann and I had split up by this time. I was living in an apartment in Georgetown, and we were headed for a divorce. Ours was not a sudden or dramatic breakup, but we were no longer making each other very happy, and, after long and heartfelt talks about it, and wrestling with our Catholic guilt and worries over the impact on the kids, we had reached a mutual decision, and I had moved out. As a practical matter, if I wanted to continue to play a role in my children's lives—and I certainly did—I had to be in Washington, where they, at ages fifteen and twelve, were both in school. I had become, as my son put it, "the Dad of Wednesday nights and every other weekend." I wasn't happy about this. Divorce seemed like a failure to me. But at the same time, I was relieved, even liberated. The weight from the tension and arguments with Ann had been lifted. We finally faced the reality that our marriage had hollowed out after nearly two decades.

The idea of leaving the *Times* felt like another divorce. For nearly two decades, my job at the paper had determined where we lived—and in many respects how we lived. Many of my closest friends were at the *Times*. On the telephone, identifying myself when calling a source, the *New York Times* had been my last name for a long time. It would not be easy to walk away from all that.

But the CBS News offer was attractive: twice the money, more visibility, and the challenge and excitement of something new. I felt I'd be doing the same thing—covering the news—but in a different medium with different priorities that reached a wider audience. At forty-six, with glasses and a hairline that had been receding since my twenties, I had no illusions that I was a future anchorman. No one would call me telegenic. But by this time I had learned the ropes of national and international news, and I hoped that some of that authority might come through. I was ready for a new chapter.

Before making a final decision, I suggested to CBS that we try me on for size. They agreed and assigned Mary Martin, one of their best Washington producers, to help me make an audition tape. Mary was funny, irreverent, whip smart, and savvy about television. If the tape I made with a gifted producer like Mary was terrible, or if CBS or even I thought it was terrible, we could bury the whole idea. I hadn't said a word to the *Times* about any of this up to that point, so no bridges had been burned; it was our little secret. I wrote a brief script, about a two-minute piece on some current Washington story, laid the narration down on tape, and Mary and I and a camera crew went to the bank of the Tidal Basin, a stock stand-up location with the Jefferson Memorial in the background, and I recorded the final twenty seconds or so of the piece on camera. Back at the CBS bureau, we screened the tape together in an edit booth. I was self-conscious watching it. I thought I looked and sounded like exactly what I was: a middle-aged, balding print reporter talking awkwardly into a camera. When it was over, I looked at Mary.

"I've seen worse," she said, and packed up the tape to ship to New York.

The CBS brass at the Broadcast Center on West Fifty-Seventh Street apparently agreed. They invited me to fly to Manhattan and meet with Ed Joyce and Howard Stringer, then president and vice president of CBS News. At that moment in time, CBS News was in the market for experienced print reporters to bolster their correspondent corps, especially in Washington. After thirty minutes, we had a deal. A four-year "talent" contract would be drawn up. (I had thought I was a reporter, but no—now I was "talent.")

Then Ed and Howard added the sweetener. Was I heading back to Washington that afternoon? Yes, I was. Well, as it happened, so were they. Why didn't I join them in the CBS plane? A limo took us out to a private hangar at White Plains, and soon the three of us were aloft in a cushy, fourteen-passenger executive jet with a personal flight attendant offering drinks and nibbles. I realized that I was being seduced, but, as the old saying goes, when it's inevitable, relax and enjoy it. What I didn't realize was that this would be the last time I would see the inside of a CBS corporate jet. The golden age of network television, if that is what it was, or at least its free-spending era, was coming to an end just as I was joining it.

The reaction of my *Times* colleagues to the news that I was leaving for CBS surprised me. It was an unusual career move in those days. The only other *Times* correspondent who had done it recently was James Wooten, who had made a success of it at ABC. Frankly, I expected my fellow *Times* reporters to snicker at the idea or dismiss it as a silly sell-out. Instead, they were curious about why I was doing it, what I would be doing, and how much I would be paid. Most of them, even the *Times* lifers, seemed to think it was an intriguing idea. A few even said they might try something similar themselves. I did wonder what my late father would have thought of my move. He'd done a fair amount of television in his day, but always as a guest, and I knew he resented the impact television had on sports. He hated, for example, how the World Series games were played at night, in prime time, to suit the demands of television. In his view, baseball was an afternoon game, best played in daylight. But television as a job, for me, in news, that would allow me to learn and expand—I think he might have applauded that.

In any event, I plunged right in, doing tape pieces for the *CBS Morning News* and conducting live interviews with Washington newsmakers three mornings a week. Other networks employed voice coaches and consultants to break in new correspondents; CBS News had a different philosophy—that is, sink or swim. I simply showed up the first morning and went on the air. That was fine with me, because, frankly, at forty-seven I was too old a dog to learn many new tricks. I had no time to learn to be a professional broadcaster. This new gig was either going to work naturally, bald pate and all, or not at all. The *Times* had been gracious as I went out the door and said I could come back any time. I was prepared to hold them to their word if my late-blooming television career turned out to be a disaster.

A disaster it wasn't, although Dan Rather, who had succeeded Cronkite by this time, was safe in his anchor chair. I made my share of mistakes, like my first stand-up interview, when I cleverly placed myself between the camera and the subject on the north lawn of the White House, interrupted him repeatedly, and rendered the whole thing useless. The producer standing beside the camera was surprisingly gentle: "You might try stepping to one side the next time," he'd said. The all-time classic newbie faux pas had been committed years earlier by Bernard Kalb, who had made the jump from the *Times* to CBS a generation before me. Doing his first stand-up interview, Kalb had held the microphone to his own mouth while he asked his first question. Then, proving that old habits die hard, he'd tucked the microphone under his arm, taken out a notebook and pen, and jotted down the answer. The muffled reply went unrecorded for posterity, or CBS News.

Cosmetic issues arose. Like my wardrobe. The blue suit was deemed okay, but the gray blended into the background on the set, and the tan made me look pale. My favorite old tweedy sports jacket was unacceptable. And what about my glasses, which I had worn since I was sixteen? Should I try contacts? Everybody had an opinion. Finally my son, Christopher, then fourteen, settled the debate when he said, "Dad, you look smarter with your glasses on." Compared to newspapers, television is a group exercise. To get a television piece on the air, a correspondent required, in those days, a producer, a two-person camera

crew, a tape editor, plus all the technicians in the control room and studio. Gathering the news is only half the task. It took a village to deliver
the product to the viewer. I was amazed at how long it took to prepare
a piece that might run a couple of minutes on the air. There was actual
work involved! No one had told me! As a panelist on *Washington Week*
or the Sunday shows, all I did was show up and opine about a topic I had
been covering that week. Producing a network tape piece on deadline
was another matter. And the writing was different: simpler, more linear,
more to the point. I wrote everything I read on the air, as did most correspondents at CBS, trying to get to the essence of a story as quickly
as possible. One thought to a sentence, thank you, and make it all fit in
a minute forty-five, or whatever length the broadcast could afford for
that piece on that day. I tried to write as conversationally as possible
and still manage the occasional turn of phrase. First-rate producers like
Mary Martin kept me from making a fool of myself and getting lost in
my own rhetoric—most of the time. As a newspaper correspondent, I
had been a one-man band in the field. Occasionally I had worked with
a photographer, but even then I had decided what the story was and
had done the reporting and writing and filing. In television, it took a
high-tech army to make air. On the road, and especially on a presidential trip overseas, the effort and size of the team multiplied. Early
on in my tenure, I was a *Morning News* correspondent accompanying
President Reagan on a swing through Europe. Producers from CBS's
Special Events unit, as professional a bunch as I had ever encountered,
had "advanced" every leg of the trip, plotting camera angles, estimating
"throw distances" (whatever they were), and pretesting the best restau-
rants. The technical arrangements were prodigious: to enable me to do
a live report from a town square in Strasbourg, France, on VE Day, a
ground station was flown in to beam the signal to the satellite. It seemed
an extraordinary production to me; everyone else treated it as routine.

Today, technology has simplified and streamlined much of the production. Cameras are smaller and lighter, portable uplinks can fit in a
suitcase, single videographers handle pictures and sound, many correspondents can and are required to shoot and edit and feed their own
material. But in the 1980s, an eon ago in TV terms, it was a team effort
with a budget to match. In those days, the networks were flush with
cash and still thought of their news divisions as first-class worldwide-
news-gathering operations. If the story was worth it, the expense was

not a problem. Need to charter a Learjet to catch up with the story after a broadcast? Dial it up. Later, as corporate conglomerates bought up the networks and insisted that the news divisions become profit centers, budgets were cut, foreign bureaus were closed, and the bottom line became a primary consideration.

A few months after I joined CBS, a story broke that brought home the respective strengths and weaknesses of print and television. It also gave me a total immersion course in the demands and possibilities of live television. On June 14, 1985, two Lebanese terrorists hijacked TWA Flight 847 shortly after takeoff from Athens, en route San Diego, with 147 passengers and crew aboard. The red and white Boeing jetliner was diverted to Beirut, then Algiers, and back to Beirut. The hijackers demanded the release of some seven hundred Arab prisoners from Israeli jails, and a standoff began that lasted nearly three days.

On a few hours' notice, I was summoned to New York to coanchor the *CBS Morning News* with Bob Schieffer to provide running coverage for two hours every morning. From the New York studio, we debriefed correspondents on the scene and conducted live interviews with officials and experts and released hostages and frantic family members. Because of the six-hour time difference between New York and Beirut, we had breaking news to report each morning. In addition, live television became a conduit for indirect communications between the Shiite terrorists, the US and Israeli officials, and the hostages and their families.

Everything was done live. One morning, I was able to get the Amal militia leader, Nabih Berri, on the phone from Beirut. I knew him from an interview I had done with him in Lebanon a year earlier. He told me on the air of his plan to release three of the hostages that day. When we checked the State Department for confirmation, it was the first they had heard of it. With developments like that, the show crackled with immediacy. The morning newspapers, coming out twenty-four hours later, seemed dated by comparison.

In the end, one of the hostages was killed. The hijackers singled out a US Navy diver, Robert Stethem, beat him, shot him in the temple, and dumped his body on the tarmac. The others were released in groups and eventually transferred to downtown Beirut and Damascus, where they were eventually let go. I flew to Frankfurt with Mary Martin to intercept some of the returning Americans and interview them as they reunited with their families. All of this aired live on the *Morning News* direct from Frankfurt Airport. It was a dramatic story, and television stayed on top of it. But it was up to the newspapers like the *Times* to dig into the background of the hijackers and the political movement behind them. Television is good at telling you what happened, sometimes even showing it to you as it happens, but it is less effective explaining why something happened and what it might mean. Not even the networks have the staff and resources and, most importantly, the motivation to do the digging that this requires.

As soon as the hostages from TWA 847 were released, the *Morning News* went back to its normal mix of news and features and cooking tips and the like. I had been warned by James Wooten, the former *Times* reporter who had already made the transition from print to television before me, "The people who tell you that television is all entertainment and no news don't know what they are talking about. But the people who say it is all news and no entertainment don't know either."

The *CBS Morning News* kept me busy that summer of 1945. In August, we did a week of live-broadcast segments from Japan commemorating the fortieth anniversary of the atomic bombings of Hiroshima and Nagasaki. The following February, I was in Manilla covering the Philippine election in which President Ferdinand Marcos held off a challenge from Corazon Aquino, largely by stealing the votes he needed in the provinces.

In each case, I traveled with a team of producers and technicians to cover the stories live. It is hard to imagine the network morning news broadcasts making that commitment today. They have the resources— all are immensely profitable programs that bring in tens of millions annually in advertising revenue—but less appetite for serious international news. Today, in the age of cable news, the broadcast network morning shows are a frothy mix of celebrity coverage, features, and, conspicuously, promotional segments about upcoming prime-time programs. One or the other will still score a major interview, a big "get" in the bookers' parlance, but as often as not it will be someone from a celebrity murder trial or kidnapping or Hollywood scandal rather than a world leader. In any event, my time as Washington correspondent for the *CBS Morning News* turned out to be brief. I'd been part of the team less than a year when Howard Stringer, who had taken over as president of CBS News, came to Washington determined to move me to the White House. He pitched it as a plum: I'd join Lesley Stahl, Bill Plante, and Jacqueline Adams to cover the second-term Reagan administration. I was flattered by the offer, but I knew enough about the all-consuming, claustrophobic life of a network-television White House correspondent to do what I could to duck the assignment. Which turned out to be not much. I protested to Howard that I had been there, done that, for the *Times* during the Carter administration. But he was insistent. Reagan had three more years in the White House and was embroiled in the Iran-Contra scandal. It was a big story, and CBS was determined to add some reporting muscle to its White House team. There would be a salary boost in it, Howard said, and a lot of airtime. Yes, I said, but . . . It didn't matter; I was on my way back to the White House.

As it developed, it was a good move, especially for a newspaperman-turned-television correspondent who still had a lot to learn about covering a fast-paced beat for television. All the news broadcasts, morning and evening, expected a piece or even two from the White House every day. Quickly, with the help of excellent producers, I learned to cover an event, turn out a script in minutes, do a stand-up on the North Lawn, and feed the package in short order. It was not high art, and certainly not literature, but I learned to write for television in that cramped CBS booth in the West Wing, and it served me well. I learned, for example, to write to the pictures, not over them. Seems obvious, but it is not instinctive—not for an ink-stained wretch trying to learn new tricks.

It was a dramatic period at the White House. President Reagan was slowing down perceptibly, but the news was not. Reagan ducked most of the consequences of the Iran-Contra mess and went on to reach a genuine rapprochement with the Soviet Union in its waning days. With summit meetings in Geneva, Reykjavík, Washington, and Moscow, he and Mikhail Gorbachev effectively ended the Cold War and took the first solid steps toward nuclear-weapons reductions. Arguably the Soviet Union would have collapsed of its own cumbersome weight anyway, and probably Reagan got more credit than he deserved for its dissolution, but it was a momentous time, nonetheless. Covering the Gipper's visit to the heart of the "Evil Empire," watching the old cold warrior strolling through Red Square with his new friend "Gorby," and shaking hands with ordinary Russians was worth the price of admission.

Say what you will about Ronald Reagan, but the man knew how to vacation. He spent one full year of his eight as president at his ranch outside Santa Barbara, with the press corps happily in tow. It wasn't strictly a vacation for us when the president was secluded at Rancho del Cielo three or four times a year for weeks at a time, but it came close. Like other correspondents, I rented a house overlooking the Pacific, played tennis at the Biltmore Santa Barbara, went sailing out of the Santa Barbara Yacht Club, and studiously sampled the wines of the Central Coast. And, oh, yes, every now and then we filed a piece to satisfy the producers back in New York. But there was very little real news, and that was fine with us.

Covering the White House for television back in Washington was infinitely more confining—and in some ways frustrating—than covering it for the *New York Times*. I was chained to the daily schedule of events and pseudoevents that the White House staged every day. If the president was greeting Boy Scouts in the Oval Office or welcoming a championship basketball team in the Rose Garden, I needed to be there with a camera crew to get the pictures and capture whatever comments Reagan might make about the news of the day. His remarks were rarely substantive; Reagan was the master of the offhand quip and empty ad-lib. But the pictures were critical. They were the video on which the day's White House story could be hung, even if they had nothing to do with the news. As a result, I would be at the White House, working out of the tiny CBS broadcast booth in the press room, elbow-to-elbow with Bill Plante or Lesley Stahl, from early morning until after the evening news. A White House correspondent for a newspaper like the *Times*, by contrast, can skip the made-for-television moments that take up much of the president's day and pick up any comments the president might make from the wires. This journalist is free to research, report, and round out the story of the day or an enterprise piece without worrying about the manufactured events that television needs to cover. No surprise, then, that you will find more original reporting in the paper than on television. In any event, my second stint at the White House came to a close with the end of the Reagan administration. The Gipper flew back to his hazy retirement in California, and I moved on to a new and intriguing assignment that opened up at CBS by happenstance.

21

CBS News Sunday Morning

The happenstance came in the person of a rumpled, avuncular, writer-storyteller and broadcasting genius named Charles Kuralt. By that time, Kuralt was the hugely popular host of television's equivalent of the Sunday *New York Times Magazine—CBS Sunday Morning*. The broadcast presented ninety minutes of news, features, and reporting on culture, the arts, music, fly-fishing, and just about anything that struck the fancy or curiosity of the anchor and its creative original executive producer, Robert "Shad" Northshield. From its sparkling opening trumpet fanfare to its closing pastoral scenes, *CBS Sunday Morning* was, and is, a unique treasure, one of the finest broadcasts on television.

As *CBS Sunday Morning* celebrated its tenth anniversary in 1989, Kuralt was looking to beef up his roster of regular correspondents. He already had onboard standouts like the great pianist Billy Taylor on jazz; flute virtuoso Eugenia Zukerman on classical music; John Leonard, the film, book, and drama critic; Bill Geist, the witty former *New York Times* columnist, who contributed essays on anything, really, that could illustrate the kookiness of the human condition—and many others.

But evidently Kuralt and Northshield still felt shorthanded when it came to correspondents to do the cover stories of the broadcast, which usually keyed off the news or focused on trends and overlooked stories. The covers were and are the first full-length piece after the headlines of the day and were and are important to set the tone of that Sunday's broadcast.

Charles and I had met a few times around CBS, and he had apparently been watching some of my work on air. Evidently he liked what

he saw. One day when I was in New York, he invited me to take a week
or two to do the cover story for an upcoming broadcast.

"You'll enjoy the extra time," he said. "You can let it breathe a little."

My first piece for *CBS Sunday Morning*, on January 8, 1989, was a
critical assessment of Ronald Reagan's eight years in the White House,
which were coming to an end in less than two weeks. We took a hard
look at his promises and his performance: the goals achieved (inflation
cut back sharply, arms reduction achieved with the Soviets) and targets
missed (the budget not balanced, the size of government not reduced,
the Iran-Contra scandal, etc.). It was a reasonably balanced summation
of Reagan's two terms but probably not a hit in the White House.

Kuralt liked the piece and told me so. He proposed that I work for the
broadcast full-time and offered to intercede with management to make
it happen, freeing me from my daily duties in the Washington bureau
and clearing my schedule to do a regular diet of stories for his broadcast. I liked the idea. I was just wrapping up my latest stint at the White
House and was open to something new. But I was skeptical that management would agree to release one of their Washington correspondents
from daily duty. Kuralt, who was the network's senior correspondent at
that point, had no doubt that he could get his way with CBS management, most of whom he held in minimum high regard.

"You leave them to me," he said. "My role around here is to persuade
them what's in their best interest." In a few weeks, good to his word,
management had seen Kuralt's wisdom, and the deed was done.

For me, that was the start of a nine-year romance with longer-form
television. Designated the broadcast's "senior correspondent," I did
cover stories, features, interviews, personality profiles, live shots from
the field—you name it—for *CBS Sunday Morning*. The cover stories and
many of the major pieces would run nine to eleven minutes, a lifetime in
network television news, versus the minute forty-five to two minutes for
the average piece on the morning or evening news broadcasts.

Kuralt was right—I did enjoy letting the pieces breathe a bit. You
could have some fun with the script, take more care with the writing,
explore different approaches to the news, and introduce some interesting characters. The pace and the rhythm appealed to me after decades of
meeting daily deadlines. I would usually produce two covers a month:
in week one, I'd set out to shoot the piece on location somewhere in the
US or abroad. During week two, I'd usually go to New York, where the

broadcast was based, to screen, write, narrate, and supervise the editing of the piece with the producer and a tape editor. That schedule involved lots of travel and not a few overnights at the Essex House or Parker Meridien in New York, CBS's preferred hotels for visiting correspondents. But I was able to continue to live in Washington, have a semblance of a normal life, and see my kids on a regular basis. An ideal arrangement.

The assignment took me everywhere.

I went to "Little Saigon" in San Jose, California, to report on how the Vietnamese boat people were faring fifteen years after the fall of South Vietnam; to Montgomery, Alabama, to interview the architect and sculptor Maya Lin on her stunning new memorial commemorating the civil-rights movement; to the Kennedy Space Center to report on NASA and the future of space travel; to Orlando, Maine, to focus a cover story on the plight of America's homeless; to Helsinki to cover a US-Soviet summit; to Israel for a piece on the unprecedented flood of Soviet Jews migrating to Israel that year; to Panama on the first anniversary of the US overthrow of Manuel Noriega; and twice to East Germany—to Torgau for a forty-fifth anniversary reunion of US and Soviet army veterans on the banks of the Elbe River where they had met in the closing days of World War II, and a second time to Dresden to report on the halting, awkward reunification of East and West Germany. All that and more in my first year or two on the broadcast.

Over the next several years, I kept traveling: I made three trips to Cuba, a first for me, to do pieces on the still-strained but slowly warming relations with the United States, a feature on the ambitious efforts to restore the handsome architecture of Old Havana, and a hard look at the precarious state of free expression and political opposition in Castro's Cuba. I made my first trip to Belfast, Northern Ireland, for a cover on the valiant and ultimately successful diplomatic efforts of George Mitchell to bring the Protestants in the north and the Catholics in the Republic of Ireland together in the Good Friday Agreement. I traveled to Haiti and the Dominican Republic for a look at the questionable history of US military interventions on the island of Hispaniola and back to Haiti three months later when the United States tried it again. I was in Mexico in 1994 to cover the closest presidential election there in fifty-five years, filing pieces for the *CBS Evening News* and *CBS This Morning* as well as *Sunday Morning*.

I pursued environmental stories that mattered, from the return of the gray whales to the waters off California to the reestablishment of wolves to Yellowstone National Park to the magnificence of North Cascades National Park—a vast wilderness of mountains, glaciers, and lakes that the American people own but don't often visit. I reported on the neglected state of the national system of wildlife refuges and examined the repair and restoration of my home waters, the endangered Chesapeake Bay, which was, and is, struggling under the pressure of the invasion of some eighteen million inconsiderate human beings who choose to live along its magnificent shores and frequently treat it like a trash bin.

I also indulged my passion for sailing, with pieces on the revival of the magnificent J boats, the accomplishments of a blind sailor who competed in regattas, and the fortunes of the first all-woman team to compete in the male-dominated Whitbread Round the World Race. Later I did a piece on the first, and to date only, all-woman's team competing to defend the America's Cup. The women didn't qualify to compete in the final, but it made a good story. In 1994, I covered the start in Charleston, South Carolina, of the BOC Challenge, a nine-month, twenty-seven thousand–mile, single-handed yacht race around the world. Each one of the solo sailors was a character. The sailing pieces may not have attracted the largest audiences, but they had drama, great visuals, and fascinating personalities—and, what the hell, I had fun doing them.

In addition to the covers, I got to do profiles of writers and artists that interested me. I traveled from New York to Los Angeles with the late, great André Previn, the classical pianist, composer, and conductor who in 1993 was resuming playing jazz for the first time in thirty years and setting off on a world tour. I did a piece on Beau Jacque, who introduced the wonderful zydeco music he learned growing up in Opelousas, Louisiana, to wildly enthusiastic concertgoers in Central Park in Manhattan.

I did a joint profile of Jimmy and Rosemary Breslin, the father and daughter authors who had published their memoirs simultaneously. I traveled for three days on horseback through the Bitterroot Mountains of Idaho with filmmaker Ken Burns and with historian Stephen Ambrose as he retraced the adventures of Lewis and Clark as recounted in his riveting best seller *Undaunted Courage*. I got to watch Kurt Vonnegut struggle with the notoriously difficult Saturday *New York Times* crossword puzzle (he wouldn't start writing on any day, he said, until he finished the puzzle) while doing a profile of his wife, Jill Krementz, the photographer, who had just published a book about the often-messy work habits of famous authors, titled *The Writer's Desk*. Jill and I had been colleagues and friends on the *Herald Tribune*. She had photographed Vonnegut years before and married him.

Not surprisingly, writers—at least good writers—made great profiles and set the broadcast apart. One of the best, and certainly the most fun, I met in November of 1996. I had read an excerpt in the *New Yorker* of a new memoir titled *Angela's Ashes* by a then-unknown Frank Mc-Court, about his early years growing up poor and hungry in the slums of Limerick, Ireland. It was poignant, witty, utterly without self-pity, and altogether delightful. I suggested to the then–executive producer Missie Rennie that I do a piece about McCourt and his book, which was quickly becoming a best seller and would go on to make millions, win the Pulitzer, and become a film. The *New York Times'* Michiko Kakutani had raved about it in her daily book review as "a classic modern memoir."

To her credit, Missie had already read and enjoyed the excerpt and immediately said yes. When I learned through his agent that Frank and his three brothers, Malachy, Michael, and Alfie, were about to return to Limerick together for the first time in forty-seven years to visit the grave of their mother, Angela, I could see a wonderful piece in the making.

Missie agreed to foot the bill, and I flew to London with a superb *Sunday Morning* producer and CBS veteran, Jim Houtrides, picked up a first-rate crew from the London bureau, and met McCourt for the first time at Filthy MacNasty's, an Irish pub in London, where Frank was about to read the opening passage of his book to an appreciative audience: "When I look back on my childhood," Frank began reading in his soft, beguiling brogue, "I wonder how I survived at all. It was, of course, a miserable childhood: the happy childhood is hardly worth your while. Worse than the ordinary miserable childhood is the miserable Irish childhood, and worse yet is the miserable Irish Catholic childhood."

With those few sentences, beautifully read, he had me hooked and the audience entranced.

It was the beginning of a delightful several days with the warm and wacky McCourt brothers in England and Ireland—and, for me, a friendship that lasted until Frank passed away in July of 2009. We flew to Dublin, where Frank scored big with television interviews and a packed reading at Waterstones, the iconic four-story bookstore on Dawson Street. The next day, we and the McCourt clan drove to Limerick, where the family had grown up desperately poor and hungry in "the lanes," a ramshackle slum of tiny, filthy houses where, Frank wrote, "from October to April the walls glistened with the damp, clothes never dried, tweed and woolen coats housed living things and sometimes sprouted mysterious vegetations."

"People everywhere brag and whimper about the woes of their early years," Frank wrote, "but nothing can compare with the Irish version: the poverty; the shiftless, loquacious alcoholic father; the pious, defeated mother moaning by the fire . . ."

Over the next three days, with the camera rolling, Frank and his brothers strolled the lanes, walked along the banks of the River Shannon, drank and sang in pubs and bars, and even climbed the windswept ruins of the Castle Carrigogunnell, where as a teenager Frank had looked out on the Shannon rolling west and dreamed of America across the sea. With his three brothers, we visited the cemetery where Angela's ashes were scattered and where the McCourts, irreverent as ever, laughed at their own stories and sang to her memory.

In a long sit-down interview one morning that we shot, appropriately, in a hotel bar, Frank marveled at the early success of his book, surprised, he said, that anyone would want to read it at all. He'd immigrated to the United States at nineteen, joined the army, gotten an education, and taught in New York high schools for forty years before retiring and finally sitting down to write his book.

"I knew this was the one thing in my life that I had to do," he told me. "I had to write this. This was the major enterprise of my life, and I had to get it out of my system. I would have died howling if I hadn't written this book; I would have begged for another few years."

Frank became a celebrity after *Angela's Ashes*. He wrote several more books, was continually in demand, and generally enjoyed life with his third wife, Ellen Frey, until he died of cancer at seventy-eight. (His first marriage, he often said, was a formality, the second a disaster, and the third, to Ellen, "perfection.") He and Ellen had met at the Lion's Head, the famous pub in Greenwich Village, when Frank had stood in the entryway and demanded, in a loud voice, "Any of my ex-wives in here?"

He and I remained friends over the years, seeing each other in New York and Washington—and once, traveling together to South Bend, Indiana, at Notre Dame, where he drew an overflow crowd delivering the annual Red Smith Lecture. My father would have loved it. The McCourts and Susy and I stayed on campus until the weekend to watch Notre Dame lose, badly, to the University of Southern California. It was the first, big-time college football game Frank had seen, and he loved it, especially when the game ball was delivered by a soldier who parachuted out of a plane and landed precisely on the fifty yard line to hand it to the referee to start the game. Frank was as amazed by all the silly hoopla as he was by his own success.

It wasn't often that I ended up close to an interview subject for years afterward, but then, not many were like Frank McCourt. Truly, one of a kind.

By 1998, after thirteen years in commercial television and nine years with *CBS Sunday Morning*, I found that I was repeating myself. The cover stories were starting to feel routine and the frequent travel tiresome. I was in the midst of negotiating my fourth four-year-contract with CBS when another option presented itself. I was contacted by Jim Lehrer, anchor of *The NewsHour with Jim Lehrer* on PBS, with an intriguing offer. It was another happenstance, and this time it led to my moving on from CBS.

22

The News Business as News

Jim Lehrer had an idea. Even better, he had secured a grant from the Pew Charitable Trusts to finance his idea.

By the end of the twentieth century—this was 1998, and Y2K was fast approaching—the news business was confronting a raft of economic, ethical, and technological challenges that would transform the nature of news and the lives of the people who cover it in print, on the air, on cable, and, increasingly, on the Internet. The world of news—my world for the previous forty years—was being turned upside-down by forces that few fully understood. Jim Lehrer's idea was to cover the news as news on his broadcast, to report and analyze the changes confronting journalism writ large. His notion was that the many controversies about how, why, and when news was reported not only affected the news but was news itself. He had the vehicle, *The NewsHour*, and the initial funding, thanks to Pew; now he needed someone to make it happen. That someone turned out to be me.

Jim first raised the idea with me when we ran into each other at a cocktail party in Washington. We were social friends but had never worked together. He suggested I come over to *The NewsHour*'s studio and offices across the Potomac in Shirlington, Virginia, meet his executive producer, Les Crystal, and talk about it. In our first session, which lasted nearly two hours, we realized that, despite the considerable differences in our backgrounds, we saw many things in similar fashion, especially news coverage. Jim had also begun his career on newspapers before moving to broadcast. With his news partner, Robert MacNeil, Jim had created *The MacNeil/Lehrer Report*, the first hour-long, national news broadcast on public television, which had evolved into *The*

193

NewsHour with Jim Lehrer after MacNeil retired. It was a sober, serious nightly summation of national and international news with a heavy dose of politics that attracted a small but devoted nightly audience of a million or more. The private, self-mocking slogan among the *NewsHour* staff, "We dare to be dull," had more than a grain of truth, but it was a respected, reliable, balanced source of public-affairs broadcasting that had a lock on the precious 6 to 7 p.m. Eastern time slot on PBS. It continues as the *PBS NewsHour*.

Jim and I were rough contemporaries; he was four years my senior. He died in 2020 at the age of eighty-five. Back in 1998, as we talked in his office, we realized we were similar in one way: we were two writers who happened to do television for a living. That cemented it. It seemed like a good match, and I liked the idea of covering the business I had been in so long as a beat. So, at the end of my CBS contract, I signed on with *The NewsHour* as a senior producer with the title of media correspondent. Overnight I moved from commercial network television to the smaller, more rarefied world of public television.

The Media Unit that Pew had agreed to fund didn't exist, so we had to create it. I would serve as senior producer and on-air correspondent, but we needed a team. I recruited Mary Beth Durkin, an outstanding producer with experience at both CBS and, a few years before, *The NewsHour*, and Morgan Till, a talented young production assistant from CBS, as associate producer, plus Ilyse Veron from *The NewsHour* staff, and we moved into *The NewsHour*'s expanding offices in Shirlington.

To announce the creation of the new unit, MacNeil/Lehrer Productions, the parent company, bought newspaper display ads headlined, "THE NEWSHOUR HAS ALWAYS COVERED THE NEWS, NOW TERENCE SMITH COVERS THE PEOPLE WHO COVER THE NEWS." With that, we were in business.

At the first 10 a.m. story conference in Jim's office on my first day, I began to appreciate the different mindset of public television. In drafting a rundown for that night's broadcast, we actually talked about the news—not just the news that might bring ratings but the news that was important for people to know.

A similar planning session at CBS would often begin with a report on the current ratings of the *CBS Evening News* and how it ranked compared to the competing broadcasts on NBC and ABC—who was up, who was down, what stories seemed likely to attract the greatest number of eyeballs, etc. There is nothing wrong with that; it was just a tacit admission of reality—namely, that the ratings were crucial to the advertisers and that ads paid the bills.

No mystery there, but the network's concern over ratings inevitably affected the news judgement and influenced what would be on the air that night. So did the footage that might be available on any given night. If there was arresting video of a car crash or collapsing crane or a cute animal doing something stupid, it made air, whether there was any real news value or not. Pictures first, content second. Ratings were king, and the ranking of the *Evening News* affected everything in the news division, from morale to budget. When the flagship broadcast was on top, life was good and production money was available. When it was second or third, the hunt for scapegoats began. When an evening-news broadcast is in trouble, the old axiom goes, the first thing network management does is change the set. If that fails to turn it around, they fire the executive producer. Still no improvement? Fire the anchor. After that? Suicide!

At the *NewsHour*, if management even knew whether the ratings were up or down one week over another, it was rarely, if ever, mentioned. They conducted periodic audience surveys, of course, but the total number of viewers was more steady than changing. To be fair, there was no direct, head-to-head competition to *The NewsHour* and, of course, no ads and no advertisers to please. At the morning meeting, we talked about what needed to be covered on that night's broadcast and the best way to cover it. We discussed the best possible guests to interview, how to advance the story if possible, and what we could add to the mix given *The NewsHour*'s very limited resources. And, of course, we had an hour of airtime, minus a few minutes of underwriter credits— say, fifty-six minutes—to devote to the news versus the twenty-two minutes of editorial time in the typical half-hour evening-news network broadcast. The extra time was luxury.

There was also a cooperative, collegial attitude among the dozen or so producers and on-air correspondents at *The NewsHour*'s morning story conferences. The staff was so small and the resources so scarce that it was usually obvious who would do what story and how. Jim would decide immediately after the meeting, and Les Crystal would dole out the day's assignments.

At CBS, producers invariably would have to compete for airtime for their stories and correspondents against similar pitches from bureaus around the country and the world. The executive producer would have to decide who and what made air and what did not: a minute forty-five for this story, a twenty-second "tell" read by the anchor for a lesser tale. The internal competition had its benefits, but the atmosphere could be cutthroat. (*CBS Sunday Morning* was an exception. Given its limited staff and more leisurely production schedule, every piece we shot made the broadcast.)

For me, the more cooperative, news-first atmosphere at *The News-Hour* was a breath of fresh air. The news mattered most, not some stupid pet trick. A worthwhile story would make the broadcast because it was worthwhile. Important international news especially would be covered. The segments largely respected the intelligence of the viewer, if not his or her patience. There were exceptions of course. Many of the longer discussions bordered on the tedious, some of the panels I could have skipped altogether, and I couldn't share Jim's passion, for example, for the extended interviews with outgoing and incoming Marine commandants that Jim, the former Marine, relished. All in all, it was a substantive, serious, important, even essential broadcast, especially compared to the hot-headline services that the evening-news shows had become on the networks. I was glad I'd made the move.

Happily, Jim and the broadcast were entirely open to story ideas and discussions from the new Media Unit. So we set to work reporting on the controversies, scandals, trends, high points, and low points of the news business. We did tape pieces, interviews, live panels—the whole gamut.

There was no shortage of subjects. Newspapers and magazines were still prospering but beginning to feel the first effects of the erosion of advertising that would crumble their economic models in the early years of the new century. Craig Newmark had launched a new Web-based service in 1996 and incorporated it as "Craigslist.com" in 1999. Its free ads and listings would go on to drain newspapers of their most reliable source of revenue, the columns of classified advertising that publishers used to refer to privately as "rivers of gold." Print, generally, was just beginning to feel the economic meltdown that would kill hundreds of smaller papers, deplete local news, and transform the industry.

At the same time, the Internet was coming into its own as the World Wide Web with its discussion forums, blogs, social networking, on-line shopping, and advertising and was a fast-rising, nearly universal marketplace of ideas and news. I had originally underestimated—dismissed—the Internet as just another medium of transmission. Wrong! With its interactive, limitless capacity and worldwide reach, it was a genuine cultural, political, economic, and communications revolution that would, with a few notable exceptions, eat the lunch of newspapers and the traditional forms of print. Understanding and reporting the Internet and its impact was a rich source of fodder for the Media Unit.

There was also no shortage of scandals, political and journalistic—from Bill Clinton's Oval Office dalliance with Monica Lewinsky to Jayson Blair's fabrications in the *New York Times*. One day I was analyzing the ethics of scandal coverage, the next I was interviewing Howell Raines, then executive editor of the *New York Times*, squirming live on *The NewsHour* set under questioning about how Jayson Blair could have gotten away with his lies for so long.

On September 11, 2001, I was about as far off base as possible, shooting a story in Grand Forks, North Dakota, about the economic and editorial challenges confronting a prize-winning small-town daily, when hijacked planes crashed into the Twin Towers of the World Trade Center, the Pentagon, and a farmer's field in Pennsylvania. With air service grounded, I had to drive the 1,500 miles back to Washington to join the coverage. Sharing the wheel with Ilyse Veron and with Anne Davenport—the excellent media unit producer who had joined *The NewsHour* from ABC and succeeded Mary Beth Durkin—we drove through a stunned, sobered country to arrive back in Washington with the Pentagon wreckage still smoldering just a couple of miles from the studio.

The aftermath of 9/11 was the central story—really, the only story—as the US invaded Afghanistan, failed to capture Osama bin Laden, and then, in a colossal blunder, turned its fire on Saddam Hussein's Iraq. It was a huge, misguided, corrupt, and deceitful foreign-policy catastrophe, the worst since Vietnam, built on lies and distorted intelligence and an absurd, neoconservative notion that the United States, by force of arms, could ignite a democratic revolution that would spread throughout the Middle East. The 2003 Iraq War would ultimately kill nearly five thousand US soldiers and more than one hundred thousand Iraqi civilians and leave that historic, oil-rich country in shambles.

The Iraq War was also a massive failure for news organizations. We—and I include myself and *The NewsHour*—fell prey to a kind of groupthink or tacit acceptance of the reality that the nation was going to war in Iraq no matter what. It was based on the widely shared suspicion that Saddam harbored weapons of mass destruction, a contention hammered home repeatedly by top administration officials, including Vice President Cheney, who deliberately misled the public. When Congress voted to authorize use of force, news organizations began to cover the coming war as a fait accompli. It was no longer a question of *if* but rather *when*. The media focus was on the preparations for the war, not where it should have been—the shaky premises on which the whole sad episode hung. News organizations spent more time and energy on how to cover a war that seemed inevitable than on questioning the rationale for the war. News organizations largely failed to challenge Bush administration talk of mushroom clouds and aluminum tubes and Saddam Hussein's nonexistent role in 9/11.

The exceptions to this media herd mentality were the Knight Ridder Washington bureau and, to a lesser extent, Walter Pincus in the *Washington Post*. In the weeks leading up to the war, their reporting began to openly question the administration's claims about Saddam and his mythical weapons. At the same time, they reported that President George W. Bush had made the decision months earlier to take the Iraqi leader down. The goal was regime change, in part as payback for Saddam's efforts to assassinate George H. W. Bush, in part so the son could claim credit for finishing the job his father had started a decade earlier. The die was cast.

At *The NewsHour*, we reported some of the skepticism, and interviewed some of the open critics of the march to war, including Senator Edward M. Kennedy, but not nearly enough. Most of *The NewsHour*'s coverage focused on the preparations and timing and likely goals of the assault, not the validity of the Bush administration's claims. The great bulk of the interviews and discussions on the broadcast were with the war's proponents, not the skeptics. Groupthink is the only explanation for this across-the-board media failure, which was shared by the networks and major organizations, bolstered by a sort of blind, unquestioning patriotism in the wake of 9/11. The government, including

Congress, had decided to go to war, and now we were going to cover it as best we could.

All in all, a pathetic performance.

Almost from the beginning of my time on the *NewsHour*, I anchored a wide range of segments, panels, and interviews that had nothing to do with media. I was sort of the fifth wheel in a repertory company of on-camera correspondents that included Jim, Judy Woodruff, the late Gwen Ifill, and Ray Suarez, jumping in whenever needed. I enjoyed the variety of subjects, especially the interviews, and after years of reporting at home and abroad was usually able to get up to speed on a few hours' notice. But I never viewed it as a career that would continue once Pew's generous underwriting of the Media Unit ran out.

The Pew Charitable Trusts made an ideal funder: they covered the bills and never interfered with the coverage. Once a year, Jim and I would take the train to Philadelphia to meet with the Pew leadership in their paneled boardroom overlooking the city. We anticipated probing questions about how we were spending their money, but mostly the board members wanted to gossip about the news from Washington and the latest media controversy. Originally they had funded the Media Unit for three years of operation. They renewed for three more years and one more after that, a generous total of seven years, more than twice the initial commitment, and that was it. Our record up to that point was impressive: we had aired 110 in-depth tape reports, and I had anchored some 250 studio discussions on media and national and international issues. In the course of the seven years, we had won eighteen national awards and honors for media criticism and analysis. I stacked them up in the corner of my office alongside the two Emmys I had won at CBS.

Pew had always described its grants as seed money. Now it was up to *The NewsHour* to continue the media coverage on its own budget or find another source of funds. The development people at MacNeil/Lehrer Productions, the parent company, beat the bushes but to no immediate avail. The most obvious and promising potential funder of the Media Unit was the Knight Foundation, which supports a broad array of journalism programs and projects and was already supporting *The NewsHour*'s online operation, but negotiations broke down over Knight's request to have a specific weekly time slot on the broadcast that they could promote. Jim Lehrer, always a bit of a control freak

when it came to his broadcast, would not agree. Other than a few regularly scheduled features, such as the political commentary of columnists
Mark Shields and David Brooks on Friday nights, Jim was adamant
about keeping the broadcast schedule clear to cover the day's news and
the segments he wanted to see on any given night. Bottom line: no deal.

The NewsHour was in no position to fund the Media Unit itself. The
broadcast was already running an annual deficit in a climate where
corporate underwriting was rapidly drying up. The major funders that
once had committed to multiyear, multimillion-dollar grants now would
only allocate a few hundred thousand dollars (or less), usually only for
a few months at a time. The whole world of corporate and nonprofit underwriting (read: advertising) was fragmenting. Knight and others were
funding innovative projects that capitalized on the Internet and other
new technologies. *The NewsHour*, with its older audience and conventional approach, was less appealing. MacNeil/Lehrer Productions,
which had never had a sophisticated development operation, was feeling the pinch. In fact, a few years later, MacNeil/Lehrer would "donate"
the entire money-losing operation to WETA, the larger and more-flush
public-broadcasting corporation of greater Washington, which had an
established, successful fundraising operation and would continue the
broadcast as *The PBS NewsHour*.

So, for me, the prospect of retirement, at least from daily journalism,
arose as a logical option. Counting print and commercial and public
television, I had been in the daily news business just shy of fifty years.
I was sixty-seven. I departed the *NewsHour* in 2005 with the essentially
meaningless title of special correspondent. I had spent twenty years in
broadcasting after becoming one of the first veteran print correspondents to make the transition from newspapers, had won two news Emmys for work on CBS's *48 Hours*, shared a Peabody at *CBS Sunday
Morning*, and collected a raft of other awards. Most important, I had
enjoyed the work and felt I had been able to maintain the same professional standards on television as in print. No regrets. I did muse about
what my father would have thought about my path through commercial
and public television and the idea of retirement from daily journalism.
He had never contemplated retirement. I think he saw it as a yawning,
empty space into which one swiftly disappeared. He did not want to
disappear. He had loved what he was doing right up to the end. I saw it
differently: something new and different, an inviting challenge.

I also had no idea what I would do next. Other than my initial position at the *Stamford Advocate* as a newbie during the summer between my junior and senior years at Notre Dame, I had never applied for a job. Something had always turned up. I assumed it would again.

Epilogue: It's a Wrap

In the almost a half-century between the day in 1958 I walked into the *Stamford Advocate* to apply for a job to the day in 2005 I walked out of the *NewsHour* a free man—at least from the demands of daily journalism—everything, of course, had changed. I had changed. The world had changed.

Most important, newspapers changed—and are still changing—most of all. Put simply, their economic models have collapsed in the face of the digital revolution. Rich, profitable display advertising and classified ads have migrated to the Internet, and subscription revenue, once a minor factor on a newspaper's balance sheet, is now vital for those papers that have survived into the third decade of the twenty-first century. The *New York Times* is an example of this drastic change: advertising in the print edition has largely vaporized, but digital revenue has soared, reaching eight hundred million dollars by early 2020, with five-million-and-counting digital subscribers worldwide. Part of this growth is the result of a discernible "Trump Bump," in which readers, appalled by the craziness of Donald Trump's presidency, were hungrily searching for reliable news and information and willing to pay for it. Every time he spoke of "fake news" or "the failing *New York Times*" or labeled the press "the enemy of the people," new subscriptions came pouring in.

Where has all the advertising gone? Google is one place. Google's ad revenue grew in two decades from a standing start to $137 billion in 2018. The combined advertising take of all US newspapers that year was sixteen billion dollars and falling. It does not take a financial genius to see where this is heading.

With their principal revenue source evaporating, newspapers have continued to shrink and close around the country, victims in most cases of the digital revolution and a head-in-the-sand refusal to embrace it successfully. Some have folded; others have cut back their print runs, slashed their staffs, and cut costs. More than forty thousand newsroom jobs were eliminated in the first two decades of the twenty-first century. In 1950 there were 1,777 daily newspapers published in the United States; seventy years later there were fewer than 1,200. The costly business of investigative reporting has been cut back sharply, especially at the state and local levels. All this has been magnified by the COVID-19 pandemic, which has shattered the economy generally and threatened the underpinnings of the news business. The exceptions today are the major national newspapers—the *New York Times*, the *Wall Street Journal*, and the *Washington Post*—that adapted to the economic demands of the digital world. Collectively, they are doing important investigative work.

With newspapers in decline, Americans have begun to get most, if not all, of their news online on smartphones and other devices. An entire generation has grown up not reading newspapers on newsprint. A diminishing number of ancients, like me, continues their ever-more-costly print subscriptions, but the newspaper on newsprint delivered to your doorstep is fast becoming an expensive, boutique product. Its days are clearly numbered.

Meanwhile, the cable news channels—Fox, MSNBC, and CNN—have become loud, argumentative voices in the national conversation, intensifying the political polarization that has paralyzed the federal government and permeated every corner of public life. Everything, even wearing masks during a pandemic, has become political.

All-digital news sites like *BuzzFeed*, *Vox*, and others have become major sources of news for millions. Twitter, Facebook, and Instagram have become central to peoples' lives. Social media has been weaponized by Russia in the 2016 US elections and since, while all manner of conspiracy theories have been exploited and promoted. The burden on the consumer to sort fact from fiction is greater than ever.

There is a great deal of hand-wringing these days about the news business. Young people don't read, don't know anything beyond what they see on their screens, and don't see the value of independent knowledge as long as they have Google and can look it up; the sky, we are told, is falling. I don't agree. My own view is that everything is changing—and will keep changing—but not everything is lost. At least, that's what I keep telling myself.

As for my retirement, I discovered, as many have before me, that after a long career in a visible industry, all sorts of propositions will present themselves. I was invited to do periodic commentaries on NPR and enjoyed it. Having moderated countless panels on PBS, I was hired as a moderator by the *Atlantic* and others to conduct deep-dive discussions of public policy at small dinners all around the country. I wrote freelance pieces for magazines, including a cover for the *Smithsonian* retracing the voyage of Captain John Smith around the Chesapeake Bay on the four hundredth anniversary in 2008. It was a great excuse to explore nooks and crannies of the Chesapeake I had never seen. Nothing but fun—all of it.

I have accepted invitations to join boards, including the Fund for Investigative Journalism. Most of the boards are nonprofits dealing with the health of the Chesapeake Bay, including the University of Maryland Center for Environmental Science, the Smithsonian Environmental Research Center, the West/Rhode Riverkeeper, and, best of all, the Chesapeake Bay Trust, a nonprofit grant-making organization with a mission to promote public awareness and participation in the protection and restoration of the Chesapeake. Susy and I had been together for ten years when we married on a sparkling, perfect fall day in 1997. We sold the house in Washington and moved full time to the western shore of the bay, so the best and worst of the Chesapeake have been right in front of our door. I served two full terms on the Chesapeake Bay Trust board and two more years as chair, a decade in which the board has approved tens of millions of dollars in grants for education and restoration projects that, I hope, have made a contribution to the improving health of the bay.

In 2014, finding the big house on the West River more than we needed, we downsized slightly to a house overlooking Spa Creek in the heart of Annapolis, the historic Maryland state capital, where I had bought my first sailboat in 1977. I ran into the editor of the Annapolis *Capital Gazette*, one of the oldest dailies in the country, and agreed to write a regular column. So, some fifty years after I started at the *Stamford Advocate*, covering city hall, I found myself writing about local news again at a similarly sized paper. After decades of covering national and international news, I was once again writing about local issues, about the city council, and the mayor's race. You *can* go home again.

Since the journalism world has become ever more digital, I have started a blog of columns and commentary at terencefsmith.com and have contributed to *The Huffington Post* and other online news aggregators. That led to an invitation from Crystal Cruises to speak on current affairs aboard their lovely ships on two-week sailings all around the world. With the cruises and separate assignments escorting *New York Times* Journeys to Berlin and elsewhere, I continued to assuage my wanderlust, which seems to be a permanent condition for which, happily, there is no cure.

So that's my journey, from hot type to cold, print to television, commercial to public, local news to international to national to local again and, now, digital. A pleasure, thank you, from beginning to end. And Pop? I'd love to hear what he thinks about sports today and the passing scene. I'd love to hear him on ballplayers signing contracts as free agents in the hundreds of millions of dollars, of players kneeling during the national anthem, of colleges fielding football teams that are as professional as the NFL. He would have thoughts on all of this and more. He would be funny, trenchant, and to-the-point. Who knows? Maybe he'd even write a column about it.

Acknowledgments

Thanks to my college roommate, Patrick Roache, and his wife, Catherine Stewart Roache, both PhD's and authors, who suggested this memoir in the first place. Admittedly, some wine had been consumed as we relaxed in the cockpit of my sailboat, Winsome, on the Chesapeake, trading old stories when they urged me repeatedly to write them down. Any and all errors are mine alone, but the Roaches are to blame for the project itself. Thanks, also to my many friends from *The New York Times*, *CBS News*, and *PBS NewsHour* and elsewhere who encouraged the process and critiqued the product. I had help as well from Ginger Vanderpool, tech wizard; and my agent, Diane Nine of Nine Speakers, Inc. of Washington, D.C. Finally, thanks most of all to Susy, who has graciously, patiently listened to all these stories once again.

Index

Note: The photo insert images are indexed as *p1, p2, p3*, etc.

About the Author

Terence Smith is an award-winning journalist who has been a political reporter, foreign correspondent, editor, and television analyst over the course of an almost five-decade career that included the *New York Times*, CBS News, and *NewsHour* on PBS. In 2013 Smith was inducted into the Society of Professional Journalists' Hall of Fame. He resides in Annapolis, Maryland.